T0406693

The Southern African Development Community and Law

Mkhululi Nyathi

The Southern African Development Community and Law

palgrave
macmillan

Mkhululi Nyathi
Independent Researcher
Bulawayo, Zimbabwe

ISBN 978-3-319-76510-5   ISBN 978-3-319-76511-2   (eBook)
https://doi.org/10.1007/978-3-319-76511-2

Library of Congress Control Number: 2018941841

Cover image: imageBROKER / Alamy Stock Photo
Cover design: Tjaša Krivec

Printed on acid-free paper

This Palgrave Macmillan imprint is published by the registered company Springer
International Publishing AG part of Springer Nature.
The registered company address is: Gewerbestrasse 11, 6330 Cham, Switzerland

ACKNOWLEDGEMENTS

A book of this nature can rarely be a product of individual effort. A number of people contributed immensely along the way and in different ways. I would be remiss if I did not sincerely acknowledge the invaluable support and guidance that I received from a number of people.

First and foremost, I would like to thank my wife Putso for standing beside me throughout the writing of this book. She graciously allowed me space and gave me the motivation to work on the book project. For that I will forever remain indebted to her and I dedicate this book to her. I also thank my children: Nomasiko, Manqoba, and Nomalungelo—the older two for their love and tolerance and Nomalungelo for her sweet trouble and companionship. You are wonderful children that any parent could ever hope for. I also thank my parents Kenneth and Margaret for their love and care during my formative years and for instilling in me the culture of hard work.

This book is based on my doctoral thesis prepared at the Centre for Human Rights, Faculty of Law, University of Pretoria. I express my profound gratitude to my thesis supervisor, Professor Magnus Killander for his guidance during my doctoral candidacy. Professor Killander continued rendering his support after my doctoral qualification in preparing this book for publication.

I would also like to thank all those who read and commented on the several versions of my draft thesis and all the reviewers, both formal and informal, who reviewed the book manuscript and offered their comments and suggestions. All the shortcomings in this book are, however, mine and mine alone.

I feel compelled to repeat the acknowledgements carried in my thesis in this and the next two paragraphs. My profound gratitude goes to the Doctor of Laws Bursary Office at the Faculty of Law, University of Pretoria, for facilitating my full-time post-graduate bursary. Ms Jeanne-Kay Goodale and all who were involved, thank you! Also to be mentioned is the Institute for International and Comparative Law in Africa at the Faculty of Law, University of Pretoria, for the research grant that enabled me, while I was still a doctoral candidate, to travel to Gaborone, Botswana, to carry out research at the SADC headquarters in March 2014.

I should also record my appreciation for the assistance and support I got from some of the officials at the Southern African Development Community (SADC) Headquarters in Gaborone, Botswana. Nthabiseng Liphapang, Legal Counsel, extended her warm welcome and gave me the assurance of assistance in case of need. The SADC librarian, Maria Tali was always ready to assist, going out of her way to help me find relevant material. Although I did not meet Inonge Kwenda (then Legal Counsel at SADC) during my research sojourn in Gaborone, I later got in touch with her and she read through the first draft of my thesis and offered her most helpful comments.

Dr Tomaz Salomão, former executive secretary of SADC, is also due my gratitude. He read the chapters of my draft thesis which deal with the institutions of SADC and agreed to share with me his knowledge and insights into the internal workings of SADC institutions. In the context of a dearth of scholarly literature on SADC institutional practice, Dr Salomão's knowledge greatly assisted me to increase my understanding of SADC governance beyond the legal instruments.

A special thank you to the entire team that worked on this book at Palgrave Macmillan, New York: Alina Yurova, Editor, Regional Politics and Development Studies; and her Editorial Assistants, John Stegner and Katelyn Zingg and the Production team for all the assistance and guidance and for making possible the production of this book.

TABLE OF CASES

TABLE OF TREATIES AND OTHER INTERNATIONAL INSTRUMENTS

Contents

ABBREVIATIONS AND ACRONYMS

AEC	African Economic Community
AU	African Union
CJEU	Court of Justice of the European Union
CoA	Committee of Ambassadors/High Commissioners (SADC)
CoM	Council of Ministers (SADC)
COMESA	Common Market for Eastern and Southern Africa
CSOs	Civil Society Organisations
EAC	East African Community
EACJ	East African Community Court of Justice
EALA	East African Legislative Assembly
ECCJ	ECOWAS Community Court of Justice
ECOWAS	Economic Community of West African States
EP	European Parliament
EU	European Union
ICM	Integrated Committee of Ministers [now Sectoral and Cluster Ministerial Committees (SADC)]
NGOs	Non-governmental organisations
OPDS	Organ on Politics, Defence and Security Co-operation (SADC)
RISDP	Regional Indicative Strategic Development Plan (SADC)
SADC	Southern African Development Community
SADCPF	SADC Parliamentary Forum
SCMCs	Sectoral and Cluster Ministerial Committees (SADC)
SCO	Standing Committee of Officials (SADC)
SEOM	SADC Election Observer Mission
SIPO	Strategic Implementation Plan of the Organ (SADC)

SNCs   SADC National Committees
TEU   Treaty on European Union
TFEU   Treaty on the Functioning of the European Union

CHAPTER 1

Introduction

The main objective of this book is to assess whether two of the principles
set out in the Treaty of the Southern African Development Community
(SADC Treaty)—democracy and the rule of law, are reflected in the institutional design of the Southern African Development Community (SADC)
and, to the extent that they may not be reflected, to proffer an alternative
model of a SADC governance framework that is democratic and anchored
in the rule of law.

SADC is a regional economic and political integration organisation
with 16 Member States from the southern tip of the African continent
right up to the Democratic Republic of the Congo and including the
Indian Ocean island states of Comoros, Madagascar, Mauritius, and
Seychelles.

The objectives of SADC are set out in article 5(1) of the SADC Treaty
and include the promotion of sustainable and equitable economic growth
and socio-economic development and the promotion of common political
values, systems, and other shared values which are transmitted through
institutions which are democratic, legitimate, and effective. The SADC
Treaty also sets out in article 4 the principles of SADC which include
respect for human rights, democracy, and the rule of law.[1]

---

[1] See Chap. 2 for a detailed discussion.

© The Author(s) 2019
M. Nyathi, *The Southern African Development Community
and Law*, https://doi.org/10.1007/978-3-319-76511-2_1

1

This book is written from an international institutional law perspective and seeks to address the following question[2]: Is the design of the institutions of SADC democratic and reflective of a desire to anchor policymaking and implementation processes in the rule of law? Flowing from this question is a related one: To the extent that the design of the institutions of SADC does not reflect the values of democracy and the rule of law, how best can these design deficits be addressed?

This book is written in a legal style and discusses legal institutional issues. However, it is intended for anyone with an interest in understanding the institutions of SADC and how these institutions relate to each other.

Before delving into the main theme of this book, it is important to first briefly sketch out SADC's institutional history and current governance structure and legal framework. The history of SADC dates back about five decades. It started in the 1960s when political leaders of newly independent African states were involved in ad hoc political and security cooperation in a bid to achieve the independence of the remaining African countries still under colonial or white minority rule.[3] In the 1970s, this political and security cooperation later evolved into yet another informal, loose grouping called the Front Line States.[4] The concrete institutional evolution of SADC began in earnest on 1 April 1980. That was the day the leaders of Angola, Botswana, Mozambique, Tanzania, Zambia, Swaziland, Lesotho, and Malawi met in Lusaka, Zambia, and adopted the Lusaka Declaration entitled *Southern Africa: Toward Economic Liberation*.[5] The Southern African Development Coordination Conference (SADCC) was subsequently established by the signatories to the Lusaka Declaration

---

[2] International institutional law is a fairly recent, stand-alone discipline falling within the broader area of public international law and concerns itself with the rules of law that govern the status, structure, and functioning of international organisations. See H.G. Schermers & N.M. Blokker *International institutional law: Unity within diversity* (2011) 4.

[3] G.H. Oosthuizen *The Southern African Development Community: The organization, its policies and prospects* (2006) 53.

[4] As above.

[5] The declaration was signed by Angola, Botswana, Malawi, Mozambique, Namibia, Swaziland, Tanzania, and Zimbabwe. See the preamble of the original SADC Treaty; see also Oosthuizen (Footnote 3 above) 70. SADC expanded in the 1990s with the joining of South Africa, Mauritius, Seychelles, the Democratic Republic of Congo (DRC), and Madagascar. Comoros is the newest member of SADC, having been admitted into membership in August 2017. See https://www.sadc.int/news-events/news/union-comoros-becomes-16th-sadc-member-state/ (accessed 31 August 2017).

through a Memorandum of Understanding signed on 20 July 1981. SADCC was later transformed into SADC in 1992 through the SADC Windhoek Declaration and Treaty establishing SADC that was ratified by the SADCC Member States.[6]

The SADC Treaty was amended on 14 August 2001. The amendment of the original SADC Treaty followed introspection by the members that culminated in a number of reports and a review by the Committee of Ministers.[7] The sectoral model used in the 1992 SADC Treaty, where Member States were given specific sector responsibilities, was initially seen as a model of decentralisation at regional level meant to provide Member States with a sense of ownership of the regional agenda and at the same time avoid a financially burdensome bureaucratisation.[8] The decentralised sectoral model was abandoned in 2001 in favour of the current centralised model, as the former was found to be unworkable.[9] Quite expectedly therefore, the amendment saw the abolition of (sectoral) commissions. The other major result of the amendment was the establishment of the Integrated Committee of Ministers (ICM) [now the Sectoral and Cluster

[6] B. Sirota 'Sovereignty and the Southern African Development Community' (2004–2005) 5#1 *Chicago Journal of International Law* 345, making reference to N. Poku *Regionalism and Security in Southern Africa* (Palgrave 2001) 99. See also C. Ng' ong' ola 'The legal framework for regional integration in the Southern African Development Community' (2008) *University of Botswana Law Journal* 3–15 for a historical overview of the evolution of the objectives and institutions of SADC. See also A. Saurombe 'An analysis and exposition of dispute settlement forum shopping for SADC Member States in the light of the suspension of the SADC Tribunal' (2011) 23 *South African Mercantile Law Journal* 393; A. Saurombe 'The role of SADC institutions in implementing SADC Treaty provisions dealing with regional integration' (2012) 15 # 2 *Potchefstroom Electronic Law Journal* 456–457 https:// doi.org/10.4314/pelj.v15i2.16 (last accessed 15 October 2014).

[7] One of the reports was the 1993 report entitled 'A framework and strategy for building the Community.' There was also a 1997 report by independent consultants entitled 'Review and rationalisation of the SADC programme of action.' Both reports criticised the decentralised model of integration. See Oosthuizen (Footnote 3 above) 100–101.

[8] Oosthuizen (Footnote 3 above) 63. Oosthuizen also identifies as part of the rationale of decentralisation the related need of safeguarding national sovereignty of the Member States. It has also been observed by others that the decentralised approach was adopted on the assumption that it would allow greater participation by ordinary people. See S. Zondi 'Governance and social policy in the SADC region: An issues analysis' (2009) *Working Paper Series No. 2* Planning Division, Development Bank of Southern Africa 15 http://www.lead-4change.org/downloads/module_2/Zondi%20DBSA%20Paper%20on%20SADC%20-%20Governance%20and%20Policy.pdf (accessed 14 December 2013); L. Nathan *Community of insecurity: SADC's struggle for peace and security in Southern Africa* (2012) 24.

[9] See Footnote 7 above.

Ministerial Committees (SCMCs)], and the SADC National Committees (SNCs).[10] However, the 2001 amendment saw the retention of such institutions as the Summit of Heads of State or Government (the Summit) and the Council of Ministers (CoM) with their powers and responsibilities largely intact.

The institutional framework of SADC is set out in article 9 of the SADC Treaty. At the apex is the Summit. This is the supreme policymaking institution of SADC.[11] As will be shown in Chap. 3, the powers of the Summit are extensive and overarching and subject to little, if any, oversight and control. Under the Summit are the CoM[12]; the SCMCs[13]; the Standing Committee of Officials (SCO)[14]; the Secretariat headed by the Executive Secretary; and the SNCs. Of these institutions, only the SNCs and the Secretariat are, to a limited extent, outside the domain of national executives of Member States.[15]

The SADC Treaty also establishes a judicial institution in the form of the SADC Tribunal. Matters to do with the SADC Tribunal's composition, jurisdiction, and rules of procedure, among other things, are dealt with in the Protocol on Tribunal and the Rules of Procedure Thereof (the Tribunal Protocol), which was adopted in 2000 and subsequently made an integral part of the SADC Treaty.[16] Despite initially submitting to the jurisdiction of the Tribunal in the earlier *Campbell* matters,[17] Zimbabwe later challenged the legality of the Tribunal (among other legal contestations), and refused to comply with its decisions, culminating in the suspension of the Tribunal and its eventual effective disbandment as resolved by the Summit.[18]

There is also the SADC Parliamentary Forum (SADCPF). However, this is an autonomous body that lies outside the SADC legal institutional

---

[10] The SCMCs and the SNCs are discussed in detail in Chaps. 3 and 4 respectively.
[11] Art 10 of the SADC Treaty.
[12] Art 11 of the SADC Treaty.
[13] Art 12 of the SADC Treaty.
[14] Art 13 of the SADC Treaty.
[15] It should be noted though that this 'executivist tilt' is not a peculiar SADC affliction but is a feature of a number of international organisations and has been viewed as the major source of their democratic deficit. See A. Peters 'Dual democracy' in J. Klabbers et al. *The constitutionalizaion of international Law* (2009) 292.
[16] See Chap. 4, Sect. 4.2 for a detailed discussion.
[17] See Chap. 4, Sect. 4.2 for a detailed discussion.
[18] See Chap. 4, Sect. 4.2 for a detailed discussion.

framework.[19] In fact, the SADCPF has been pushing for its transformation into a regional parliament.[20]

With regard to the legal framework, at the top of the hierarchy of legal instruments is the SADC Treaty. While the SADC Treaty provides in article 6(5) that 'Member States shall take all necessary steps to accord [the SADC] Treaty the force of national law,'[21] there is no framework set out in the Treaty for the direct automatic applicability of any of its provisions (or decisions taken pursuant thereto) in Member States. Although article 6(5) is couched in peremptory language, the domestication of the SADC Treaty is left to the discretion of individual Member States. The other legal instruments are protocols which may be adopted by the Summit, subject to their ratification by Member States and binding only on the Member States that are parties to that particular protocol.[22] There is thus no general, SADC-wide legal framework for the direct applicability and enforceability of the provisions of the protocols in Member States. As the comparative study in Chap. 6 will show, there is now a trend in some African regional economic communities (RECs), such as the East African Community (EAC) and the Economic Community of West African States (ECOWAS), that prefer lawmaking through community acts, regulations, and other instruments, with generally direct applicability in Member States, instead of norm setting through protocols.[23]

In addition to 'law' making through the adoption or amendment of the above legal instruments, there are provisions in the Treaty, as shall be discussed in detail in Chap. 3, for norm setting through decisions of the Summit, mostly on the recommendations of the CoM. As shall be shown in Chap. 3, the latter has its own decision-making powers, but largely on administrative and operational matters, but even so, within the overarching control of the Summit.

While the 2001 amendment of the SADC Treaty was no doubt informed by past failures, and the jettisoning of the decentralised model was intended to improve and streamline the SADC governance structure, the 2001 SADC 'makeover' did not address the fundamental problems of

[19] See Chap. 4, Sect. 4.4 for a more detailed discussion.
[20] See Chap. 4, Sect. 4.4 for a more detailed discussion.
[21] Art 6(5) of the SADC Treaty.
[22] Art 22 of the SADC Treaty.
[23] See Chap. 6.

democracy and the rule of law.[24] Too much power remains vested in a single institution—the Summit, with no concomitant framework for the balancing and control of the Summit's powers by the other institutions.

It should be noted that the SADC Treaty does not define or set out the elements of democracy or those of the rule of law. Indeed, with regards to democracy it has been noted that this is a term that is difficult to define as it is ever-changing.[25] With regards to democracy, therefore, this book does not engage in an unbounded discussion of all the elements of democracy but assesses the SADC institutional framework against a single dimension of democracy—separation of powers.[26]

While this book assesses SADC's institutional architecture against the normative values of democracy and the rule of law, other related concepts, including constitutionalism and good governance, will unavoidably come up for discussion. This should not be viewed as digression or broadening of the scope of this book but rather as something that is unavoidable in light of the interrelationship of these concepts and the manner they are dealt with in some of the literature and legal instruments. What is proffered in this book, therefore, is a 'constitutional' appraisal of the SADC institutional framework from the perspective of democracy (narrowly defined) and the rule of law.[27] It needs stating therefore that this book is not concerned with the assessment or review of the achievements of or challenges faced by SADC, something that would need a different (and empirical) study (or studies based on different integration areas) backed by relevant and credible methodological tools. However, the challenges to do with democracy and the rule of law are covered at length. Although these form part of the principles and objectives of SADC, this should not

---

[24] For a discussion of democracy and the rule of law in the context of the SADC legal framework, see generally Chap. 2 below.

[25] R.A. Dahl 'Can international organisations be democratic? A skeptic's view' in I. Shapiro & C. Hacker-Cordon (eds) *Democracy's edges* (1999) 20.

[26] The rationale for the choice of this single dimension of democracy is set out in Chap. 2.

[27] While the terms 'constitution' and 'constitutional appraisal' might readily be understood to be linked to the domestic order, it has been observed that there is no valid reason why this should be so, since the term 'constitution' can also be used to 'describe the fundamental legal order of any autonomous community or body politic.' See for example E. de Wet: 'The international constitutional order' (2006) 15 *International Comparative Law Quarterly* 52. In fact, there is a view that international institutional law is in an international organisation what constitutional law and administrative law is in a state, and to some, 'international constitutional law' is the preferred name of the discipline. See Schemers & Blokker (Footnote 2 above) 7, 14.

be viewed as a selective appraisal of one area of integration provided for in the SADC Treaty. These challenges are highlighted primarily because they assist in the broader constitutional analysis of the institutions of SADC, since they are directly linked to the major theme of this book.

This book is narrowly focused on the question of institutional design—it seeks to assess whether the institutional design of SADC is in sync with the SADC Treaty principles and objectives, specifically those of democracy and the rule of law. In other words, the enquiry is whether, having set out what they wanted to achieve, the Member States of SADC were/have been able to create the right mix of institutions to carry out the mandate of the organisation?

What this book focuses on is the analysis of the formal powers and functions of the institutions of SADC as set out in the SADC Treaty. The rationale for this largely 'text-bound' approach is that the composition and powers of international institutions are ordinarily matters of treaty law. Therefore, the design of the constitutive and subsidiary legal instruments of international organisations is of primary significance since it is bound to inform the subsequent behaviour of the organisation.[28]

However, international organisations do not always act in terms of the letter of their constitutive documents. Experience has shown that at times international organisations or some of their institutions or organs would, for better or worse, act in a manner not originally anticipated by their treaties.[29] However, the primacy of treaties at international institutional law cannot be easily contested.

[28] This is not to say that the practices of international organisations do not matter. Indeed, with regards to treaty interpretation, in addition to interpreting the terms of a treaty in their context and in light of the objects and purposes of the treaty, subsequent practice of an international organisation in the application of the treaty which establishes the agreement of the parties regarding its interpretation is also taken into account. See art 31(3)(b) of the 1969 Vienna Convention on the Law of Treaties, adopted on 22 May 1969; *Legality of the Use by a State of Nuclear Weapons in Armed Conflict (Request by the World Health Organisation), Advisory Opinion of 8 July 1996*, ICJ Reports 1996, p. 66 at p. 75, para 19 and the list of previous cases therein cited.

[29] A good example is the United Nations General Assembly (UNGA) *Uniting for Peace* Resolution of 3 November 1950. This resolution was to the effect that in the event that the United Nations Security Council (UNSC) was constrained to discharge its primary responsibility of the maintenance of international peace and security owing to lack of unanimity amongst its permanent members, the UNGA could intervene instead. See De Wet (Footnote 27 above) 65.

The discussion of the primacy of treaties in international organisations would not be complete without the mention of the doctrine of implied powers of international organisations. The International Court of Justice has held, in the context of the United Nations, that to the extent that an organisation acts in a manner that is 'appropriate for the fulfilment of one of (its) stated purposes' there is a presumption that such an action is not *ultra vires*. Thus, in order to achieve its objective, an international organisation may exercise powers not expressly provided for in its constitutive document.[30] Such an exercise of power would not be held to be *ultra vires* as long as there is a connection between such exercise of power and the fulfilment of the purposes of the organisation.[31]

However, even with implied powers, the centrality of the constitutive document of an international organisation cannot be overemphasised—it is the starting point in the determination of the existence or otherwise of such implied powers, since the purposes of an international organisation can only be ascertained by reference to its constitutive treaty. In any case, in the absence of a categorical pronunciation by a competent judiciary authority, the question of the existence or otherwise of implied powers would always remain liable to contestation.

The other reason for avoiding putting too much emphasis on practice, especially from the perspective of democracy, is that it might only serve to undermine it as a normative value. Governance of public institutions, be they domestic or international, should generally be anchored in formally and legally entrenched democratic, transparent, and accountable institutions not on the benevolence of public officers whose powers are unlimited and the exercise of which is unconstrained.[32] Indeed, any practice of

---

[30] *Certain Expenses of the United Nations (Article 17, para 2, of the Charter), Advisory Opinion of 20 July 1962*: ICJ Reports 1962, p. 151, at p. 168; *Legality of the Use by a State of Nuclear Weapons in Armed Conflict (Request by the World Health Organisation)* (Footnote 28 above) at p. 79, para 25.

[31] According to Klabbers, constituent documents of international organisations should be expected and do in fact have 'gaps.' This is either because of the reality that drafters of international instruments cannot be expected 'to think of every contingency'; or that the drafters deliberately leave a space for flexibility in order to allow international organisations to evolve. See J. Klabbers *An introduction to international institutional law* (2009) 58.

[32] There is indeed the view that where there is an exercise of public power, there should be public justification for the exercise of such power, and that it matters not if such exercise of power leads to the production of binding norms or decisions. See N. Krisch & B. Kingsbury 'Introduction: Global governance and global administrative law in the international legal order' (2006) 17 # 1 *European Journal of International Law* 13.

an international organisation not based on clearly set out treaty provisions, even if it has unquestionable democratic credentials, can easily be changed, even for worse, as opposed to treaty provisions.

The same largely text-bound approach that this book uses with regard to SADC is adopted in the analysis of institutional design of organisations chosen for comparative analysis.[33] The limited focus on practice is therefore deliberate and should be understood in this context. As will be seen in Chap. 7 which carries the institutional model for SADC as envisioned in this book, the same approach is used when it comes to the recommendations, as what is proposed is treaty reform as opposed to merely change in practice based on, for example, mere political will.

Having positively set out the objectives and scope of this book, it may be necessary to state at this point what this book is not about. This book is not about whether democracy, the rule of law, and related principles should be applicable to SADC.[34] The constitutional analysis of the SADC institutional design carried in this book proceeds on the basis that these principles are applicable to and in SADC since the SADC Member States signed up to them.[35]

This book is limited to the core institutions of SADC as explicitly established by the SADC Treaty—the article 9 institutions; and those that have come to be understood by some as forming part of the article 9 institutions. For ease of both analysis and presentation, these have been divided into two broad classes—norm-setting/rule-making and oversight institutions. This does not imply that there is rigidity in terms of these different roles.[36]

One article 9 institution is not covered in detail. This is the Organ on Politics, Defence, and Security Co-operation and its institutional appendages. This institution forms the slightly 'autonomous' although 'integrated' peace and security architecture of SADC.[37] However, for the sake of completeness, especially the need to present a clear picture of the whole

---

[33] See generally Chap. 6.
[34] As will be briefly shown in Chap. 2, there is no consensus in scholarship on the applicability of these principles at international law in general and also at international institutional law.
[35] See Chap. 2.
[36] See introduction section of Chap. 3 for a detailed discussion.
[37] For a discussion of how the two-tier SADC evolved, combining economic cooperation that evolved from SADCC and the largely political/diplomatic-cum security-oriented peace and security cooperation which is said to have evolved from the Frontline States, see

SADC institutional architecture and its internal linkages, a relatively detailed 'outline' of the SADC peace and security architecture is presented in Chap. 3.

As has already been intimated, an in-depth debate about linking democracy and the rule of law to policy effectiveness and efficiency is eschewed in this book. There is no suggestion that democratisation of the SADC governance framework would overnight result in the realisation of SADC's objectives. In fact, it would be difficult (although perhaps not necessarily impossible) to measure the success of a regional integration scheme especially in the areas of economic and social development, since there could be a number of other factors at play that are external to and delinked from the regional integration project.

But what exactly is the nature of this international organisation called SADC? To answer this question, a brief overview of international organisations would suffice first. International organisations are diverse in nature. There are those that deal with single subjects like the North Atlantic Treaty Organisation (NATO) whose focus is security. Another example is the World Trade Organisation (WTO) which deals with international/multilateral trade matters. On the other hand, there are some organisations that have a broad range of objectives including trade and related matters, security, environmental matters, migration, and so on. Regional economic communities (RECs) or even more appropriately, regional economic and political integration organisations, including the East African Community (EAC), the Economic Community of West African States (ECOWAS), the European Union (EU) and SADC, fall under this latter category. The process of states coming together under the latter arrangement has come to be generally understood as the process of regional integration. Regional integration thus goes beyond matters to do with trade and economic relations between states. As already intimated, it can and in fact does play a role in a number of other areas including democratic participation; political and security cooperation; respect for human rights and social development matters like education and poverty reduction; among others.[38]

E.N. Tjønneland 'Making sense of the Southern African Development Community' (2013) 22 # 3 *African Security Review* 192–193.

[38] See R. Robert 'The social dimension of regional integration in ECOWAS' (2004) *Working paper No. 49* Policy Integration Department, International Labour Office 1–3 http://staging2.ilo.org/wcmsp5/groups/public/---dgreports/---integration/documents/publication/wcms_079141.pdf (last accessed 4 August 2014).

In the current state of affairs at international institutional law, RECs are invariably defined by the geographical proximity of their Member States and the shared interests of such states.[39] RECs are a fairly recent phenomenon at international law and started to take a well-defined shape in mid-twentieth century in the form of the precursors to the European Union (EU) and the East African Community (EAC). These organisations are discussed in detail in Chap. 6. As will be shown in that chapter, RECs continue to accommodate more and more objectives, including, as indicated above, promotion of democracy and protection of human rights. Some, like the EU, have integrated so much that they now occupy some grey area between the classical nation state and the traditional treaty-based international organisation.[40]

Within Africa, the continuing development of RECs has seen, particularly in the last two decades, the development and transformation of EAC and ECOWAS, respectively, at least in terms of treaty design, into 'communities' that are subject to community laws of a general nature which are directly applicable in their respective Partner/Member States.

While it may not be possible to predict the next evolutionary stage and form of regional integration in all the current RECs, what is apparent at the time of this study is a continuing trend of ever deeper integration, although admittedly, the pace of integration is generally slow.[41] There is a gradual transfer of sovereignty (even if at times such transfer is limited) by nations over matters that have traditionally been within the exclusive domain of the nation state to regional organisations.

These RECs exist (and are developing) within the context of an ongoing academic discourse on the subject of democratisation of international

---

[39] This is indeed the case with regard to SADC and the three RECs that have been chosen for comparative analysis in this book.

[40] M. Horeth 'The European Commission's White Paper on Governance: A "tool kit" for closing the legitimacy gap of EU policymaking?', a paper presented at the Workshop *Preparing Europe's future: The contribution of the Commission's White Book on Governance*, Center for European Integration Studies Bonn & Europe 2020, in cooperation with the Representation of the North Rhine Westphalia to the European Union in Brussels, November 2001 available at https://www.zei.uni-bonn.de/dateien/discussion-paper/dp_c94_hoereth.pdf (accessed 14 June 2013).

[41] For example, it is envisaged that the realisation of the African Economic Community, an Africa-wide economic integration process (of which African sub-regional RECs are said to be the building blocks), will be done in six stages spanning some thirty four years. See art 6 of the African Economic Community Treaty available at http://www.wipo.int/wipolex/en/other_treaties/text.jsp?file_id=173333 (last accessed 9 June 2014).

law.[42] This discourse generally falls outside the scope of this book, save for those themes that are substantially linked to it. The democratisation of international law, however called, has attracted multifaceted and growing scholarly attention covering diverse themes, including the desirability and practicability or otherwise of a democratic hierarchical world order[43]; and the extent of the democratisation/constitutionalisation of certain international organisations, including RECs, among other things.[44]

The discourse on the democratisation of international law continues to attract the attention of scholars from diverse backgrounds such as political science, international relations, and international law.[45] Only a broad sketch of this discourse, backed by a limited selected 'overview' literature outlining its contours will suffice for the purposes of his book.

Some scholars such as Dahl are sceptical about the applicability of democracy beyond the state. Dahl's scepticism is based on the large size of the international community and the related challenges.[46] Moravcsik's 'anti-global democracy' thesis, on the other hand, sees no need for democracy at the global level because of what he perceives as the technical nature of international institutions which in his view should be protected from democratic inroads.[47]

---

[42] The choice of this descriptive term is a deliberate one. It is broad enough to cover the various sub-themes that may fall within this discourse some of which may be synonyms, while others may be held to be distinct theoretical conceptions.

[43] Marchetti, for example, argues that the current system is not democratic as it excludes global citizens from participating in the making of decisions that affect them. He proposes a federalist global democratic system that is multi-layered and underpinned by representative participation. See generally R. Marchetti (2008) *Global democracy: For and against: Ethical theory, institutional design and social struggles.*

[44] See for example, N. Walker 'Reframing EU constitutionalism' in J.L. Dunoff & J.P. Trachtman (eds) *Ruling the world? Constitutionalism, international law and global governance* (2009) 149–176; J.L. Dunoff 'The politics of international constitutions: The curious case of the World Trade Organization' in J.L. Dunoff & J.P. Trachtman (eds) *Ruling the world? Constitutionalism, international law and global governance* (2009) 178–205; J.P. Trachtman 'Constitutional economics of the World Trade Organization' in J.L. Dunoff & J.P. Trachtman (eds) *Ruling the world? Constitutionalism, international law and global governance* (2009) 206–229.

[45] See K. Dingwerth 'Global democracy and the democratic minimum: Why a procedural account alone is insufficient' (2014) 20 # 4 *European Journal of International Relations* 1126.

[46] Dahl (Footnote 25 above) 19–36. See also Dingwerth (Footnote 45 above) 1140.

[47] A. Moravcsik 'Is there a "democratic deficit" in world politics? A framework for analysis (2004) 39 # 2 *Government and Opposition* 336–363; A. Moravcsik 'In defence of the

There is also the pro-democracy league. Some of the advocates of the democratisation of international law are Held and Archibugi.[48] Through their cosmopolitan democratic model, they challenge the theory that democracy is and should be bounded within the classical Westphalian territorial state. To them, democracy should exist in a multi-level network of the nation state, regional and international organisations. They argue, among other things, for the democratisation of existing regional organisations and institutions,[49] including global institutions such as the United Nations.[50]

However, it should be noted that beyond the 'anti' and 'pro' global democracy scholarship,[51] there is some empirical reality that may not be ignored—international organisations themselves, or at least some of them, appear to be democratising.[52] For those organisations that are acquiring democratic credentials, the reasons behind such acquisition may be difficult

---

"Democratic deficit": Reassessing legitimacy in the European Union' (2002) 40 # 1 *Journal of Common Market Studies* 603–624; A. Moravcsik 'The myth of Europe's "Democratic deficit"' (2008) *Intereconomics: Journal of European Public Policy* 331–340.

[48] See generally, D. Archibugi 'From the United Nations to Cosmopolitan Democracy' in D. Archibugi & D. Held (eds) *Cosmopolitan democracy: An agenda for a new world order* (1995) 121–162; D. Held 'Democracy and the new international order' in D. Archibugi & D. Held (eds) *Cosmopolitan democracy: An agenda for a new world order* (1995) 96–120; D Archibugi 'Principles of Cosmopolitan Democracy' in D. Archibugi et al. (eds) *Re-imagining political community: Studies in cosmopolitan democracy* (1998) 198–228; D. Held 'Democracy and globalisation' in D. Archibugi et al. (eds) *Re-imagining political community: Studies in cosmopolitan democracy* (1998) 12–27; D. Archibugi (2008) *The global commonwealth of citizens.*

[49] Held, for example, argues for the creation of regional parliaments in Latin and North America and the strengthening of those that are already in existence like in the EU. See Held 'Democracy and the new international order' (Footnote 48 above) 108.

[50] With regard to the UN, some of the reform proposals include the creation of a global parliament; reforming the Security Council to reflect a fair regional representation; establishing compulsory jurisdiction by the International Court of Justice; and the creation of a global military.

[51] The tag 'anti' may not be a proper one here, since there are some who are not so much against the idea, but are rather of the view that it is not practically feasible. See for instance, Dahl (Footnote 25 above).

[52] See Dingwerth (Footnote 45 above) 1126, 1127, 1130, 1131. See also Krish & Kingsbury (Footnote 32 above) 4. The latter make specific reference to the following organisations: the World Bank which has established an Inspection Panel whose role is to make sure that the bank's internal policies are complied with; the Organisation for Economic Cooperation and Development (OECD) which has introduced the notice and comment procedure; and the Codex Alimentarius Commission which has brought on board NGOs.

to establish—it may be through giving in to scholarly pressure or other forms of advocacy; or it may be a result of organisational strategic objectives; or merely a consequence of trying to conform to democratic norms, or some other reasons.[53]

The democratisation of international institutions has mainly to do with institutional design—reforming the institutions (for those that are already in existence) so that they acquire democratic credentials. This could be either through, for example, opening up participatory spaces for civil society; providing for access to the organisation's information; or the creation of a parliamentary body.[54] However, to some, these formalistic institutional design responses are not enough in and by themselves to democratise global governance, since, in their view, structural inequalities tend to result in the exclusion of the disempowered—the poor, the uneducated and those without access to healthcare, hence their view that there is the need to move beyond formalistic institutional design in order to address the issue of social and economic inequalities.[55]

Institutional design of RECs will no doubt continue to engage the interests of lawyers and political scientists, among other scholars and interested players. As will be seen from some of the literature referred to in this book, current pro-democracy scholarship in international institutional law (including studies on RECs) can be said to be largely preoccupied with two related issues—the so-called democratic deficit of international organisations and the constitutionalisation of international organisations in order to reduce this deficit.[56]

There will therefore most likely be a continuing academic discourse on what should constitute an acceptable democratic framework for the governance of RECs. As is evident from above, some of the literature on democracy in international organisations seems to be mainly concerned with the accommodation of the interests of, and participation by the citizen in the governance framework of international organisations. This book seeks to contribute to the broad democratisation discourse, although from a narrow perspective as already indicated above, and focusing on SADC. It offers a critique of the institutional design of SADC and

---

[53] See Dingwerth (Footnote 45 above) 1130 and the references thereunder.
[54] Dingwerth (Footnote 45 above) 1125.
[55] As above.
[56] With regard to RECs, the EU seems to have attracted most of the academic attention so far.

suggests an alternative institutional model that focuses on addressing the 'internal democratic deficit' inherent in SADC as contextualised in this book.

A clarification should be made immediately as to what constitutes democracy at the international level, more specifically in the governance of RECs, in the context of this book. There appears to be basically two broad conceptions of democracy at the international level. There is democracy that some view as a norm (or at least an emerging norm) recognised by the international community (or at least by a good number of actors at the international level, including states) demanding respect and protection of democracy and its related principles at the national level[57]; and democracy as a norm that should permeate the governance not only of nation states but international institutions as well—the global democracy discourse referred to above. It is under the latter conception of democracy that this book generally falls.[58] However, even so and as has already been pointed out above and as illustrated in detail in Chap. 2, this book does not seek to argue whether or not there should be democratic governance at SADC as this is a matter that the SADC Treaty itself has adequately addressed.

The discussion on the continuing development of RECs (and their institutional characteristics) would not be complete without discussing briefly the theory of institutionalisation. This theory, whose roots are in the EU integration model, was crafted by some scholars to explain the emergence and form of regional integration.[59] This theory sees the

---

[57] See for example, T. Franck 'The emerging right to democratic governance' (1992) 86 *American Journal of International Law* 46; G.H. Fox & B.R. Roth 'Democracy and international law' (2001) 27 *Review of International Studies* 327; S. Wheatley (2010) *The democratic legitimacy of international law* 212; S. Marks 'What has become of the emerging right to democratic governance?' 2011 (22) # 2 *The European Journal of International Law* 507; J. d' Aspremont 'The rise and fall of democratic governance in international law: A reply to Susan Marks' 2011 (22) # 2 *The European Journal of International Law* 550.

[58] This is not to say however that the earlier conception of democracy should be ignored. As has already been indicated and as is elaborated on in Chap. 2, the SADC Treaty itself seeks to promote democratic institutions in Member States. Both of these conceptions of democracy are thus clearly complementary and in the context of SADC, are both specifically accommodated in the SADC Treaty.

[59] The outline of this theory carried in this and the following directly related paragraphs is a reconciled summary of the largely congruent and cumulative contributions of the following: W. Sandholtz & A. Stone Sweet 'Integration, supranational governance, and the institutionalization of the European polity' in W. Sandholtz & A. Stone Sweet (eds) *European integration and supranational governance* (1998) 1–26; M.L. Volcansek 'Courts and regional integration' in F. Snyder (ed.) 2002 *Regional and global regulation of international*

emergence of regional integration as a direct product of the pressure applied by transnational economic actors on their national governments to enter into economic transnational relations with other states in order to reduce the cost of doing cross-border business through the standardisation of trading rules, among other cost reduction measures.

The theory of institutionalisation posits that owing to the desire for sovereignty (state autonomy and control) preservation, there would initially be some reluctance on the part of national political actors to enter into transnational arrangements. However, over time, the need to see wealth creation within their borders will force national political actors to give in to the pressure exerted by the economic actors leading to a convergence of interests between national politicians and economic and social actors. The theory of institutionalisation sees the development of these transnational arrangements as an evolutionary process, initially emerging in the form of soft regionalism which is characterised by intergovernmental dialogue over largely economic cooperation matters. Disputes, if any, are settled diplomatically. Overtime, so the theory goes, there is progression from soft regionalism to hard regionalism, with the latter implicating political cooperation. This progression is said to be influenced by the production of more rules which require, among other things, a supranational institution like a third party independent regional court, for their adjudication. Thus, soft regionalism gradually transforms into hard regionalism with an integrated supranational infrastructure that can handle the continued production of rules at the regional level.

It should be noted, however, that the distinction between soft regionalism/inter-governmentalism and hard regionalism/supranationalism is a hard one to maintain since it is, as is persuasively argued by some scholars, a matter of degree and the use of either of these as a tool of governance is informed by the policy area involved. This is even the case in a highly 'supranationalised' polity like the EU, where foreign policy, for example, still remains under an intergovernmental governance framework.[60] According to Volcansek:

> most interstate relationships do not fit neatly into one or the other category, for the distinction is really a matter of degrees between the two poles. As

---

trade 166–180; M.L. Volcansek 'Courts and regional trade agreements' in J.F. Stack Jr & M.L. Volcansek (eds) *Courts crossing borders: Blurring the lines of sovereignty* (2005) 23–41.

[60] Volcansek 'Courts and regional integration' (Footnote 59 above) 167.

various regional arrangements mature and change, different aspects of the interstate relationships may fit more closely to one or the other.

Also, Schemers and Blokker who set out what they call the 'characteristics' of intergovernmental organisations and those of supranational organisations, rightly acknowledge that the term 'supranational' has so far only been used 'descriptively and has not acquired a distinct legal meaning'; and when the term is used 'in a relative sense, the distinction between supranational and intergovernmental organizations becomes blurred.'[61] The same authors argue further that even the EU, which they call an organisation 'with most supranational features' still 'depends to a considerable extent on intergovernmental cooperation,' hence their conclusion that there is no perfectly supranational organisation currently in existence.[62] Stone Sweet and Sandholtz also point out the futility of trying to characterise the EU as either intergovernmental or supranational.[63] Another author who questions the 'value' of the distinction between intergovernmentalism and supranationalism is Klabbers. According to Klabbers, even in instances where member states are deprived of the power to regulate behaviour at the domestic level in some areas, decision-making procedural strictures such as the requirement of unanimity or consensus ensure that 'the organisation does not rise above its members, but remains between its members (intergovernmental).'[64]

As intimated above, one of the elements of an 'institutionalised' regional integration polity is invariably an independent regional judiciary since it is easier for stakeholders in a regional integration set up to repose their faith in an independent third party judiciary than in uncertain political/diplomatic resolution of disputes. Indeed, Volcansek argues that a formal dispute settlement system that uses a forum such as a court is an imperative in the maintenance of 'stable and durable' regional economic cooperation.[65]

The theory of institutionalisation views the increased growth of transnational exchange as a push factor for increased transnational rules instead of national ones, leading to pressure on the (already existing) suprana-

[61] Schermers & Blocker (Footnote 2 above) 56–57.
[62] Schermers & Blocker (Footnote 2 above) 57.
[63] Stone Sweet & Sandholtz (Footnote 59 above) 7.
[64] See Klabbers (Footnote 31 above) 24–25.
[65] Volcansek 'Courts and regional integration' (Footnote 59 above), at p. 166.

tional institutions (the Commission and the Court of Justice of the European Union [CJEU], for example, in the context of the EU) to extend the reach of supranational rules to other domains of regional cooperation. With time, the theory posits, the transnational economic actors thus do not only exert pressure on their national political players but target the supranational institutions themselves either through political lobbying or litigation.

But again, just like in relation to the global democracy discourse above, the scope and focus of this book does not justify an in-depth engagement with the theory of institutionalisation.[66] The validity or otherwise of this theory, let alone its general applicability, is a matter not worth pursuing in the context of a book whose narrow focus is whether the design of the SADC institutions is in harmony with the normative values of democracy and the rule of law.

This book provides a holistic constitutional appraisal of all the major institutions of SADC and it seeks to proffer a wholesale, treaty-based reform proposal. So far, as Chaps. 3 and 4 will show, scholars and policy analysts, although not denying that SADC faces serious challenges of democracy, have in the main concentrated on limited institutions and themes, for example, SNCs; civil society participation; establishment of a regional parliament; the SADC Tribunal; elections; and the security architecture. Some scholars have in fact gone to the extent of suggesting that SADC has no capacity to engage in such a broad regional integration scheme and neither can it manage or sustain its institutional infrastructure.[67]

---

[66] These are not the only theories in the study of international organisations. For a brief but nonetheless lucid discussion of the other theories like the realist/neo-realist; functionalist/neo-functionalist; democratic peace; and republican liberalism, see Klabbers (Footnote 31 above) 25–29. These latter theories seek to explain more the reasons behind the establishment of international organisations, than the form of cooperation which is also the subject of the theory of institutionalism. As Klabbers quite rightfully asserts (at p. 31), these theories belong in the social sciences domain. He cautions against the lawyer (he uses the term legal theorist) getting involved in the discussion of theories of state cooperation, as legal scholarship should concern itself instead with matters to do with the rules of international organisations.

[67] For an extensive study of SADC, see Oosthuizen (Footnote 3 above). Oosthuizen has attempted to cover a number of aspects of SADC including its historical background; institutions; and what he perceives as the challenges and prospects of the organisation. Oosthuizen concludes that the fundamental weaknesses of SADC are general lack of capacity and human failure both at the national level in Member States and at the regional level; the consensus

Those of the scholars and policy analysts who have suggested reforms have not gone as far as suggesting institutional changes in the form of a wholesale SADC Treaty amendment or overhaul. Rather, the proposals have in the main been 'practice' oriented, based on a shift in political will—for example, opening up more space for civil society participation, funding SNCs, and improving democratic practice in Member States, and so on. The only notable treaty-based reform proposal has been with regard to the issue of the SADCPF. With regards to the SADCPF, as Chap. 4 will show, there have been explicit calls for specifically making it a SADC Treaty institution.[68]

Outside of scholarship, however, particularly in civil society advocacy, there is currently the 'SADC We Want' campaign. This campaign includes a call for a SADC institutional architecture that comprises a SADC court of justice; a regional parliament with significant oversight powers; and a revamped and empowered secretariat (the campaign wants the proposed new look secretariat to be called the 'SADC Regional Authority') 'with full competences to develop policies and direct program implementation,

decision-making process; absence of a stable and durable alliance to drive the SADC agenda; and overlapping memberships. Oosthuizen does not question the institutional makeup of SADC which he holds, at p. 320, to be 'suitable for the job at hand.' This last view is also shared by Draper who in fact advocates an even less grand framework with limited focus on trade facilitation matters and security arrangements that is 'primarily intergovernmental, with a minimum of supranational aspirations. See P. Draper 'Breaking free from Europe: Why Africa needs another model of regional integration' (2012) 47 # 1 *The International Spectator: Italian Journal of International Affairs* at p. 82. According to Draper, sub-regional groupings in Africa, including SADC, are not doing themselves any good by copying the European regional integration model that is formal and institutionally intensive. On the allegation that SADC (and Africans generally) have the tendency of emulating European institutions, Draper is not alone. See also L. Nathan 'Solidarity triumphs over democracy – The dissolution of the SADC Tribunal' (2011) 57 *Development Dialogue* 134.

[68] This does not mean that there has not been critical assessment of the SADC institutional architecture. One scholar who makes a well-articulated criticism of the SADC institutional framework (with reference particularly to the Summit and SCMCs) and the SADC lawmaking regime is Ng'ongo'la. See C. Ng'ongo'la 'The framework for regional integration in the Southern African Development Community' (2008) *University of Botswana Law Journal* 3. There has also been a limited and general call for the reduction or limitation of the powers of the Summit, in the wake of its suspension of the SADC Tribunal. See A. Saurombe 'The role of SADC institutions in implementing SADC Treaty provisions dealing with regional integration' (2012) 15 # 2 *Potchefstroom Electronic Law Journal* 476 https://doi.org/10.4314/pelj.v15i2.16 (last accessed 15 October 2014).

staffed with highly competent and skilled people, accountable to the Regional Parliament.'[69]

This book has eight chapters. Chapter 2 seeks to locate democracy and the rule of law in the SADC legal framework. It starts by examining SADC's primary legal document—the SADC Treaty. It also discusses relevant judicial decisions of the SADC Tribunal that address the relevance of these normative values in SADC. Chapter 2 also provides a general overview of the place of democracy and the rule of law in international organisations.

Chapter 3 sets out in detail the composition and functions of the norm-setting institutions of SADC: the Summit; the CoM; the SCMCs; the SCO; and the Secretariat. An effort has been made to ensure that as much detail as possible is extracted from the relevant Treaty provisions so that a clear institutional picture is depicted. This is important because any alternative institutional design that is proposed should be informed by what is currently obtaining. The classification of the norm-setting institutions as such is not so much informed by whether there is empirical evidence that indeed all such institutions are involved in the production of norms in SADC. Their inclusion is based on the positive provisions and spirit of the SADC Treaty.

Chapter 4 basically follows the same structure as Chap. 3, the only difference being that Chap. 4 focuses on those institutions that this book classifies as oversight institutions. Two of these institutions do not readily fall into this classification, either because of lack of well-defined functions in the Treaty or because the Treaty does not explicitly provide for such an institution. These two institutions are, respectively, the SNCs and the SADCPF. Their location in Chap. 4 is therefore more of an exercise of value judgment based on the spirit of the Treaty (in the case of the SNCs); and, with regards to SADCPF, the rationale is to expose its true status in the SADC scheme of things, since its place in or relationship to SADC is currently not very clear.

While domestic constitutional law in democratic states can be said to be anchored in separation of powers, there appears to be no generally

---

[69] This campaign is led by the Apex Alliance, a regional civil society organisation that was established in 2010 and comprises the SADC Council of NGOs, the Southern African Trade Unions Co-ordination Council (SATUCC), and the Fellowship of Christian Councils in Southern Africa (FOCCISA). See http://sadc-we-want.org/current-campaign/regional-court-of-justice/ (accessed 2 December 2015); http://sadc-we-want.org/about/campaign-organisations/ (accessed 2 February 2016).

acceptable institutional framework or theory on which to construct regional economic and political integration organisations. This book anchors its reform proposals in the theory of shared governance. Shared governance as an organisational theory is introduced in Chap. 5. Chapter 5 seeks to highlight the core normative elements of shared governance, rather than embark on a discussion of the concept's genealogy and its strengths and challenges in the various fields where it has been applied. In a way, what is included are shared governance's 'active ingredients' that could be of value to international institutional law. In order not to entirely divorce this study from other democracy-enhancing theories, and at the same time endeavouring to set out shared governance as a distinct concept of governance, Chap. 5 starts by briefly discussing two related democratic theories of participatory and deliberative democracy. The reason is to clearly demonstrate shared governance's distinguishing features. However, the similarities between the different theories are also highlighted, the idea being to illustrate that all these theories do in fact complement one another within the broader discourse of constitutionalism. Chapter 5 also sets out how shared governance has been differently contextualised in relation to international organisations, specifically in the EU. Coming after Chaps. 3 and 4, it is easy to appreciate the theoretical relevance of the concept of shared governance in the context of the SADC's institutional framework.

The book's comparative analysis is carried in Chap. 6. Chapter 6 sets out, in three different sections dedicated to the EAC, EU, and ECOWAS, each of these chosen organisations' institutional architecture covering the core norm-setting and oversight institutions.

Chapter 7 carries the book's recommendations. It seeks to demonstrate the applicability of the shared governance model to SADC. In a sense, Chap. 7 carries a 'model' of the alternative SADC institutional structure as envisioned by this study. However, this model covers only the main institutions as proposed in this book and how they should relate to each other in terms of norm setting, implementation, and oversight. But even then, not every pedantic detail is covered. The chapter provides only a broad outline of the composition and functions of the proposed institutions. Not only does Chap. 7 seek to demonstrate the applicability of shared governance to SADC and its democracy and the rule of law enhancing normative force—it also illustrates that shared governance is not an exclusive, alternative democratic theory as such, but rather complements (and also encompasses) other constitutionalist principles including the related principles of separation of powers and the rule of law. Following Chap. 7 is the concluding chapter—Chap. 8.

It is hoped that after reading this book, readers, in addition to grasping the core theme of the book, would have been assisted in answering these questions: What exactly is SADC in legal terms? What are its institutions? How are these institutions constituted and structured to relate to each other and to the Member States? Is there 'SADC law' that is applicable in Member States? What happens if there are any breaches of SADC law if there is in fact such law? Do SADC citizens have a legally guaranteed way of relating to SADC institutions? How are the other organisations 'similar' to SADC constituted?; and what can be learnt from them and vice versa?

CHAPTER 2

The Place of Democracy and the Rule of Law in SADC

2.1 INTRODUCTION

The objectives of SADC can be divided into three broad integration dimensions of economic and social integration; peace, security, and defence cooperation; and democracy and good governance protection and development. In this chapter, relevant provisions of the SADC Treaty on democracy and the rule of law, which are both part of the democracy and good governance dimension, are set out and discussed.

Section 2.2 looks at the provisions on democracy and the rule of law in the SADC Treaty and how they have been interpreted by the SADC Tribunal. In Sect. 2.3 a broad outline of the literature on the democratisation of international organisations is surveyed, the idea being to show that democracy as a general 'governance ideology' is now appreciated beyond the post-national setting, and that the legal framework of SADC on democracy and related constitutionalist values should be understood in this broader context.

© The Author(s) 2019
M. Nyathi, *The Southern African Development Community and Law*, https://doi.org/10.1007/978-3-319-76511-2_2

2.2   LOCATING DEMOCRACY AND THE RULE OF LAW IN THE SADC LEGAL FRAMEWORK

As indicated in Chap. 1, the SADC Treaty sets out various objectives of the organisation. These are located in Chap. 3 of the Treaty which sets out other related matters including the principles and the general undertakings.[1] In terms of article 4(c), SADC and its Member States are obligated to act in accordance with the principles of human rights, democracy, and the rule of law. By specifically mentioning SADC alongside its Member States, article 4(c) leaves no doubt that these principles are meant not just for adherence by SADC Member States at their respective domestic levels but should permeate SADC processes as well.

Not only is article 4(c) clear in its own right as regards the addressees of the principles of human rights, democracy, and the rule of law, but it is further buttressed by article 5 which sets out the objectives of the Treaty. For instance, article 5(1)(b) sets out the objective of the promotion of common political values, systems, and other shared values which are transmitted through institutions that are democratic, legitimate, and effective. It should be noted that the equivalent article in the original 1992 Treaty was very limited, only providing for the objective of '[evolving] common political values, systems and institutions.' There was no reference at all to democracy or any of the related concepts in the whole of then article 5 in which all the objectives of SADC were set out. The objective of the development of democratic, legitimate, and effective institutions introduced by the 2001 amendment was clearly a break with the past and was unquestionably intended to infuse these values into the whole regional integration scheme.[2]

While article 5(1)(b) does not specifically tie this objective to SADC and its Member States in the same manner that article 4(c) categorically states that the principles of human rights, democracy, and the rule of law apply to both SADC and its Member States, this is undoubtedly the case.

---

[1] The principles are set out in art 4; the objectives in art 5; and the general undertakings in art 6.

[2] Another provision worth mentioning is art 5(1)(c). It provides as one of the objectives of SADC the consolidation, defence, and maintenance of 'democracy, peace, security and stability.' This provision substituted the original 1992 SADC Treaty art 5(1)(c) which was limited to the promotion and defence of 'peace and security.' Art 5(1)(c) however seems to be tied to the peace and security dimension of SADC. What is important to note though is the deliberate effort to formally infuse the democratic element even in this integration area.

A contrary interpretation of article 5(1)(b) would clearly lead to an absurdity. Such an interpretation, other than unduly narrowing the scope of the objective, would have the awkward result of suggesting that SADC as an organisation can legitimately promote democratic and related values and practices in its Member States, while its own institutions and processes are not democratic. Indeed, any couching of article 5(1)(b) along the same line as article 4(c) would only have been a result of overkill in draftsmanship.

The principles in the SADC Treaty, buttressed as they are by the article 5(1)(b) objective, are not mere aspirations, but legally protected values. In addition to being cast in peremptory terms, there is an additional protective wall (at least at the domestic level, but arguably at the level of SADC as well) built around the principles (and the objectives). Article 6(1) of the SADC Treaty provides that Member States are under an obligation:

> to adopt adequate measures to promote the achievement of the objectives of SADC, and shall refrain from taking any measure likely to jeopardise the sustenance of its principles, the achievement of its objectives and the implementation of the provisions of (the) Treaty.

The SADC Tribunal had occasion to pronounce itself on articles 4(c) and 6(1) in some of cases that came before it. In the *Campbell* matter,[3] it held that Member States, by virtue of articles 4(c) and 6(1) of the SADC Treaty, are under an obligation to respect, protect, and promote what it called the 'twin fundamental rights' embraced by the concept of the rule of law—access to the courts and the right to a fair hearing.[4] While the Tribunal was in that case dealing with a Member State's obligations under the SADC Treaty, its reasoning clearly applies with equal force to SADC as an organisation especially with regard to article 4(c). In fact, in a related matter dealing with an application for interim measures pending the determination on the merits in the 'main' *Campbell* matter,[5] the Tribunal affirmed the reach of article 4(c) by categorically holding that:

> This means that SADC as a collectivity and as individual member states are under a legal obligation to respect and protect human rights of SADC

---

[3] *Mike Campbell (Pvt) Ltd and others v Republic of Zimbabwe* SADC (T) 2/2007) (decided on 28 November 2008). The judgment is discussed in detail in Chap. 4, Sect. 4.2.

[4] See particularly para 36 of the Campbell judgment, Footnote 3 above.

[5] Footnote 3 above.

citizens. They also have to ensure that there is democracy and the rule of law within the region.[6]

In another case, *Barry L.T. Gondo and 8 others v the Republic of Zimbabwe,*[7] applicants had been awarded various damages against the government of Zimbabwe in various courts in Zimbabwe owing to violence inflicted upon them by the members of Zimbabwean Republic Police and/or the Zimbabwean National Army. The government of Zimbabwe did not comply with the judgments nor could applicants execute against the government of Zimbabwe because of a provision in the State Liabilities Act which protected the property of the government of Zimbabwe from execution and attachment or any other process to satisfy a judgment debt. The Tribunal ruled that the relevant section of the State Liabilities Act breached the rights to an effective remedy, access to an independent and impartial court or tribunal and fair hearing. The Tribunal also held that the impugned provision contravened the right to equality before the law and the right to equal protection of the law and accordingly incompatible with Zimbabwe's obligations under Articles 4(c) and 6(1) of the SADC Treaty.

In *Luke Tembani v Republic of Zimbabwe,*[8] the Tribunal was asked to make a determination on the legality of a certain Zimbabwean statute and the then Constitution of Zimbabwe that authorised a contractual creditor (a parastatal bank) to dispose of a debtor's property pledged as security without recourse to courts of law. In the Tribunal's view, the contractual creditor:

> had acted against the principles of natural justice in that the Applicant was not only denied the right of a hearing before an independent and impartial court or tribunal where he could contest the amount of the debt allegedly owed by him and the value of his farm which he claimed had been sold by ABZ at little more than half of its actual price, but that ABZ also became a judge in its own cause.[9]

The Tribunal found in favour of applicant in these terms:

---

[6] *Mike Campbell (Pvt) Ltd and another v Republic of Zimbabwe* SADC(T) 2/2007 (decided on 13 December 2007).

[7] SADC (T) 05/2008 (decided on 9 December 2010).

[8] SADC (T) 07/2008 (decided on 14 August 2009).

[9] Para 41 of the judgment.

We consequently hold that the Applicant has been denied access to the courts and deprived of a fair hearing, in contravention of Articles 4(c) and 6(1) of the Treaty, when his mortgaged property was seized and sold ... since both section 38(2) of the Act and section 16(7)(d) of the Constitution of the Respondent, which sanctions that provision of the Act, contravene Articles 4(c) and 6(1) of the Treaty.[10]

In arriving at its decision, the Tribunal referred to and affirmed the decision of the South African Constitutional Court in *Chief Lesapo v North West Agricultural Bank and Another.*[11] In that case, the Constitutional Court of South Africa had this to say:

A trial or hearing before a court or tribunal is not an end in itself. It is a means of determining whether a legal obligation exists and whether the coercive power of the State can be invoked to enforce an obligation, or prevent an unlawful act being committed. It serves other purposes as well, including that of the resolution of disputes, and preventing remedies being sought through self-help. No one is entitled to take the law into her or his own hands. Self-help, in this sense, is inimical to a society in which the rule of law prevails....[12]

A far more elucidated rationale of having a fair trial and a court sanctioned execution process is however found in the following South African Constitutional Court's dictum which was embraced by the SADC Tribunal:

Execution is a means of enforcing a judgment or order of court and is incidental to the judicial process. It is regulated by statute and the Rules of Court and is subject to the supervision of the court which has inherent jurisdiction to stay the execution if the interests of justice so require. If the debt itself is disputed, the seizure of property in execution of the debt must equally be disputed. To permit a creditor to seize property of a debtor without an order of court and to cause it to be sold by the creditor's agent on the condition stipulated by the creditor to secure payment of a debt denies to the debtor the protection of the judicial process and the supervision exercised by the court through its Rules over the process of execution.[13]

---

[10] Para 44 of the judgment.

[11] 2001 (1) SA 409 CC.

[12] Para 11 of the *Chief Lesapo* judgment (Footnote 11 above) and para 36 of the SADC Tribunal judgment.

[13] Paras 13 and 14 of the *Chief Lesapo* judgment (Footnote 11 above) and para 36 of the SADC Tribunal judgment.

In a way, in addition to the SADC Tribunal seeking to protect and advance the values of democracy and the rule of law set out in the SADC Treaty, it also tried to establish itself as an agent of legal harmonisation in the SADC region. Indeed, after setting out that the issue for determination was whether the impugned statutory provisions conformed to articles 4(c) and 6(1) of the SADC Treaty, the SADC Tribunal indicated that it would be guided in its determination by sub-articles (4) and (5) of article 6 of the SADC Treaty which provide, respectively, that Member States shall take all steps necessary to ensure the uniform application of the SADC Treaty; and that they shall take all necessary steps to accord the Treaty the force of national law. Unfortunately, the SADC Tribunal did not use the opportunity presented by the case to set out what these provisions fully entailed. One gets the feeling that the SADC Tribunal maybe hoped that SADC Member States would either proactively try to align their legal regimes with the SADC Treaty or do so after clarification/affirmation of SADC law by the Tribunal's judicial interpretation in different fields on a case by case basis.

The above are not the only provisions on democracy and the rule of law in the SADC Treaty. Among the preamble recitals is the 'need to involve the peoples of Region centrally in the process of development and integration, particularly through the guarantee of democratic rights, observance of human rights and the rule of law.'

Over and above the treaty provisions on the place of human rights, democracy and the rule of law in SADC, these principles have also been taken on board in programme implementation activities. The Regional Indicative Strategic Development Plan (RISDP), the strategic programmatic long-term blue print meant to provide time-framed strategic direction to SADC programmes,[14] makes several references to democracy, human rights, and the rule of law and other principles such as good governance and transparency. By way of example, item 1.5.3 of the RISDP which deals with prerequisites for deeper integration and poverty eradication boldly asserts that '[g]ood political and economic governance, entrenched in a culture of democracy, transparency and respect for the rule of law, represent the bedrock upon which (the) RISDP is premised.'

---

[14] This is touted as a 'comprehensive development and implementation framework guiding the regional integration agenda over a period of fifteen years from 2005–2020.' See http://www.sadc.int/about-sadc/overview/strategic-pl/regional-indicative-strategic-development-plan/ (last accessed 13 April 2014).

While SADC's legal framework can be consulted to locate the values of democracy and the rule of law, this does not lessen the difficulty of assessing whether the design of the institutions of SADC itself is democratic. This is because the SADC legal instruments do not set out the elements of these values which could be used to benchmark institutional design. Lack of consensus in scholarship on the status (and nature) of democracy and the rule of law at the international level, including in the governance of international organisations, does not help matters. However, through the use of comparative analysis, a fair assessment and benchmarking of SADC's institutional design can be made by looking at how other RECs have designed their institutions to take into account these values.

It is necessary to note that the letter of the SADC legal instruments with regard to the values of democracy and the rule of law, undefined as they are, is generally in line with the evolving trend in which constitutionalism is now advocated by many as a central part of the governance of international organisations. For example, the International Law Association has advocated the improvement of accountability of international organisations through a number of ways—adherence to the principles of constitutionality and institutional balance; respect for such other principles as stating reasons for decisions; procedural regularity; objectivity and impartiality; and the observance of related principles and practices that fall under the principle of good governance such as transparency in decision-making and implementation processes; participatory decision-making; access to information, and a well-functioning international civil service.[15] The following sub-section provides an overview of the subject of democracy and the rule of law in international organisations.

---

[15] International Law Association Berlin Conference (2004) on Accountability of International Organisations Final Report. See also A. Peters 'Membership in the global constitutional community' in J. Klabbers et al. (2009) *The constitutionalization of international law* 211. Also, the United Nations General Assembly has recently adopted a resolution which makes the rule of law part of the governance of international organisations as well. See the 24 September 2012 United Nations General Assembly Resolution A/RES 67/1- Declaration of the High-level Meeting of the General Assembly on the Rule of Law at the National and International Levels. The Resolution is available at http://www.un.org/en/ga/67/resolutions.shtml (accessed 18 January 2015).

2.3   DEMOCRACY AND THE RULE OF LAW
IN INTERNATIONAL ORGANISATIONS

Democracy is now seen by a number of scholars as a central concern of transnational governance.[16] Some of the scholars also acknowledge, based on empirical evidence, the link between policy failures at the international level and absence of democratic governance.[17] While it may sound presumptuous to categorically state that there can be no sustainable development in the absence of democracy, it cannot be denied that there is a link between sustainable development (one of the objectives of SADC) and the existence of effective, strong, accountable, and legitimate institutions of governance.[18]Therefore, efforts to democratise regional economic communities like SADC should not cease simply because their constituent members or the majority of such members may not be democratic.[19]

---

[16]See, for example, G. de Búrca 'Developing democracy beyond the state' (2007–2008) 46 *Columbia Journal of Transnational Law* 226; R. Marchetti (2008) *Global democracy: For and against: Ethical theory, institutional design and social struggles.*

[17]De Búrca (Footnote 16 above) 225.

[18]S. Zondi 'Governance and social policy in the SADC region: An issues analysis' (2009) *Working Paper Series No. 2* Planning Division, Development Bank of Southern Africa 15 http://www.lead4change.org/downloads/module_2/Zondi%20DBSA%20Paper%20 on%20SADC%20-%20Governance%20and%20Policy.pdf (accessed 14 December 2013) 5. Although Zondi makes reference to literature dealing mainly with the role of the state in development, the views he expresses seem to apply with equal to governance at the regional level.

[19]Some scholars view the reluctance to embrace democracy in SADC as reflective of what obtains at the national level in Member States where there are generally undemocratic regimes. See P. Draper 'Breaking free from Europe: Why Africa needs another model of regional integration' (2012) 47 # 1 *The International Spectator: Italian Journal of International Affairs* 71; L. Nathan 'Solidarity triumphs over democracy – The dissolution of the SADC Tribunal' (2011) 57 *Development Dialogue* 133; M. Killander 'Legal harmonization in Africa: Taking stock and moving forward' in L. Fioramonti (ed.) *Regionalism in a changing world: Comparative perspectives in the new global order* (2013) 95. Indeed, only a third of SADC Member States have been classified as liberal democratic (Botswana, Mauritius, Namibia, Seychelles, and South Africa), with others falling under different classifications like electoral democratic; electoral authoritarian; and closed authoritarian. See K. Matlosa 'Elections and conflict management' in C. Saunders (ed.) *Region-building in Southern Africa: Progress, problems and prospects* (2012) 79 and the references thereunder. According to Nathan, the lack of political congruency in SADC means there would never be shared community norms, except that of 'strict respect for sovereignty.' See L. Nathan 'The disbanding of the SADC Tribunal: A cautionary tale' (2013) 35 # 4 *Human Rights Quarterly* 872.

It is indeed difficult to deny that a framework of governance that provides for concentration of power in the hands of a few without accountability and checks and balances can only lead to a weak system of governance which cannot efficiently (and sustainably) deliver public goods, resulting in poverty and underdevelopment.[20] The development and promotion of democracy at the regional level in SADC through the creation of democratic regional institutions, in addition to being part of the principles and objectives of SADC, is thus clearly an endeavour worth pursuing in its own right, as it serves to guarantee the attainment of the other goals set out in the SADC Common Agenda.

Democracy (and constitutionalism) is no longer relevant only in relation to the 'bounded' nation state, but can be transposed onto the international plane. International organisations are thus seen as also subject to 'constitutional guarantees such as political accountability, the rule of law and protection of human rights.'[21]

According to Ulfstein

Democratic control over law-making is fundamental in national constitutions. Likewise, international 'legislation' in the form of decisions binding on member states should ideally be adopted by democratic organs composed of directly elected representatives, and supported by public debate, transparency, and the participation of actors from civil society.[22]

Ulfstein makes a similar argument about the rule of law:

While the respect for the rule of law traditionally has been a requirement addressed to the domestic legal order, the relevance of the principle is increasingly acknowledged also as part of international law.[23]

There certainly does not appear to be any compelling reason to limit the force of democratic control to the domestic sphere. It may be important to point out here that any intergovernmental project involves public goods. The participants are public agents seized with public time. The meetings and all their related costs are met by public resources financed,

---

[20] Zondi (Footnote 18 above).

[21] G. Ulfstein 'Institutions and competencies' in J. Klabbers et al. *The constitutionalizaion of international Law* (2009) 51. See also, generally, De Búrca (Footnote 16 above) 221–278.

[22] Ulfstein (Footnote 21 above) 55.

[23] Ulfstein (Footnote 21 above) 59. See also the many references thereunder.

in most cases, by the individual Member States. Over and above this, and particularly with regard to RECs, their establishment is directly linked to the need to maximise the welfare and happiness of their respective citizens. This on its own is enough justification for the proposition that democracy should be embedded in all the processes of the organisation, be they of a decision-making or of implementation nature.

Whilst there are growing calls for the need for democracy at the international level, including among the states themselves,[24] there are some within the broad pro post-national democracy scholarship who are reluctant to push for democratic decision-making in all international organisations, or the general control of decision-making powers at the international level. There is an argument for relative democratic control of decision-making at the international level that is confined to only those organisations that make 'authoritative' or 'binding' decisions. This argument for a limited approach is made by, among others, De Búrca. De Búrca's concern is the need for democracy in those international organisations that make 'authoritative rules and policies outside the state and which lie beyond the control of national democratic and constitutional structures.'[25] There is thus an evident reluctance on the part of some scholars to embrace democracy beyond the state as a general governance norm.

While it is not the intention of this book to fully engage the subject of the relative application of democracy in international organisations, it is necessary to point out that differentiating between authoritative rule-making organisations and (to the extent that they are different) those that make binding decisions on the one hand, and those that do not make authoritative or binding rules on the other hand, is problematic in two major respects: first, it quite clearly constrains rather than enhance democracy as a general governance ideal; and second, it rests on a tenuous assumption that it is always apparent, at the time of decision-making, that

---

[24] See Resolution A/RES 67/1 (Footnote 15 above).

[25] De Búrca (Footnote 16 above) 221. See also Ulfstein (Footnote 21 above); S Wheatley (2010) *The democratic legitimacy of international law* 92, 95. A similar argument is also made by H.G. Schermers & N.M. Blokker (2011) *International institutional law: Unity within diversity*. According to Schermers & Blokker, '[o]rgans for advice and control (in international organisations) are necessary, particularly when policy-making organs have the power to take binding majority decision.' They also state, writing in the context of the need for judicial control (discussed in detail in the introductory part of Sect. 4.2 in Chap. 4), that '[t]he need for judicial control is **strongest** where international organizations may take binding decisions by majority vote' (own emphasis). See pp. 407, 436 respectively.

a decision is either authoritative/binding or non-authoritative/non-binding. Once a decision is made, it can play itself out in a way that was not initially anticipated by the decision maker. For example, a supposedly authoritative/binding decision made by an international organisation may simply be ignored by national actors; while on the other hand, an apparently unauthoritative/non-binding decision may in due course assume such a far-reaching influence resulting in its transformation into an 'authoritative'/'binding' norm.[26]

That the distinction between authoritative/binding and non-authoritative/non-binding lawmaking international organisations may be difficult to sustain is evidenced by an apparent concession by De Búrca on the need for democracy as a general normative value in international organisations, although admittedly her focus is on the International Monetary Fund (IMF) and the World Bank. While discussing the efforts to reform such transnational organisations as the IMF and the World Bank, she argues:

> So far, most reform proposals have been directed towards improving the efficiency, effectiveness and output of such bodies. Although these are laudable goals ... a core dimension of what is at stake is democracy. On the one hand, the very existence of these arenas of decision making implies a 'felt need' for regulation at the transnational level, suggesting that the problems to which they aim to respond are not adequately addressed by state based and local decision making.[27]

There is therefore a good case for the development of a feasible alternative democratic institutional model which should address, among other things, SADC's current main Achilles' heel—unbridled executivism, which, as the sections that discuss various institutions of SADC in Chaps. 3 and 4 show, not only leads to absence of control in decision-making and accountability,

---

[26] As noted by Krisch and Kingsbury, some regulations emanating from the exercise of global governance 'may be highly effective despite (their) predominantly non-binding forms.' See N. Krisch & B. Kingsbury 'Introduction: Global governance and global administrative law in the international legal order' (2006) 17 # 1 *European Journal of International Law* 1, 4. See also J. Klabbers (2009) *An introduction to international institutional law*, p. 182, who shares the view that 'non-legally binding instruments may be quite as effective (or ineffective) as legally binding ones.' See also the reference thereunder, which is in fact a different work by Kingsbury.

[27] De Búrca (Footnote 16 above) 103–104.

but stifles conversation and debate and is at odds with SADC's principles and objectives.

But establishing that the legal framework of SADC accommodates the normative values of democracy and the rule of law and that these values are now seen as forming part of the governance matrix of international organisations is, as has already been indicated, itself not enough to address the question of democratic institutional design. What elements of democracy should be reflected in an international organisation, in particular an REC? This question is even more relevant because, as has already been stated, the SADC Treaty does not define what democracy is. With regards to the rule of law, if indeed there is controversy on the exact nature of the elements of this principle, it does not come close to that which pursues democracy.

But a brief digression to discuss the rule of law may suffice here. The principle of the rule of law has traditionally come to be accepted as comprising the following elements: no one and no organ is beyond the law, that is, the use of power is subject to the constraints imposed by the law; the absence of arbitrary power; equality before the law; and protection of rights by independent courts.[28] The rule of law is thus closely tied to, or inseparable from, constitutionalism.[29]

Built into the framework of the rule of law, and as identified by Nollkaemper,[30] is the element of legal accountability of those public powers/authorities that contravene their legal obligations. As Nollkaemper asserts, while legal accountability is on its own a feature of good governance and can be used as a tool for the control of the exercise of public power, it is not enough to guarantee that those who wield public power will act in terms of the set rules; and thus instead of the rule of law being solely preoccupied with guaranteeing or insisting on positive prior compliance with the law by those who occupy public office, it also stands to provide 'protection in those cases where those who wield public power choose not to comply with their obligations.'[31] Thus, in the event of non-compliance, those that are aggrieved have recourse to the law. In other words, the rule of law is as much about the guarantee of legal remedies as

---

[28] G. Ulfstein (Footnote 21 above) 60.

[29] See J. Klabbers 'Setting the scene' in J. Klabbers et al. *The constitutionalization of international law* (2009) 3.

[30] A. Nollkaemper (2012) *National courts and the international rule of law* 5.

[31] Nollkaemper (as above).

it is about ensuring positive compliance with the law. Understood in this way, the rule of law can thus only thrive where judicial review is guaranteed. Therefore, there is no rule of law to talk about in the absence of an independent, impartial, and effective judiciary.

The rule of law is inseparably linked to and should emanate from democratic infrastructure and processes.[32] Conversely, in the event of questions surrounding adherence or otherwise to democratic practice, it is the rules of law that are invoked in order to arrive at the relevant determination.[33] The rule of law is thus an integral part of democracy in the absence of which there is no democracy to talk about.[34]

While ordinarily the rule of law has been considered a matter of domestic law, it is, as already pointed out above, becoming more and more relevant at the international level, largely due to the increase in decision-making powers of international organisations thereby necessitating the control of such powers.[35] The relevance of the rule of law at the international level has also not escaped the attention of the United Nations, where the rule of law is now seen as relevant both at the national and international levels.[36] This position coincides with that of Ulfstein, who considers domestic constitutional guarantees such as separation of powers, procedural safeguards, and judicial review (themselves a *sine qua non* of the rule of law) as relevant at the international level.[37] The primary concern of the rule of law therefore is the prevention of arbitrary power and the circumscription and limitation of discretion.[38]

---

[32] J.H.H. Weiler 'The geology of international law—governance, democracy and legitimacy' (2004) 64 *ZaöRV* 547.

[33] As above.

[34] Weiler (Footnote 32 above) 562. On the relationship between (and inseparability of) democracy, rule of law, and human rights, see also R.A. Dahl 'Can international organisations be democratic? A skeptic's view' in I. Shapiro & C. Hacker-Cordon (eds) *Democracy's edges* (1999) 32; UNGA Resolution A/RES 67/1 (Footnote 15 above); A. Timmer et al. 'Critical analysis of the EU's conceptualisation and operationalisation of the concepts of human rights, democracy, and rule of law (2014), a report prepared under the *Fostering human rights among European policies (Frame)* project running from 1 May 2013 to 30 April 2017, available at http://www.fp7-frame.eu (accessed 23 June 2015).

[35] Ulfstein (Footnote 21 above) 59–60; Wheatley (Footnote 25 above) 194, 195; Nollkaemper (Footnote 30 above).

[36] See generally, UNGA Resolution A/RES/67/1 (Footnote 15 above).

[37] Ulfstein (Footnote 21 above) 80.

[38] Peters (Footnote 15 above) 174.

The rule of law is thus part of constitutionalism. But what exactly is constitutionalism, and of what relevance are constitutionalist principles in international institutional law? Again, a brief overview would suffice here. In domestic law, a constitutional order is basically a system of governance that sets out the rules to be followed and controls exercise of governmental power. It is thus both a 'prescriptive' and 'proscriptive' system of governance.[39] Among the elements of a constitutionalist framework of governance are the protection of fundamental rights of citizens and a system of separation of powers between the courts and other institutions.[40] In other words, a constitutional order does not end with the creation of public authorities, but limits and controls the powers of such authorities through predetermined rules.[41] Some define constitutionalism as 'a commitment on the part of any given political community to be governed by constitutional rules and principles.'[42]

Constitutionalism in the context of international organisations is not very different from a constitutionalised domestic order: it provides for separation of powers not only between an organisation and its member states, but also among the institutions or organs of the organisation; and it also provides for judicial review by an independent judiciary.[43] Separation of powers is 'essential to the efficacy of the [organisation], to its ability to adjust to changing priorities and issues, and to prevent it from growing into a Leviathan.'[44] Thus, the same reasons that underlie the need for constitutionalism at the domestic level are applicable at the international level.

The constitutionalisation of international organisations seems to be linked to the ever-evolving nature of international law. While in the past, international law was the 'law of nations' and only affected the individual in exceptional circumstances like criminal liability for war crimes and

[39] See Klabbers (Footnote 29 above) 9. See also J.J. Worley 'Deliberative constitutionalism' (2009) *Brigham Young Law Review* 436 for a similar view.

[40] Klabbers, as above.

[41] As above.

[42] A. Stone Sweet 'Constitutionalism, legal pluralism, and international regimes' (2009) 16 # 2, *Indiana Journal of Global Legal Studies* 626. According to Stone Sweet, 'international law and politics' and 'law and politics in general' are similar concepts and thus there is no need to devise or design new concepts specifically for international law and politics.

[43] T.M. Franck 'International institutions: Why constitutionalize?' Preface to J.L. Dunoff & J.P. Trachtman (eds) *Ruling the world? Constitutionalism, international law, and global governance* (2009) xiv.

[44] As above.

genocide,[45] this position is slowly changing—international law now affects individuals directly, and at times in ways that are comparable to domestic law.[46] This change in the nature and reach of international law indeed provides an additional basis for constitutionalism on the post-national stage.

While the legal constraints on the exercise of public power resulting from the constitutionalisation of international law have usually tended to be associated with the interests of the individual, even states are protected by the same principles of constitutionalism, for example, the need for an independent judiciary, in their interstate relations.[47] Adherence to principles of constitutionalism by international organisations is also important to avoid the danger of marginalisation/exclusion and abuse of less powerful states by the more powerful ones.[48]As is the case at the domestic level therefore, the normative value of constitutionalism on the international plane basically entails legal constraints on the exercise of the powers of international organisations.[49]

The scholarship on the constitutionalisation of international law is now rich and appears to be still growing. Many scholars have contributed to this

---

[45] I. Brownlie *Principles of public international law* (1972) 38. The choice of this older volume has been deliberate—it largely represents conceptions of classical international law.

[46] A good example is the *Kadi* case [CFI, case T-315/O1, Kadi v Council and Commission, ECR 2005, 11–3649, ECJ (21 September 2005) http://curia.europa.eu/juris/showPdf.jsf ;jsessionid=9ea7d2dc30db101497068bf4402a9819f049fe2889f1.e34KaxiLc3qMb40Rch0 SaxuNaNf0?text=&docid=65739&pageIndex=0&doclang=en&mode=req&dir=&occ=first &part=1&cid=28212 last accessed 12 September 2014); case C-402/05 P, Kadi v Council and Commission, (Grand Chamber, 3 September 2008] in which both chambers of the CJEU had to deal with the question of the legality of a Security Council resolution directing the freezing of assets of individuals residing in the European Union without regard to due process.

[47] For example, the border dispute between Botswana and Namibia over the Kasikili / Sedudu Island in the Chobe River was resolved judicially by the International Court of Justice. See *Case Concerning Kasikili/Sedudu Island (Namibia/Botswana)*: ICJ Reports 1999, judgment of 13 December 1999. See also G.H. Oosthuizen *The Southern African Development Community: The organization, its policies and prospects* (2006) 85.

[48] Peters (Footnote 15 above) 211; Ulfstein (Footnote 21 above) 60. See also Schermers & Blocker (Footnote 25 above) 7 who note that 'to some extent, in the horizontally structured international society, international institutional law is what constitutional and administrative law is in the vertically structured domestic society.'

[49] As above.

discourse. They include, among many others, Dunoff and Trachtman[50]; Kennedy[51]; Paulus[52]; Doyle[53]; Fassbender[54]; Walker[55]; Dunoff[56]; Trachtman[57]; Gardbaum[58]; Kumm[59]; Halberstam[60]; Maduro[61]; and Besson.[62]

The scholarship on constitutionalism (at the international level) presented by the scholars mentioned in the above paragraph is multifaceted,

[50] J.L. Dunoff & J.P. Trachtman 'A functional approach to international constitutionalization' in J.L. Dunoff & J.P. Trachtman (eds) *Ruling the world? Constitutionalism, international law and global governance* (2009) 3–35.

[51] D. Kennedy 'The mystery of global governance' in J.L. Dunoff & J.P. Trachtman (eds) *Ruling the world? Constitutionalism, international law and global governance* (2009) 37–68.

[52] A.L. Paulus 'The international legal system as a constitution' in J.L. Dunoff & J.P. Trachtman (eds) *Ruling the world? Constitutionalism, international law and global governance* (2009) 69–109.

[53] M.W. Doyle 'The UN Charter – A global constitution?' in J.L. Dunoff & J.P. Trachtman (eds) *Ruling the world? Constitutionalism, international law and global governance* (2009) 113–132.

[54] B. Fassbender 'Rediscovering a forgotten constitution: Notes on the place of the UN Charter in the international legal order" in J.L. Dunoff & J.P. Trachtman (eds) *Ruling the world? Constitutionalism, international law and global governance* (2009) 133–147.

[55] N. Walker 'Reframing EU constitutionalism' in J.L. Dunoff & J.P. Trachtman (eds) *Ruling the world? Constitutionalism, international law and global governance* (2009) 149–176.

[56] J.L. Dunoff 'The politics of international constitutions: The curious case of the World Trade Organization' in J.L. Dunoff & J.P. Trachtman (eds) *Ruling the world? Constitutionalism, international law and global governance* (2009) 178–205.

[57] J.P. Trachtman 'Constitutional economics of the World Trade Organization' in J.L. Dunoff & J.P. Trachtman (eds) *Ruling the world? Constitutionalism, international law and global governance* (2009) 206–229.

[58] S. Gardbaum 'Human rights and international constitutionalism' in J.L. Dunoff & J.P. Trachtman (eds) *Ruling the world? Constitutionalism, international law and global governance* (2009) 233–257.

[59] M. Kumm 'The cosmopolitan turn in constitutionalism: On the relationship between constitutionalism in and beyond the state' in J.L. Dunoff & J.P. Trachtman (eds) *Ruling the world? Constitutionalism, international law and global governance* (2009) 258–324.

[60] D. Halberstam 'Constitutional heterarchy: The centrality of conflict in the European Union and the United States' in J.L. Dunoff & J.P. Trachtman (eds) *Ruling the world? Constitutionalism, international law and global governance* (2009) 326–355.

[61] M.P. Maduro 'Courts and pluralism: Essay on a theory of judicial adjudication in the context of legal and constitutional pluralism' in J.L. Dunoff & J.P. Trachtman (eds) *Ruling the world? Constitutionalism, international law and global governance* (2009) 356–379.

[62] S. Besson 'Whose Constitution(s)? International law, constitutionalism and democracy' in J.L. Dunoff & J.P. Trachtman (eds) *Ruling the world? Constitutionalism, international law and global governance* (2009) 381–407.

ranging from 'unravelling' the 'mystery of global governance'[63] to such diverse topics as human rights and international constitutionalism[64]; and courts and pluralism[65]; with a lot of other subjects in between. Indeed, the constitutional lens seems to be now a popular tool used by some scholars in looking at international organisations including organisations as diverse as the World Trade Organisation and the United Nations.[66] Whether the organisation viewed through this constitutional lens is finally determined to be a constitutionalised entity, or it fails the constitutional test, is another matter altogether.[67]

But back to the question of what elements of the normative values of democracy and the rule of law should be infused into institutional design and how? With regards to democracy, lack of its definition in the SADC Treaty and lack of consensus in scholarship on such matters as its applicability at international institutional law and what elements of it should be accommodated in international organisations are matters with little bearing on the focus of this book. With the benefit of comparative analysis,[68] one dimension of democracy—separation of powers, now seems to permeate a number of RECs. The institutional design of SADC can thus be easily assessed through the lens of this single dimension. This is not to say that other elements of democracy cannot be used as institutional design benchmarks. They can, and in fact they should. But that should depend on a particular research focus.

What exactly constitute separation of powers as a concept of democracy? The doctrine of separation of powers is a concept that originates from domestic governance whereby the state is divided into different branches each with separate and independent powers and areas of

---

[63] Kennedy (Footnote 51 above).

[64] Gardbaum (Footnote 58 above).

[65] Maduro (Footnote 61 above).

[66] Dunoff (Footnote 56 above); Trachtman (Footnote 57 above); & Doyle (Footnote 53 above) respectively.

[67] Different conclusions are sometimes reached by different scholars. For example, while Trachtman (Footnote 57 above) views the World Trade Organisation as a constitutionalised international trade regime, Dunoff reaches a different conclusion. According to the latter, there is 'little evidence that, at present, the trade system should properly be considered a constitutionalized regime.' According to Dunoff, the WTO has, among other things that he notes as negating a constitutionalised order, 'no constitutional court, no constitutional assembly, and no readily available constitutional moment.' See Dunoff (Footnote 56 above) 180, 181.

[68] See generally Chap. 6.

responsibility and competence, although in practice, these different branches interrelate.[69] The separation of powers doctrine is meant to prevent any one branch of the state from having more power than the other branches. This generally enduring doctrine espouses the notion of splitting power between several bodies, specifically the legislature; the executive; and judicial arms of state, with the hope that each will check the excesses of the others.[70]

The doctrine of separation of powers is however no longer confined to the domain of domestic constitutional law. The applicability of this doctrine at international law, especially at the regional level, has been recognised, with some arguing, for example, that it is at the core of the EU institutional framework.[71]

[69] D.P. Kommers *The constitutional jurisprudence of the Federal Republic of Germany* (1997) 116.

[70] J. Alder *Constitutional and Administrative Law* (1989) 53.

[71] See generally G. Conway 'Recovering a separation of powers in the European Union' (2011) 17#3 *European Law Journal* 304–322. According to Conway, the doctrine of institutional balance, which has been developed by the CJEU as a substitute for the separation of powers doctrine, is not a good alternative since it is 'too vague and indeterminate.' See also H.P. Hestermeyer 'The implementation of European Union law,' an unpublished and unpaginated paper presented at the workshop *The Implementation of International Law in South Africa – Strengthening the Rule of Law by Following the German Model?* 16–17 May 2014, Faculty of Law, University of Pretoria in cooperation with the Max Planck Institute for Comparative Public and International Law, the Konrad Adenauer Stiftung/Foundation & the Alexander von Humboldt Stiftung/Foundation. Without referring to the term 'separation of powers,' Hestermeyer succinctly describes the makeup of the EU today thus: 'Roughly speaking, Parliament and Council are the legislature, the Commission the Executive and the Court the judiciary of the Union.' See also A. Moravcsik 'In defence of the "Democratic deficit": Reassessing legitimacy in the European Union' (2002) 40 # 1 *Journal of Common Market Studies* 609. Moravcsik does not struggle to assert that the EU framework of governance is subject to the doctrine of separation of powers. He points out: 'Yet the EU's ability to act, even in those areas where it enjoys clear competence, is constrained by institutional checks and balances, notably the separation of powers, a multi-level structure of decision-making and a plural executive.' Also, as the comparative analysis in Chap. 6 will show, there is, in both the EAC and ECOWAS, relative separation of powers, to varying degrees, between the executive political organs/institutions and the parliamentary and judicial bodies.

2.4   CONCLUSION

In addition to setting out the provisions of the SADC Treaty that deal with democracy and the rule of law, this chapter has gone further to illustrate that over and above being accommodated in the SADC legal framework, these normative values are now generally being seen as part of the governance of international organisations, although there still remains contestation with regards to their exact nature (this is particularly so with regards to democracy) and the extent of their accommodation in post-national settings.

Having established therefore that the SADC Treaty has as part of its principles, objectives and general undertakings, the protection and development of the normative values of democracy and the rule of law, both in collective SADC processes and at the level of individual SADC Member States; and having illustrated that this is very much in accordance with developments in international institutional law in general; it now remains to discuss and critique the institutional design of the SADC institutions, starting with those that have been designated as 'rule-making/norm-setting' institutions. This is what Chap. 3 below is about.

CHAPTER 3

Rule-making/Norm-Setting Institutions in SADC

3.1 INTRODUCTION

Article 9 of the SADC Treaty establishes various institutions of SADC.[1] These institutions can be divided into rule-making/norm-setting and oversight institutions. Of these, the Summit; the Council of Ministers (CoM); the Sectoral and Cluster Ministerial Committees (SCMCs); the Standing Committee of Officials (SCO); and the Organ on Politics, Defence and Security Co-operation (OPDS) are clearly endowed, to varying degrees, with rule-making or norm-setting powers. The Secretariat, although largely an administrative institution, is to some limited degree as shall be shown in the section dealing with it below, part of SADC's norm-setting infrastructure as well. It should be noted, however, that to a large extent, these norm-setting institutions have implementation powers as well.

The distinction between norm-setting and oversight institutions is not an apparent textual distinction but rather derives from the content of the powers accorded to the different institutions by the Treaty. It should also be noted (as will be demonstrated in Chap. 4) that some of the institutions that this study has designated as oversight institutions have, to some extent, norm-setting powers as well.

This chapter discusses the integral norm-setting institutions of SADC, including their composition, mandates and, where they are clearly outlined, their procedures. Not only does this chapter seek to establish the extent of

---

[1] SADC Treaty as amended in 2001 available at http://www.sadc.int/ (accessed 8 July 2013).

© The Author(s) 2019
M. Nyathi, *The Southern African Development Community and Law*, https://doi.org/10.1007/978-3-319-76511-2_3

43

the powers of the individual SADC rule-making/norm-setting institutions—it also seeks to establish whether there are mechanisms for inter-institutional balancing and constraint between and among the various institutions around norm setting. Linked to this appraisal is the question whether there are treaty mechanisms meant to guarantee transparency and accountability in SADC's decision-making processes. In short, this chapter seeks to establish whether norm setting in SADC is a shared responsibility that is subjected to meaningful inter-institutional conversation. However, the interconnected nature of the whole institutional framework is such that the assessment of the rule-making/norm-setting institutions does not end in this chapter, but continues with the discussion of oversight institutions in Chap. 4. In the following six sections, each of the rule-making/norm-setting institutions is discussed.

The chapter discusses the following organs in turn: the Summit, the CoM, the SCMCs, the SCO, the Secretariat, and the OPDS.

3.2   The Summit of Heads of State or Government

The Summit is the highest decision-making body of SADC.[2] As the name implies, and as confirmed by the letter of the Treaty itself, it consists of the Heads of State or government of all Member States.[3] The SADC Treaty provides that the Summit shall meet at least twice a year.[4] The Treaty further provides, in article 10(9) that the decisions of the Summit shall be by consensus, unless there is provision to the contrary in the Treaty. It may be important at this stage to explain what consensus decision-making entails. Taking decisions by consensus is not the same as adopting decisions by unanimity. Where a decision has to be taken by unanimity, all those participating would have to be in positive agreement. On the other hand, a consensus decision-making procedure implies not an agreement, but rather that none of the parties is seriously opposed to the taking of the proposed decision. Taking decisions by consensus has been linked to the conclusion of package deals, that is, 'buying off' those not in agreement by giving in to the latter's other demands.[5]

---

[2] In fact, art 10(1) of the SADC Treaty puts the powers of the Summit in more grandiose terms—it is the 'supreme policy-making Institution of SADC.'

[3] Art 10(1) of the SADC Treaty.

[4] Art 10(5) of the SADC Treaty.

[5] For a detailed discussion of consensus decision-making and its implications, see J. Klabbers *An introduction to international institutional law* (2009) 207–209. For a different view of

The Summit elects the chairperson and deputy chairperson of SADC from among its members for one year on the basis of rotation. The powers of the Summit include responsibility for overall policy direction and control of the functions of SADC and the adoption of legal instruments for the implementation of the provisions of the Treaty.[6]

As will be demonstrated in the following sections where the other norm-setting institutions are discussed and analysed, the Summit is the ultimate decision and norm maker in SADC: it approves the budget of the organisation[7]; it appoints the executive secretary and the deputy executive secretaries[8]; it appoints the members of the SADC Tribunal[9]; and it determines admission of new members into SADC.[10]

With regard to the admission of new members, the decision of the Summit must be unanimous.[11] Although the Treaty gives the Summit the power to determine the procedures for the admission of new members and for accession to the Treaty by such new members,[12] the Treaty does not set out criteria for membership nor does it set out broad guidelines to be followed by the Summit in coming up with procedures for the admission of new members and for accession to the Treaty. Although subsequent membership of an international organisation is a privilege rather than right, objective criteria for membership clearly spelt out in the Treaty itself would reduce the incidence of discretion and improve the transparency and legitimacy of admission decisions.

what consensus entails, see P.C. Osode 'The Southern African Development Community in legal historical perspective' (2003) 28 # 3 *Journal for Juridical Science* 7 (and the reference thereunder). According to Osode, the practical effect of a consensus decision-making procedure is that it gives a veto power to a member state, enabling it to block a decision that it does not agree with. This latter view is erroneous and is in fact descriptive of a unanimity procedure.

[6] Arts 10(2) & 10(3) respectively of the SADC Treaty.

[7] Art 28(3) of the SADC Treaty.

[8] This is very much unlike, for example, what obtains in the European Union where the appointment of the president of the European Commission is not a matter that is decided by a single institution. For a detailed discussion of the EU governance framework see Chap. 6, Sect. 6.4.

[9] The members of the Tribunal are appointed by the Summit upon recommendation of the CoM. A more detailed discussion of the SADC Tribunal is found in Chap. 4, Sect. 4.2.

[10] Art 10(8) of the SADC Treaty.

[11] Art 8(4) of the SADC Treaty.

[12] Art 8(2) of the SADC Treaty.

Another area where the Summit plays an overarching role is the amendment of the SADC Treaty. In terms of article 36(1) of the Treaty, three-quarters of members of the Summit are needed to pass an amendment. There is no mention of ratification by Member States. The only procedural requirement provided in article 36 of the Treaty is that a proposal for the amendment of the treaty may be made to the executive secretary by any Member State for preliminary consideration by the CoM, provided that the proposed amendment shall not be submitted to the CoM for preliminary consideration until all Member States have been duly notified of it, and a period of three months has elapsed after such notification. It should be noted however that the term 'member state,' defined in article 1 as meaning 'a member of SADC,' has no 'new' definition in the context of Treaty amendment. The practical implication of this is that proposals may be received by the executives of Member States and decided upon by them without involving the Member States' legislatures, let alone the generality of the populations of SADC Member States.[13] The provisions on amendment clearly do not envisage the involvement of the whole domestic constitutional machinery in SADC Member States, but vests the final say on an institution of SADC—the Summit. Members of the Summit thus not only have the last say at the national level on their respective Member State's input into the amendment process but also have the ultimate say on the adoption of the amendment at the regional level as Summit, with the only measure of control being the three-quarters majority needed.

The procedure for the amendment of the SADC Treaty is very much unlike, for example, the amendment of the Treaty Establishing the East African Community which has a more detailed amendment procedure (set out in article 150 of the Treaty), including that an amendment shall enter into force only when ratified by all the Partner States. Similar provisions apply to the amendment of the Treaty of ECOWAS (articles 89 and 90), which provide for ratification by all Member States in accordance with their respective constitutional procedures. However, in ECOWAS, amendments come into force upon ratification not by all the ECOWAS Member States (ECOWAS has 15 Member States at the time of the finalisation of

---

[13] For a discussion on the provisions of the SADC Treaty on the involvement of SADC citizens and other stakeholders in SADC processes, see Chap. 4, Sect. 4.3.

this book)[14] but by at least nine of the signatory states. Even assuming the predominance of the executive arm in treaty ratification processes at the domestic level in some jurisdictions, a treaty provision that clearly predicates entry into force of a treaty on ratification by Member States, as opposed to the one that gives such authority to one of the institutions of an organisation, might be read to imply a more inclusive process at the domestic level. The procedure for the amendment of the SADC Treaty quite clearly puts the destiny of SADC in the hands of the Summit to the exclusion of other institutions and stakeholders, including at the domestic level in SADC Member States.

The procedure for the amendment of the SADC Treaty outlined above is however not applicable to the adoption of protocols since article 22 of Treaty requires ratification of the latter by Member States.[15] The difference in the procedures for the adoption of protocols and amendment of the SADC Treaty creates a procedurally awkward situation where 'subsidiary' legal instruments in SADC (in the form of protocols) undergo a ratification process yet the same procedure is not applicable to the amendment of the primary constitutive document—the Treaty, upon which they are based. This creates the real possibility of legitimacy-deficit not only of the SADC Treaty itself but also of other legal instruments and decisions adopted pursuant to the Treaty. This is more so since the Treaty gives some of the institutions, especially the Summit, far-reaching norm-setting powers. This clearly justifies the need for democratic legitimation of the Treaty through ratification of its amendments by Member States, especially since all the other secondary instruments will have to be tested against it. It would actually make better sense to subject amendments to the SADC Treaty to a ratification procedure and free the adoption and amendment of protocols (or any other legal instrument adopted pursuant to the Treaty) from same.

---

[14] http://www.ecowas.int/about-ecowas/basic-information/ (accessed 25 January 2016).

[15] Regarding the amendment of protocols, it is not clear if such should be subjected to a ratification procedure as is the case with their adoption. For example, article 38(3) of the SADC Protocol on Gender and Development [adopted in Johannesburg on 17 August 2008 and available at http://www.sadc.int/files/8713/5292/8364/Protocol_on_Gender_and_Development_2008.pdf (last accessed on 5 June 2016)] simply provides that '(a)n amendment of this Protocol shall be adopted by a decision of three quarters of the Member States that are Parties to the Protocol.' There is no requirement, let alone an explicit one, for ratification as is the case with the adoption of the protocol as set out in article 40.

Admittedly, the SADC Treaty enjoins the Summit to act on the recommendations of the CoM in the exercise of some of its powers, for example, in the appointment of the executive secretary and the deputy executive secretaries[16]; in the admission of new members; and in the approval of protocols.[17] But that is as far as the Treaty goes. The SADC Treaty does not set out a framework for inter-institutional bargaining involving various institutions of SADC in these significant policy areas. In fact, even acting on the recommendations of the CoM is not something that is cast in peremptory terms. The Summit can thus ignore the recommendations of the CoM since not only is it not obligated to take its decisions on the basis of such recommendations, but it also has no legal obligation to state the reasons for not acting on the CoM's recommendations. The CoM thus largely plays the role of loyal servant and adviser of the Summit.

To argue that power is centralised in the Summit is not the same as saying that the other institutions of SADC do not get involved in the formulation of SADC policies in practice. As one scholar has observed with regard to protocols, it is the SADC Secretariat, working with relevant technical and legal experts, that comes up with the initial drafts which are then subjected to hierarchical considerations and negotiations by the other institutions comprising senior officials and ministers (these other institutions are discussed below) until they are finally adopted by the Summit, subject of course to ratification by the Member States. The argument presented here is simply that at the end of the day, it is the decision of the Summit that matters. Also, the general attitude (or rather, general political position) of the Summit on any issue would likely influence the decision of the subordinate political institutions that are supposed to make recommendations to it.[18]

[16] Article 10(7) of the SADC Treaty.
[17] Article 22(2) of the SADC Treaty.
[18] See L. Nathan 'The disbanding of the SADC Tribunal: A cautionary tale' (2013) 35 # 4 *Human Rights Quarterly* 872. To illustrate the predominance of the Summit in policymaking in SADC, Nathan (at p. 881) gives an example of the 1996 far-reaching proposed terms of reference developed by the Secretariat which would have given the OPDS power to monitor SADC Member States' compliance with democracy, human rights, and the rule of law. According to Nathan, this proposal was rejected at ministerial level since it was viewed as an attack on Member States' sovereignty; and the ministers instead proposed a watered-down version which would have given the OPDS the power to monitor not compliance by Member States, but rather the latter's ratifications of international human rights instruments. Interestingly, even this watered-down version (which clearly betrayed the ministers' knowledge of the general attitude of the Summit on the issue) did not make it into the OPDS

There is, therefore, absolutely no mechanism provided for in the SADC Treaty for checks and balances in the arena of norm setting and decision-making. When it comes to ultimate decisions in the areas referred to above, the Summit acts alone, since the province of CoM, let alone that of the other subordinate institutions, is only the making of recommendations. As shall be shown in Chap. 6, other RECs have established 'cooperative' frameworks where decisions on significant matters are not left to the discretion of a single institution.

The unbridled formal powers of the Summit given to it by the SADC Treaty have been used to effect (and even overstepped) in practice. The actions of the Summit in the suspension and eventual dissolution of the SADC Tribunal briefly referred to in Chap. 1 and discussed in detail in Chap. 4 is a good example of the democratic deficit inherent in the SADC governance framework. As things currently stand, the SADC integration project is a legal framework effectively without an adjudicator and thus free from enforceable legal constraints. As has been aptly put by Kumm, '[a]n international community that makes do without the resource of a well-developed legal system in which the authority of law is generally recognized is impoverished.'[19] As things stand, the Summit is the overall law and policymaker, implementer and adjudicator in SADC. Crudely put, the Summit is SADC and SADC is the Summit.

So pervasive and overarching is the Summit's role in SADC affairs that some scholars are in such awe and despair that they actually see the creation of a democratic institutional framework at the regional level in SADC as, at least in the current state of affairs, impossible. According to Nathan, '[t]he crux of the matter is that the SADC states (read heads of state or government) will not relinquish sovereignty to regional institutions.'[20] He goes on to state, in an equally categorical fashion:

Protocol that was subsequently adopted in 2000. The protocol instead carries a bald provision which simply provides that the OPDS should encourage Member States to observe universal rights enshrined in the United Nations and the Organisation of African Unity (now African Union) instruments.

[19] M. Kumm 'The legitimacy of international law: A constitutionalist framework of analysis' (2004) 15 # 5, *The European Journal of International Law*, 918.

[20] Nathan (Footnote 18 above) 872. It is debatable though if it is indeed sovereignty that is at stake or it is merely the general disregard for democracy, human rights, and the rule of law.

The Summit demonstrated unequivocally that it is not subordinate to the Treaty. In an international system in which state sovereignty is a paramount factor, the Summit and its member states (sic) are constrained only if, and to the extent that, they consent to be constrained. Such consent has not been given in Southern Africa and will not be forthcoming for the foreseeable future.[21]

Over and above the Summit being the ultimate institution in SADC's decision-making processes, it does so within a treaty framework that does not provide for internal constraints even within the Summit itself, save for the requirements of consensus or unanimity, and a three-quarters majority in the case of the amendment of the SADC Treaty, which on their own are not enough to guarantee transparency and accountability. This is more so in the absence of judicial review mechanisms underpinned by the right to access to information which is applicable even to international organisations, or at least some of them.[22]

The overarching role of the Summit in SADC can be traced to the Front Line States and the days of SADCC. During that era, the Heads of State of the now SADC Member States were ultimately in charge of the affairs of these organisations and were apparently reluctant to share their policymaking roles with other institutions. The mood was that of anti-institutionalism. As remarked by the then Mozambique's President Samora Machel on the day of the formation of SADCC:

> It is not through the creation of institutions that we will develop multilateral co-operation. Some of us have experience of the inefficiency of creation of heavy and expensive structures which contribute little or nothing to the main objectives that were achieved [sic]. The institutions should appear in order to respond to the objective needs and not conceived as an end in themselves.[23]

Similar sentiments were expressed by the then president of Botswana, Seretse Khama who criticised 'grandiose schemes' and 'massive bureaucratic

---

[21] Nathan (Footnote 18 above) 891–892.

[22] A more detailed discussion of access to information in SADC is found in Chap. 7, Sect. 7.10.

[23] President Samora Machel, Lusaka, 1 April 1980 as quoted in SEA Mvungi 'Constitutional questions in the regional integration process: The case of the Southern African Development Community with reference to the European Union' unpublished doctoral thesis, Hamburg University (1994) 87.

institutions' and instead favoured an approach focusing on common projects and specific programmes.[24] Needless to say, it is difficult to see how 'common projects' and 'specific programmes' cannot be effectively pursued by bureaucratic institutions. Also, bureaucratisation does not necessarily translate to a large number of people and 'expensive structures.' The attitude of the founders of SADCC seems to have been that of charting the course of regional integration on their own, as it were, under the guise of efficiency. This thinking is reflected not only in SADC's current institutional design but, as will be demonstrated in detail in Chap. 3, in the operations of the Summit as well.

3.3   The Council of Ministers

Just like the Summit, the CoM was carried over from the old SADC, that is to say, the pre-2001 amendment structure. The lawmaking authority of the CoM derives from article 10(3) of the SADC Treaty which grants the Summit the authority to delegate its authority to adopt instruments for the implementation of the provisions of the treaty 'to the Council or any other institution of SADC as the Summit may deem appropriate.' This is quite a broad and general authority to delegate. However, this is not a delegation of the Summit's primary powers as set out in the SADC Treaty, but rather of secondary powers for the implementation of the treaty.

Article 10(3) of the SADC Treaty thus clearly vests the CoM with secondary lawmaking/norm-setting powers, but only if so delegated by the Summit.[25] What is implicit in this provision is that not only are the powers of the Summit confined to those of primary norm setting set out in the SADC Treaty, but they extend to the adoption of implementation frameworks as well, a power that has come to be traditionally accorded to subordinate institutions in similar organisations as will be shown in Chap. 6.

The CoM consists 'of one Minister from each Member State, preferably a Minister responsible for Foreign or External Affairs.'[26] The Member

---

[24] Mvungi (Footnote 23 above).

[25] A recommendation is made in Chap. 7 that, for purposes of effectiveness, the authority to come up with secondary or implementation of legal instruments should vest in the reformed Secretariat (as proposed in this study).

[26] Article 11(1) of the SADC Treaty. Under the old Treaty, a similarly worded provision [the old article 11(1)] gave preference to ministers responsible for economic planning or finance. In the current practice of the CoM, there is no limit as to the number of ministers who attend CoM meetings. Member States usually send between two and five ministers.

States holding the chairpersonship and deputy chairpersonship of SADC appoint, or rather hold, the chairperson and deputy chairperson of the CoM respectively.[27] The CoM reports and is responsible to the Summit.[28] It meets at least four times a year and reaches its decisions by consensus.[29]

However, with the majority of the Member States, the 'head of delegation' is usually a minister of foreign affairs. When the executive secretary sends out a notice of meeting and the agenda, s/he directs these to each Member State's SADC National Contact Point (on SADC National Contact Points, see Sect. 3.5 below) and it would be up to the Member States to decide who to send to the meeting in question. For example, in the case of an extraordinary Summit meeting dealing with a specific integration area or theme, it is not unheard of that 'heads of delegation' in the CoM meeting preceding that of the Summit are ministers in charge of the relevant national ministerial portfolio. For this and other 'practice insights' below, the author is indebted to the former executive secretary of SADC, Dr. Tomaz Salomão who availed his time to peruse some of the draft material on which this book is based; and also agreed to meet with the author (at the University of the Witwatersrand School of Governance, No. 2 St David's Place, Parktown, Johannesburg, South Africa on 23 March 2015) and share his knowledge and experience on the internal workings of SADC. At the time of the meeting/discussion, Dr. Salomão was a Visiting Research Fellow at the Wits School of Governance. While some of these practices may be clearly *ultra vires* the SADC Treaty, for example, the numerical composition of the CoM, caution must be exercised before one draws the conclusion that the Member States are willingly acting in common accord to disregard the terms of the treaty, or for that matter that they believe the practices are functionally beneficial to SADC. It could well be that they have not benefited from proper legal guidance and they believe that their practice is per the strict letter of the treaty. Indeed, when it comes to a relatively small organisation like SADC which has so far not attracted the same level of legal scholarly attention like the UN and the EU for example, and arguably does not benefit from a large pool of competent legal counsel (the need for competent legal minds, even if few in number, cannot be overemphasised) it would be too quick to reach such a conclusion. In any case, to the extent that additional 'members' may only participate in deliberations and not in actual decision-making, this could be legally tolerated although the possibility that having an unfixed number in CoM meetings could be a nuisance especially to those Member States with smaller delegations is high. It is still very possible that someone might one day successfully challenge some of the practices. The absence of a competent judicial organ with wide powers of review, a matter discussed in detail in Chap. 4, clearly constrain the legal development of SADC in this regard.

[27] Art 11(3) of the SADC Treaty.

[28] Art 11(5) of the SADC Treaty.

[29] Art 11(4) and 11(5) of the SADC Treaty respectively. In terms of article 11(4) of the old Treaty, the CoM was obligated to meet at least twice a year. In practice (per Salomão, Footnote 26 above) the CoM has two 'major' meetings in a year: the February meeting for the adoption of the budget and the August meeting immediately preceding the meeting of the Summit. With regard to the February meeting, although the majority of the Member

In addition to the exercise of authority delegated to it by the Summit, article 11 of the SADC Treaty vests the Council with its own primary responsibilities. These responsibilities are

- overseeing the functioning and development of SADC
- overseeing the implementation of the policies of SADC and the proper execution of its programmes
- advising the Summit on matters of overall policy and efficient and harmonious functioning and development of SADC
- approving policies, strategies, and work programmes of SADC
- directing, coordinating, and supervising the operations of the institutions of SADC subordinate to it
- recommending to the Summit the establishment of directorates, committees, other institutions and organs
- creating its own committees as necessary
- recommending to the Summit persons for appointment to the posts of executive secretary and deputy executive secretaries
- determining the terms and conditions of service of the staff of the institutions of SADC
- convening conferences and other meetings as appropriate, for purposes of promoting the objectives and programmes of SADC
- performing such other duties as may be assigned to it by the Summit or the treaty

The above responsibilities are set out in article 11(2) of the SADC Treaty. Other than perhaps the powers to coordinate and supervise the operations of its subordinate institutions; recommend to the Summit persons for appointment to the posts of executive secretary and deputy executive secretaries; determine the terms and conditions of service of the staff of the institutions of SADC; and convene conferences and other meetings for the specified purpose, these largely operational responsibilities are couched in overly broad terms; and while the number of responsibilities gives an appearance of an institution with a lot of work to do in its own 'autonomous' areas, on closer analysis, there are a lot of similarities and overlaps in the literal framing of some of the responsibilities, for example, the functions of overseeing the functioning and development of SADC;

States' delegations would be led by ministers of foreign affairs, the 'main' people involved in the budget adoption process are usually the ministers of finance or their deputies.

and overseeing the implementation of the policies of SADC and proper execution of its programmes are similar responsibilities that can be streamlined and reduced without compromising the overall substantive responsibilities of the CoM.

3.4   The Sectoral and Cluster Ministerial Committees

Initially called the Integrated Committee of Ministers (ICM), the Sectoral and Cluster Ministerial Committees were born out of the 2001 SADC Treaty amendment which got rid of the decentralised model based on (sectoral) Commissions.[30] These committees consist of ministers from each Member State.[31]

It may be important to briefly highlight the pre-SCMCs position in order to understand what might have informed the amendment of the Treaty. With the exception of some few matters, there really is not much of a difference between the then ICM and the current SCMCs in terms of both functions and composition.

Notwithstanding the fact that the functions of the ICM were clearly outlined in the Treaty, and that their composition was clearly stated—two ministers from each Member State, the ICM's functions and composition were further elaborated on, and quite clearly without any Treaty basis, by an ordinary decision of the Summit of 25–26 August 2003, Dar es Salaam, Tanzania.[32] In terms of that decision, which was informed by, among other things, the recommendation of the CoM and also by the Report on the Review of Operations of SADC Institutions, the ICM was obligated to

- convene meetings at the integrated committee level. Such meetings were to comprise officials and ministers.[33] At this so-called integrated

---

[30] The SCMCs replaced the ICM through the Agreement Amending the Treaty of SADC signed by the SADC Heads of State or Government on 17 August 2008 at Johannesburg, South Africa, available in the SADC library, Gaborone (accessed 10 March 2014).

[31] Article 12(1) of the SADC Treaty.

[32] Item 4.3 of the minutes of Summit proceedings available in the SADC library (accessed 10 March 2014).

[33] It would appear from a holistic reading of the decision of the Summit that the officials referred to here were not the senior officials who constitute the SCO, since these are specifically referred to as 'Senior Officials' elsewhere in the minutes. However, it is not clear if such

committee level, issues that were to be deliberated on were those from all directorates and 'other programme-related issues.'

• convene meetings at cluster level as defined by the composition of the four directorates. Such meetings were to be held at senior officials and ministerial levels.

• meet in May each year at the integrated level in three sessions: session one being a plenary meeting to consider cross-cutting issues; session two to consider cluster issues; and session three to consolidate issues and decisions.

The Secretariat was mandated to further reflect on the need to clearly spell out the decision-making mandate of the ICM in order to clarify which decisions were to be taken by the ICM and which ones would be referred to the CoM and also on the need to rationalise meetings of the ICM at both the integrated and cluster levels.

Apparently, the ICM had, prior to the decision of the Summit discussed above, adopted its Rules of Procedure which became effective on 5 March 2003.[34] Quite clearly, the confusion surrounding the predecessor of the SCMCs speak not only to the need for SADC institutions to respect the letter of the Treaty but also to the need for a detailed treaty framework clearly setting out the responsibilities of each institution and the relationship of each institution to the other institutions.[35]

Chairpersonship and deputy chairpersonship of the SCMCs replicate that of the Council, and by extension, that of the Summit.[36] The

officials were officials in the employ of the Member States or those in the employ of the Secretariat.

[34] This appears from item 7.2.2 of the minutes of CoM meeting of 9–10 March 2003 available in the SADC library, Gaborone (accessed 10 March 2014). Unfortunately, these Rules of Procedure could not be located by the author. It is also not clear if these were inherited by the new SCMCs.

[35] Also, in terms of item 7.3.3 of the minutes referred to in Footnote 32 above, the two ministers from each Member State were expected to 'bring inputs from their respective SADC National Committees.' This was quite contrary to article 16A (10) of the SADC Treaty which provides that each national secretariat [an institution in each SADC Member State that is supposed to 'facilitate' the operation of the SNC in that Member State (the SNCs are discussed in detail in Chap. 4, Sect. 4.3)] 'shall produce and submit reports to the Secretariat at specified intervals.' As will be shown in Chap. 6 where the institutions of the EU are also discussed, the EU treaty framework is quite clear and heavy on detail.

[36] See Article 12(4) of the SADC Treaty.

Committees take their decisions by way of consensus.[37] Instead of consisting of just two ministers from each Member State, as was the case under the ICM, the SCMCs consist 'of ministers from each member state.'[38] This broader casting of the composition of the SCMCs is apparently meant to make the SCMCs an 'institution' with different configurations, with the composition of each meeting being determined by the 'integration' areas under discussion.

Article 12(2) of the Treaty lists the responsibilities of the SCMCs. These include

- overseeing the activities of the core areas of integration which are stated as trade, industry, finance, and investment; infrastructure and services; food, agriculture, natural resources, and environment; social and human development and special programmes (these are said to include health and HIV and AIDS; education, labour, employment; and gender); politics, defence, and security; and legal and judicial affairs
- monitoring and controlling the implementation of the Regional Indicative Strategic Development Plan (RISDP) in the areas of their respective competences
- providing policy advice to the CoM
- creating such permanent or ad hoc sub-committees as may be necessary

It should be noted that although similar, these functions are narrower in scope than the ones originally given to the ICM, since the latter included the powers to provide policy guidance to the Secretariat; make decisions on matters pertaining to the directorates; and monitor and evaluate the work of the directorates.[39]

The SCMCs are also endowed with decision-making powers to 'ensure rapid implementation of programmes approved by the Council.'[40] These powers should not be confused with the power to adopt instruments for the implementation of the provisions of the Treaty as is the case with the

---

[37] Article 12(8) of the SADC Treaty.

[38] Article 5(1) of the Agreement Amending the Treaty of SADC (Footnote 30 above).

[39] Article 12(2)(c) & (d) of the 'original' 2001 amended SADC Treaty.

[40] Article 12(3) of the SADC Treaty as further amended by the 17 August 2008 amendment of the SADC Treaty (Footnote 30 above).

Summit's power to delegate such powers to the CoM or any other institution of SADC. Had the framers of the Treaty so intended, they would have used similar language. The implementation powers of the SCMCs are thus clearly of a second-tier administrative, rather than lawmaking nature. Be that as it may, the requirement that the CoM meets at least four times a year and the SCMCs, which are supposed to 'ensure' rapid implementation of programmes approved by the CoM, meet at least once a year, surely defeats the purpose of this treaty intent of rapid implementation of programmes approved by the CoM.[41] This would be so even if one were to remain alive to the possibility of these Committees meeting more than once in a year as the treaty only provides a mandatory minimum; since the four meetings of the Council per year are also a mandatory minimum.

In terms of the SADC institutional ranking order, the SCMCs are subordinate to the CoM. A few pointers would suffice to buttress this observation: as has been stated elsewhere in this chapter, the Summit, in the exercise of some of its powers, acts on the recommendations of the CoM. The SCMCs are also clearly subordinate to the Council, since they provide policy advice to CoM and are obligated to make decisions to ensure rapid implementation of programmes approved by the CoM. Further, the SADC Treaty explicitly provides that the SCMCs report and are answerable to the CoM.[42]

In terms of the letter of the SADC Treaty, there is not much of a distinction between the responsibilities or powers of the CoM and those of the SCMCs.[43] In other words, there is nothing that the SCMCs are empowered to do that the CoM cannot do within its broad and overlapping powers. In fact, some of these responsibilities, as is indicated in detail in Chap. 7, can vest in the Secretariat, more so because they are mostly to do with the adoption of implementation instruments, thus needing a continuous and sustained attention, rather than being dealt with on the basis of ministerial meetings. For purposes of operational effectiveness and to ensure clear lines of responsibility, only one institution at ministerial level with various configurations, as suggested in detail in Chap. 7, would

---

[41] The same concern appears to be raised by C. Ng'ongo'la in 'The framework for regional integration in the Southern African Development Community' (2008) *University of Botswana Law Journal* at p. 25.

[42] Article 12(6) of the SADC Treaty as further amended by the 17 August 2008 amendment of the SADC Treaty (Footnote 30 above).

[43] Ng'ongo'la (Footnote 41 above) makes a similar observation.

suffice. Such need is clearly borne out of the unclear status of the SCMCs within SADC as illustrated above and also because there is a clear disjunction between the letter of the SADC Treaty and practice.[44]

3.5   THE STANDING COMMITTEE OF OFFICIALS

Just like the Summit and the CoM, the Standing Committee of Officials (SCO) is an old institution of SADC that was a carry-over from the pre-2001 amendments. Membership of the SCO consists of one permanent secretary or an official of equivalent rank from each Member State.[45] Such a permanent secretary or official must be from the ministry that is the SADC National Contact Point.[46] The SCO is said to be a technical advisory committee to the CoM and is responsible and reports to the CoM.[47] As is the case with the CoM, the SCO meets at least four times a year[48] and its decisions, again like is the case with the CoM, are by consensus.[49] The

---

[44] Ng'ongo'la (Footnote 41 above, at p. 25) is of the view that the (now) SCMCs (which he views as a 'surplus' institution) have no business in the SADC institutional makeup. However, his suggestion is that the size of the CoM could have been increased to include those ministers who sit on the SCMCs, or alternatively, the CoM could have used its treaty powers to establish sub-committees of junior officials. In fact, in practice, the SCMCs act as sub-committees of the CoM. The latter is actually referred to as 'full Council.' The composition of each SCMC meeting ('CoM committee meeting') is invariably influenced by the integration area under discussion. Decisions taken at SCMC level are taken to the CoM for 'noting.' The reports that go to the Summit are prepared at the CoM/ 'full Council.' The Summit usually either adopts or suggests revision. For purposes of efficiency, sometimes the meetings of SCMCs are held close to the CoM meeting so that they feed into the latter. They are usually held four days before the CoM/ "full Council' meeting. See interview/discussion with Salomão (Footnote 26 above).

[45] Art 13(1) of the SADC Treaty. In South Africa, for example, the equivalent of a permanent secretary is a director general.

[46] Art 13(1) of the SADC Treaty. This is an 'institution' that is not expressly defined in the SADC Treaty. However, according to art (13) (1) of the Treaty, it is clearly the ministry whose minister sits on the CoM, although in practice it is a 'desk' within such ministries. In South Africa, the SADC National Contact (Focal) Point is in the Department of International Relations and Cooperation. See http://www.sadc.int/member-states/south-africa/ (accessed 6 August 2014). See also E.N. Tjønneland 'Making SADC work? Revisiting institutional reform' in Hansohm D. et al. (eds) *Monitoring regional integration in Southern Africa yearbook* (2005) 5, 171.

[47] Articles 13(2) and 13(4) respectively of the SADC Treaty.

[48] Article 13(6) of the SADC Treaty.

[49] Article 13(7) of the SADC Treaty.

appointment of the chairperson (and the deputy chairperson) of the SCO replicates that of the Summit.[50]

While there is nothing wrong with establishing a body that would perform an advisory role to the CoM, a much more effective and less costly way would be to vest this advisory role in the Committee of Ambassadors from the SADC Member States that are accredited to Botswana.[51] In fact, this is the trend in a number of international organisations including the African Union and the EU. A fuller argument in support of this position is made in Chap. 7.

3.6   THE SECRETARIAT

Although in the text of the SADC Treaty two different articles are dedicated to the Secretariat and the executive secretary, in this section, the two are dealt with as a single institution, although the specific powers of the executive secretary will be clearly distinguished.

Article 14(1) provides that the Secretariat is the 'principal executive' institution of SADC and some of its many responsibilities are[52]

- strategic planning and management of the programmes of SADC
- implementation of decisions of the Summit; Troika of the Summit; OPDS; Troika of the OPDS; CoM; Troika of the CoM; the SCMCs; and Troika of the SCMCs[53]
- organising and managing SADC meetings
- financial and general administration
- representation and promotion of SADC

---

[50] Article 13(5) of the SADC Treaty.

[51] The Committee of Ambassadors is not specifically provided for in the SADC Treaty but was established by a decision of CoM. See Chap. 7, Sect. 7.6 for a detailed discussion.

[52] The responsibilities of the Secretariat are carried in sub-paras (a)–(p) of art 14(1) of the SADC Treaty.

[53] The troika system was made part of the SADC Treaty by the 2001 amendment. Under this system, leadership of the political institutions—the Summit; the CoM; the SCMCs; and the OPDS comprises the current chairperson, the outgoing (immediate past) chairperson, and the incoming chairperson. However, the system was already operational and had been adopted by the Summit's decision that was taken in Maputo in August 1999. See para 6.2 of the Report on the Review of the Operations of SADC Institutions, April 2001, available in the SADC library, Gaborone (accessed 10 March 2014).

- preparation of administrative regulations, standing orders and rules for management of the affairs of SADC, and their submission to the CoM for approval
- coordination and harmonisation of the policies and strategies of Member States

The Secretariat also initiates the budgetary process by preparing the budget,[54] although ultimately the budget of SADC is adopted, or rather approved, by the Summit. As is the case with the Summit's absolute power with regard to the admission of new members, there is nothing in the Treaty to suggest that the budget adoption process is a matter that should be subjected to inter-institutional conversation and bargaining.[55] While significant, the role of the Secretariat in the budgetary process is more of a technical support rather than of a policy nature.

The head of the Secretariat is the executive secretary and there is provision for the appointment of deputy executive secretaries who shall assist the executive secretary in the discharge of his or her duties.[56] The executive secretary is responsible for[57]

- consulting and coordinating with the governments and other institutions of Member States
- undertaking measures aimed at promoting the objectives of SADC and enhancing its performance, either on own initiative or pursuant to the direction of the Summit or the CoM
- promoting cooperation with other organisations for the furtherance of the objectives of SADC
- organising and servicing meetings of the Summit, the CoM, the SCO, and any other meetings convened on the direction of the Summit or the CoM
- custodianship of SADC property
- appointment of the staff of the Secretariat
- general and financial administration of the Secretariat

[54] Preparation of the budget and audited accounts are functions of the executive secretary specifically, not of the Secretariat generally. This is in terms of article 15(1) (i). Operationally, however, this is a distinction without a difference.

[55] Even the role of the CoM in relation to the budget adoption process is that of a loyal servant and adviser to the Summit as indicated in Sect. 3.3 above.

[56] Article 14(2) of the SADC Treaty.

[57] Paras (a) to (i) of art 15(1) of the SADC Treaty.

- preparation of annual reports on the activities of SADC and its institutions
- preparation of the budget and audited accounts of SADC for submission to CoM
- diplomatic and other representations of SADC
- public relations and promotion of SADC
- performing any other functions that may be assigned to him or her by the Summit or the CoM

The executive secretary is responsible to the CoM for the above duties.[58]The term of office of the executive secretary (and the terms of office of the deputy executive secretaries) is four years and he or she is eligible for appointment for another period not exceeding four years.[59]

As currently constituted, the Secretariat is an administrative institution of the political institutions (comprising executives of SADC Member States) of SADC whose decisions it is supposed to implement. When it comes to matters of policy formulation, the Treaty does not give the Secretariat any powers at all. The only exception, to some extent, is in the area of budget initiation. This does not mean however that the Secretariat does not play an effective role in policy formulation. For example, with regards to policy formulation, especially in the core areas of integration, it is ordinarily the Secretariat that initiates the process. The relevant Directorate in the Secretariat prepares a background/issues paper, sends this to Member States which would be expected to arrange consultative meetings with relevant stakeholders. Resources and time allowing, officials from the Secretariat may attend such meetings to gather information. After these consultative meetings, the Secretariat then prepares a consultative paper (it would appear that this could be a draft protocol as well) which it sends to the SCO. From there the matter goes to the SCMC and then to the CoM before being finally taken to the Summit where it can either be adopted or sent back for revision.[60] However, in the absence of clearly set out treaty powers, the involvement of the Secretariat will remain legally tenuous.

---

[58] Article 15(1) of the SADC Treaty.

[59] Article 15(3) of the SADC Treaty.

[60] For the roles (in practice) of individual institutions outlined here, see interview/discussion with Salomão (Footnote 26 above). The practice with regard to draft legal documents (including draft protocols) that have reached and been approved by the relevant SCMC appears to be that such documents should be 'cleared' by the Committee of Ministers of Justice/Attorneys General (the legal status of this committee is unclear) first before ultimately reaching the Summit. See item 9.2.2 of the record of the meeting of the Summit of

3.7   THE ORGAN ON POLITICS, DEFENCE, AND SECURITY COOPERATION

Like the ICM (read SCMCs), the OPDS came about through the 2001 amendment of the SADC Treaty. However, as far back as 28 June 1996, the intention to create the OPDS had already been made public by SADC through the Gaborone Communiqué.[61] The chairperson and deputy chairperson of the OPDS are elected by the Summit on a rotational basis. However, the chairperson of the Summit cannot be the chairperson of the OPDS at the same time.[62] The term of office of the chairperson of the OPDS is one year.[63]

The chairperson of the OPDS is obligated to consult with the Troika of the Summit and to report to the Summit.[64]The other institution of the OPDS is the Ministerial Committee comprising ministers from each member state responsible for foreign affairs; defence; public security; state security or police.[65] Needless to say, the SADC Treaty framework creates the possibility of overlapping memberships of various committees by certain ministers. Like the other norm-setting institutions of SADC, with the limited exception of the Summit, decisions of the organ are taken by consensus.

The SADC Treaty confines itself to just the creation of the OPDS and its composition. The functions, powers, and procedures of the OPDS and other related matters are deferred to a protocol. The stated textual basis of the OPDS is Chapter VIII of the United Nations Charter which 'recognizes the role of regional arrangements in dealing with such matters relating to the maintenance of international peace and security as are appropriate for regional action.'[66]

16–17 August 2011, Luanda. The record is available in the SADC library, Gaborone (accessed 10 March 2014). However, as the example of the OPDS protocol above demonstrates, the Summit can reject some of the proposals from the subordinate institutions. See Footnote 18 above.

[61] See the preamble to the OPDS Protocol.
[62] Art 10A (1) of the SADC Treaty.
[63] Art 10A (2) of the SADC Treaty.
[64] Art 10A (3) of the SADC Treaty.
[65] Art 10A (4) of the SADC Treaty.
[66] Preamble to the OPDS Protocol.

The preamble to the OPDS Protocol also seeks to locate the ratio-nale for the establishment of the OPDS within the broader regional integration agenda. It states that 'peace, security and strong political relations are critical factors in creating an environment that is conducive for regional co-operation and integration.' The OPDS is said to consti-tute 'an appropriate institutional framework by which Member States could co-ordinate policies and activities in the areas of politics, defence and security.'[67] The OPDS itself has several institutions, in addition to the chairperson, deputy chairperson, the Troika, and the Ministerial Committee. There is the Inter-State Politics and Diplomacy Committee (ISPDC) and also the Inter-State Defence and Security Committee (ISDSC).[68]

Although the OPDS is meant to contribute to formulation of SADC norms and policies in the peace, security, and defence dimension of the SADC integration project, it does not form part of the norm-setting infra-structure of SADC that forms the focus of this book. The brief outline of the OPDS carried here is merely for the sake of sketching a complete structure of SADC. Setting up a peace, security, and defence mechanism within an REC is not unique to SADC, but by and large, these institutions remain in the realm of 'high politics' and are managed and coordinated in the main by the 'intergovernmental' political institutions of the respective organisations.[69]

Because of the scope of this book, Chap. 6 on comparative analysis does not cover institutions of a similar nature in the selected organisations. Neither does Chap. 7 (which carries the recommendations) proffer any suggestion on reform with regard to the OPDS. This is not to say that the SADC peace, security, and defence institutional framework is perfect and needs no reform, it is a broad area in its own right that needs a separate study.

One passing remark needs to be made about the peace, security, and defence architecture of SADC though: more attention should be paid to what is more fundamental—promotion and protection of democracy,

---

[67] Preamble to the OPDS Protocol.
[68] Art 3 of the OPDS Protocol.
[69] See Chap. 6, Sect. 6.4 which discusses the EU institutional set-up.

since it is democracy that is the guarantor of peace.[70] In other words, it is more often the violation of the principles of democracy, human rights, and the rule of law that generates insecurity instead of the other way round.[71] Economic (and social) development is thus directly linked to the respect of democratic principles of governance, human rights, and the rule of law, since in the absence of these, peace cannot be guaranteed. Indeed, there is enough empirical evidence to prove that election-related conflicts, for example, would most likely occur is non-democratic and less-democratic countries than they would in liberal democratic states.[72]

3.8   CONCLUSION

This chapter has identified different rule-making/norm-setting institutions in the SADC Treaty and has sought to highlight the shortcomings of the treaty framework. The Summit clearly has overarching and unconstrained powers in the affairs of SADC. Also, while the SADC Treaty attempts to give the various institutions under the Summit different roles, some of the roles and responsibilities are not narrowly defined and on closer analysis, are shared by different institutions, with serious implications on institutional coherence, efficiency, and effectiveness.

As has already been intimated, a leaner, clearly articulated, and hopefully more efficient institutional framework would be ideal. For example, having two institutions at ministerial level in the form of CoM and SCMCs is an unnecessary duplication, and so is having two institutions in the form of the SCMCs and the SCO (both of which comprise executives of Member States) answerable to the CoM. Since the SADC Common Agenda clearly lays out the different areas of integration, there should in fact be one CoM with different configurations. This is likely to result in more informed and well-coordinated policy formulation in the various areas that constitute the Common Agenda. In fact, the shift in preference from ministers of finance to those of foreign affairs conveys a message that SADC's emphasis is more on matters of regional diplomacy than other equally important aspects of regional integration.

---

[70] K. Matlosa 'Elections and conflict management' in C. Saunders (ed.) *Region-building in Southern Africa: Progress, problems and prospects* (2012) 80.

[71] L. Nathan *Community of insecurity: SADC's struggle for peace and security in Southern Africa* (2012) 25.

[72] Matlosa (Footnote 70 above).

There is therefore an evident need to streamline the norm-setting structures of SADC to come up with a leaner structure to improve efficiency in the areas of policymaking and implementation. However, a much more sustained argument for institutional realignment covering all the SADC institutions is made in Chap. 7. The shared governance institutional model proposed and illustrated in Chap. 7 provides an alternative overall SADC governance framework, including the realignment of the policymaking architecture.

The next chapter is related to the present. It deals with what this study designates as oversight institutions of SADC and how they relate to the norm-setting institutions. It addresses structural as well as operational challenges faced by the SADC oversight institutions. It also seeks to explore oversight opportunities that lie ahead.

CHAPTER 4

Oversight Institutions of SADC

4.1   INTRODUCTION

Oversight organs in international organisations are essential because their control of decision-making processes helps to increase the confidence in such processes.[1] In the absence of enforcement mechanisms or of the legitimacy brought by the control exerted by oversight institutions, decisions made by norm-setting institutions may lose their value and significance, since they are likely to be not complied with.[2] Thus, the legitimating effect of oversight control serves to increase the incidence of compliance.

In addition to norm-setting institutions, the SADC Treaty also establishes various oversight institutions. As indicated in the previous chapter, the SADC Treaty does not carry the norm-setting-oversight distinction. This distinction is a construct of this study designed mainly to illustrate the different roles of various institutions in SADC. The oversight institutions include the SADC Tribunal and the SADC National Committees (SNCs). Another institution with oversight potential in the SADC framework is the SADCPF but it is not (at least expressly) created by the SADC Treaty. In light of this book's narrow focus on separation of powers and the rule of law, the discussion in this chapter (and in Chap. 7 which sets

---

[1] H.G. Schermers & N.M. Blokker *International institutional law: Unity within diversity* (2011) 407.
[2] As above.

© The Author(s) 2019
M. Nyathi, *The Southern African Development Community
and Law*, https://doi.org/10.1007/978-3-319-76511-2_4

out the proposed SADC alternative institutional model) is limited to these already existing institutions.

This chapter seeks to identify the different roles of these three oversight institutions and also to establish the extent to which the SADC institutional structure and other challenges constrain them in the discharge of their mandates.

The following three sections discuss in detail the above three oversight institutions and their challenges and opportunities. But before the oversight institutions are separately discussed, it is important to locate their collective value in the SADC integration process, especially the governance processes—decision-making and the implementation of such decisions. While the promotion and protection of the normative values of democracy, human rights, and the rule of law are concerns that should preoccupy all SADC institutions, it is even more critical in light of the state of democracy in the region for the SADC oversight institutions to be always alive to these values in order to ensure that the SADC good governance agenda (broadly and liberally construed) is a lived reality in the region.

A research carried out by the Centre for Peace Studies, while focusing specifically on SNCs but commenting generally on the state of good governance in the SADC region came up with this observation:

> The issue of good governance in SADC has come under immense scrutiny over the past few years. Good governance is hinged on the promotion of democratic values, accountability and transparency, which illustrates a people-centred leadership as well as the broad based participation of the people and civil society in governance. These attributes necessitate the establishment of strong independent and democratic institutions with the responsibility of ensuring transparent and accountable leadership.[3]

The same research goes on to give specific examples that illustrate the deficit of good governance in SADC:

> However, the decisions made by SADC on pressing democratic and governance issues, such as the decisions of the Summit after the controversial 2002 and 2008 Zimbabwe elections as well as the attitude of SADC heads

[3] O. Nzewi & L. Zakwe, 'Democratising regional integration in Southern Africa: SADC National Committees as platforms for participatory policy making' (2009) (Research Report 122) Centre for Policy Studies, Johannesburg 7–8.

of states to strengthening regional good governance institutions, such as the SADC Parliamentary Forum, have contributed to questions being raised about the level of commitment of SADC heads of state to good governance principles.[4]

It is particularly in the context of the promotion, protection, and development of the normative values of democracy and the rule of law, which norms form part of SADC's objectives and principles, that the SADC oversight institutions are discussed.[5]

4.2   THE SADC TRIBUNAL

There appears to be a changing role for judicial organs at the international level. Schermers and Blokker present a somewhat classical attitude of international law—the dominance of the state in international relations, with the role of the international judiciary seen as primarily the settlement of disputes between states.[6] Thus, the interests of the individual in relation to the international judicial organ are generally peripheral. Even as between states, international judicial organs are not cast as adversarial arenas in the mould of municipal courts. They are there to 'promote friendly co-operation between states by helping them solve their mutual conflicts.'[7]

Schermers and Blokker provide four roles of international judicial organs: judicial control of the legality of decisions of the organisation; administrative jurisdiction over staff members of the organisation; interpretation of rules of the international organisation to promote their uniform application by national courts; and the determination of rules of private law where it is not possible for any national legal system to be applied. In their view, the most important of these roles is the judicial control of the legality of decisions of the organisation, with the major rationale being the need to ensure that the powers of an international organisation are not abused to the detriment of the organisation's primary constituents—the states.[8]

---

[4] Nzewi & Zakwe (Footnote 3 above) 8.
[5] These normative values are also reflected in some of SADC's subsidiary documents, for example, the RISDP. See Chap. 2.
[6] Schermers & Blokker (Footnote 1 above) 435.
[7] A above.
[8] Schermers & Blokker (Footnote 1 above) 435–436.

Schermers and Blokker are of the view that when it comes to the control of the legality of decisions of an international organisation, the need for judicial control is 'strongest' in those international organisations where 'binding' decisions may be taken by majority vote.[9] One of the reasons advanced is the need to safeguard minority interests.[10] Implicit in this argument for the need for 'stronger' judicial control where an international organisation may take a binding decision by majority vote, is the acknowledgment, or rather admission, that even where the outcome of the decision-making process of an international organisation may not be a 'binding decision,' it is still imperative that such a decision is taken within the confines of legality.

The rationale for the establishment of judicial organs with administrative jurisdiction over staff members appears to be straightforward. The justification is that the occasional conflicts between employer and employee need an internal judicial review mechanism.[11] The need for the harmonisation of the interpretation of an international organisation's binding rules is, as indicated above, also one of the justifications advanced for the establishment of international judicial organs. Decisive interpretation of the rules by a single judicial institution prevents a situation whereby different member states give their own interpretations which may result in fractured and irreconcilable interpretations.[12]

Klabbers' view on the role of the international judiciary is more contemporary and pointed.[13] His view seems to go beyond merely the member states, staff members, or private law disputes with third parties. Klabbers recognises '[a] general interest in seeing that the rule of law is upheld, which then translates into an interest in organizations acting strictly in conformity with their constituent documents.'[14] He goes further to argue that:

---

[9] Schermers & Blokker (Footnote 1 above) 436. See also G. de Búrca 'Developing democracy beyond the state' (2007–2008) 46 *Columbia Journal of Transnational Law* 221. De Búrca's concern is the need for democracy in international organisations in general (not just judicial control) especially in those organisations that make 'authoritative rules and policies outside the state and which lie beyond the control of national democratic and constitutional structures.' See a related discussion in Chap. 2.

[10] J. Klabbers in *An introduction to international institutional law* (2009) 205 points out two ways of protecting a minority of members against the wishes of a majority—the decision-making procedure itself and judicial review.

[11] Schermers & Blokker (Footnote 1 above) 437.

[12] As above.

[13] Klabbers (Footnote 10 above).

[14] Klabbers (Footnote 10 above) 206.

[t]he very legitimacy of the organization and its organs is often judged at least partly by the extent to which the organization can be seen to be working in accordance with established procedures and within the parameters of its constitutional document.[15]

Implicit in Klabbers' argument is the view that adherence to the rule of law should be one of the major preoccupation of an international judiciary, thus entitling other stakeholders than just states to seek legal accountability where the organisation (or its constituent members) fails to act in terms of its own rules. This appears to be a far more pronounced role than the one expressed by Schermers and Blokker outlined above which, although recognising the primary role of an international judiciary as the judicial control of the legality of decisions of the organisation, seems to project this role as falling within the narrow confines of interstate relations.

The world is experiencing a significant increase in the establishment of international tribunals.[16] This increase has meant that more and more substantive areas of law are being brought under international law.[17] In addition to purely classical international law issues, new fields that have traditionally been viewed as matters falling within the purview of domestic law are slowly coming within the jurisdiction of international tribunals.[18] The nation state is thus gradually losing its hitherto absolute control over traditional matters of national competence to the international tribunal, leading to the blurring of the distinction between international and national issues.[19] One of the results of these developments has been a growing tendency by some international organisations (including RECs) to establish compulsory human rights jurisdiction at the regional level.[20]

While states may choose to join or leave treaties or to abide by the judgments of international courts, they remain better off if they tag along and comply so as to reap the benefits of membership and to avoid the legal and

---

[15] As above.

[16] See generally C. Baudenbacher & M. J. Clifton 'Courts of regional economic and political integration agreements' in C. P. R. Romano et al. (eds) *The Oxford handbook of international adjudication* (2013) 250–276.

[17] G. Ulfstein 'The international judiciary' in J. Klabbers et al. *The constitutionalization of international law* (2009) 126.

[18] As above.

[19] As above.

[20] Ulfstein (Footnote 17 above) 126–127.

other consequences associated with non-compliance.[21] It is in the context of these recent global developments in the area of international dispute settlement that the SADC Tribunal is discussed below.

The provisions on the Tribunal in the SADC Treaty are as follows:

Article 16
The Tribunal

1. The Tribunal shall be constituted to ensure adherence to and the proper interpretation of the provisions of this Treaty and subsidiary instruments and to adjudicate upon such disputes as may be referred to it.
2. The composition, powers, functions, procedures and other related matters governing the Tribunal shall be prescribed in a Protocol, which shall, notwithstanding the provisions of Article 22 of this Treaty, form an integral part of this Treaty, adopted by the Summit.[22]
3. Members of the Tribunal shall be appointed for a specified period.
4. The Tribunal shall give advisory opinions on such matters as the Summit or the Council may refer to it.
5. The decisions of the Tribunal shall be final and binding.

The Protocol on Tribunal and the Rules of Procedure Thereof (the Tribunal Protocol) was adopted by the Summit on 7 August 2000, prior to the 2001 amendment of the SADC Treaty. However, at the time of the 2001 amendment, the Tribunal Protocol had only been signed and ratified by Botswana.[23] Lesotho, Mauritius, and Namibia ratified the Tribunal Protocol after the adoption of the 2001 amendment.[24] These latter ratifications were, in view of article 16(2) of the SADC Treaty quoted above, obviously only of academic interest.[25]

---

[21] Ulfstein (Footnote 17 above) 127.

[22] While art 22(2) of the original 1992 SADC Treaty provided that any protocol became an integral part of the Treaty, the 2001 amendment, through arts 18 and 21(a) (the amending articles) changed this position by making only the Tribunal Protocol an integral part of the Treaty and thus freeing it from the art 22 protocol ratification procedure applicable to ordinary protocols.

[23] http://www.tralac.org/wp-content/blogs.dir/12/files/2011/uploads/20060621_status_SADC_protocols.pdf (accessed 1 October 2013).

[24] As above.

[25] See Footnote 22 above.

To bring it into line with the Treaty, the Summit subsequently amended the Tribunal Protocol in Luanda on 3 October 2002.[26] Unlike other protocols, amendments to the Tribunal Protocol, just like those of the SADC Treaty itself, are adopted by three quarters of all the members of the Summit and become effective within 30 days after their adoption.[27]

The Tribunal Protocol covers a number of areas on the functioning of the Tribunal, including organisational and administrative matters,[28] jurisdiction, and procedure.[29] The Tribunal Protocol has, in its Part III which deals with jurisdiction, two related articles: article 14 deals with the basis (substance) of jurisdiction of the Tribunal and article 15 deals with the scope of the Tribunal's jurisdiction. In terms of article 14, the Tribunal has jurisdiction over all disputes referred to it in terms of the Treaty and the Tribunal Protocol relating to the interpretation and application of the Treaty; interpretation, application, and validity of the protocols, all subsidiary instruments adopted within the framework of the Community[30]; acts

[26] The Agreement Amending the Tribunal Protocol is found at http://sadc-tribunal.org/wp-content/uploads/2013/03/AgrementAmendingProtocolTribunal.pdf (last accessed 20 August 2014).

[27] Art 18 of the Agreement Amending the Tribunal Protocol. See also L. Nathan 'Solidarity triumphs over democracy – The dissolution of the SADC Tribunal' (2011) 57 *Development Dialogue* 128. While the provisions on the amendment of the SADC Treaty and the Tribunal Protocol appear to be straightforward, there are some who believe that they are so ambiguous as to require judicial elucidation or legislative amendment. For rather overstretched and convoluted alternative interpretations of these and other related provisions (on the Tribunal's human rights jurisdiction, discussed below) see generally, S.T. Ebobrah 'Tackling threats to the existence of the SADC Tribunal: A critique of perilously ambiguous provisions in the SADC Treaty and the Protocol on the Tribunal' (2010) 4 # 2 *Malawi Law Journal* 199.

[28] These include nomination, selection, and appointment of members of the Tribunal.

[29] The status of the SADC Tribunal at the time of the finalisation of this study is a complex legal issue. Pending the coming into force of the recently adopted 'new' protocol, the Tribunal is still *de jure* as constituted in terms of the SADC Treaty and the original protocol as later amended in 2002, hence the deliberate use of the present tense in referring to the 'old' Tribunal that has de facto been disbanded.

[30] It should be noted that in terms of the Agreement Amending the Protocol of the Tribunal adopted at Lusaka, Zambia, on 17 August 2007, the Tribunal's jurisdiction was 'extended' to include determination of appeals arising from the decisions of panels constituted in terms of the Protocol on Trade. See C. Ng'ongo'la in 'The framework for regional integration in the Southern African Development Community' (2008) *University of Botswana Law Journal* who at p. 28 makes reference to art 5 of the Agreement Amending

of the institutions of the Community; and all matters specifically provided for in any other agreements that Member States may conclude among themselves or within the Community and which confer jurisdiction on the Tribunal.

The scope of the Tribunal's jurisdiction is set out in article 15 and includes jurisdiction over disputes between Member States, and between natural or legal persons and Member States. The jurisdiction over natural or legal persons is limited in that no such persons shall bring an action against a Member State unless they have exhausted all available remedies or they are unable to proceed under their domestic jurisdiction.[31] It may be important to also mention that the Tribunal's jurisdiction is not consent based. Where a dispute is referred to the Tribunal by any party, the consent of other party or parties to the dispute is not required.[32]

The remainder of Part III (articles 16–22) deals with such matters as preliminary rulings; disputes between the Community and Member States; disputes between natural or legal persons and the Community; and disputes between the Community and its members of staff related to the latter's conditions of employment; advisory opinions; applicable law; and the Tribunal working languages.

The Tribunal is enjoined by the Tribunal Protocol to apply the SADC Treaty; the SADC Tribunal Protocol and other protocols that form part of the Treaty; and all subsidiary instruments adopted by the Summit, by the CoM or by any other institution or organ of the Community pursuant to the Treaty or protocols.[33] Ironically, the Tribunal is also given a jurisprudential blank cheque, as it were—it 'shall develop its own Community jurisprudence having regard to applicable treaties, general principles and rules of public international law and any rules and principles of the laws of Member States.'[34]

---

the Protocol of the Tribunal, inserting a new art 20A in the Tribunal Protocol. It can be argued though that art 14 of the Tribunal Protocol is broad enough and would have bestowed such appellate jurisdiction on the Tribunal anyway. However, the 2007 amendment could be defended on the basis that an explicit conferment of appellate jurisdiction in trade matters in the Tribunal Protocol itself was necessary for purposes of clarity especially on the exact nature of the Tribunal's jurisdiction.

[31] Art 15(2) of the SADC Tribunal Protocol.

[32] Art 15(3) of the SADC Tribunal Protocol.

[33] Art 21(a) of the SADC Tribunal Protocol.

[34] Art 21(b) of the SADC Tribunal Protocol. The application of rules and principles of the laws of Member States is well established in international adjudication. See, for example,

Overall, the Tribunal's quantitative jurisprudence, developed over a period of just three years (2007–2010) is a limited one. For its small size though, it is relatively diverse in scope, covering employment disputes, trade matters, and human rights cases. The labour cases include *Mtingwi*, *Kethusegile-Juru*, *Mondlane*, and *Kanyama* cases.[35] The Tribunal also had an opportunity to pronounce itself on its rules of procedure, for example, in the *Swissbourgh Diamond Mines*; the *United Republic of Tanzania*; and the *Zimbabwe Human Rights NGO Forum* cases.[36] Some of the cases that came before the Tribunal involved significant substantive human rights issues.[37] The Tribunal was also called upon to review the discretionary exercise of power by an agent of one of the institutions of SADC—the Summit.[38]

Political developments in Zimbabwe starting from the late 1990s not only led to the development and growth of the Tribunal's human rights jurisprudence, but, ironically, marked the demise of the Tribunal. In brief, the ZANU-PF government of Zimbabwe embarked on a populist and largely unplanned land reform programme. This constituted in the main encouraging and assisting sections of black Zimbabweans to forcibly occupy white-owned farms. White farmers were murdered, assaulted, and dispossessed not only of their land but of everything on the farms including crops, animals, farm equipment, and other movables.[39] While these actions

---

D. Freestone 'The European Court of Justice' in J. Lodge (ed.) *Institutions and policies of the European Community* (1983) 47.

[35] *Ernest Francis Mtingwi v SADC Secretariat* SADC (T) 1/2007 (decided on 27 May 2008); *Bookie Monica Kethusegile-Juru v the Sothern African Parliamentary Forum* SADC (T) 02/2009 (decided on 5 February 2010); *Mondlane v SADC Secretariat* SADC (T) 07/2009 (decided on 5 February 2010); *Kanyama v SADC Secretariat* SADC (T) 05/2009 (decided on 29 January 2010).

[36] *Swissbourgh Diamond Mines (Pty) Ltd and Others v Kingdom of Lesotho* SADC (T) 04/2009 (11 June 2010); *United Republic of Tanzania v Cimexpan (Mauritius) Ltd and Others* SADC (T) 01/2009 (11 June 2010); *Zimbabwe Human Rights NGO Forum v Republic of Zimbabwe* SADC (T) 05/2009 (decided on 1 January 2008).

[37] *Barry L.T. Gondo and 8 others v the Republic of Zimbabwe* SADC (T) 05/2008 (decided on 9 December 2010). See Chap. 2 for a summary of the salient facts and the reasoning of the Tribunal in this case; *Luke Tembani v Republic of Zimbabwe* SADC (T) 07/2008 (14 August 2009).

[38] *United People's Party v Southern African Development Community and others* SADC (T) 12/2008 (14 August 2009).

[39] See, for example, http://www.dailymail.co.uk/news/article-132504/Zimbabwe-white-farmers-fight-flee.html (accessed 1 October 2013); http://www.voanews.com/content/white-zimbabwe-farmer-killed-105789778/156393.html (accessed 1 October 2013).

clearly amounted to criminal offences including murder, assault, trespass, and theft, the police largely turned a blind eye to the events.[40]

These events and related legal developments led to the *Campbell* case.[41] The applicants filed an application with the SADC Tribunal on 11 October 2007 challenging the acquisition by the government of Zimbabwe of a certain piece of land. Pending the determination of their challenge, they sought and were granted an interim order protecting their possession of, and interests in that piece of land.[42] Seventy-seven other applicants applied to intervene in the proceedings and also sought the protection of interim measures pending the determination of the main matter. The applications were subsequently granted—the interim measures were granted and all the related matters were consolidated into one case. The Tribunal found in favour of applicants on all jurisdictional and substantive grounds, including that the applicants had been discriminated against on the grounds of race in breach of article 6(2) of the SADC Treaty.

Zimbabwe was directed to take all necessary measures to protect the possession, occupation, and ownership of applicants' lands. Only three applicants were not covered by this portion of the order since they had already been evicted from their lands.[43] Zimbabwe was, however, directed to pay fair compensation by a specified date to these applicants.[44]

With the government of Zimbabwe having refused to abide by the decisions of the Tribunal on interim measures, some of the applicants approached the Tribunal complaining about the conduct of the Zimbabwean government and sought an order for the referral of Zimbabwe to the SADC Summit in terms of article 32(5) of the SADC Tribunal

---

[40] In one of the cases, the government of Zimbabwe deposed to an affidavit to the effect that there was a state of lawlessness prevailing in Zimbabwe at the relevant time and that the authorities had difficulty in addressing the problem of intimidation and violence committed by certain people. See *Mike Campbell (Pvt) Limited and others v the Republic of Zimbabwe* SADC (T) 11/2008 (decided on 18 July 2008) para 4.

[41] *Mike Campbell (Pvt) Ltd and others v Republic of Zimbabwe* SADC (T) 2/2007 (decided on 28 November 2008). The full judgment of the Tribunal in this case, like in all the cases decided by the Tribunal dealt with in this Chapter, is available at www.salii.org (last accessed 9 September 2013); http://www.worldcourts.com/sadct/eng/index.htm (last accessed 13 September 2014).

[42] The order has been paraphrased.

[43] It is not clear on what basis the Tribunal did not order a return to the *status quo ante*.

[44] The judgment does not state if the fair compensation was for improvements effected before acquisition or it was fair compensation for the actual value of the lands.

Protocol.[45] Having established failure on the part of Zimbabwe to comply with the decisions of the Tribunal, the Tribunal referred Zimbabwe's intransigence to the Summit.

Not only did the government of Zimbabwe fail or refuse to comply with the decisions of the Tribunal, it also sought to prosecute applicants in the *Campbell* case through a law that made it a criminal offence for owners or occupiers of gazetted lands to remain on their lands.[46] In fact, Zimbabwe's Deputy Attorney General (Crime)[47] at the time, Mr Johannes Tomana, wrote a letter to applicants' lawyers indicating that his office was proceeding with the prosecution of the applicants since the interim order of the SADC Tribunal could not and had not suspended the constitutional responsibility of his office to prosecute violators of Zimbabwe's existing criminal laws.[48]

In another subsequent matter, *William Michael Campbell & another v the Republic of Zimbabwe*,[49] applicants approached the Tribunal also complaining about the failure by the government of Zimbabwe to comply with the Tribunal's decisions. The Tribunal again referred the matter to the Summit.

The uncontroverted evidence placed before the Tribunal in support of the application included that the Deputy Attorney General of Zimbabwe, just like in the above case, had written a letter to applicant's lawyers stating that:

> the policy position taken by the Government of Zimbabwe to the judgment handed down by the SADC Tribunal on the 28th November 2008 is that all prosecutions of defaulting farmers under the provisions of the Gazetted Lands (Consequential Provisions) Act should now be resumed.[50]

[45] *Mike Campbell (Pvt) Limited and others v the Republic of Zimbabwe* (Footnote 40 above).

[46] Gazetted Lands (Consequential Provisions) Act.

[47] This was the designation of the Deputy Attorney General responsible for criminal prosecutions at the time. At the time of the finalisation of this study, there is now a separate constitutional institution,—the Prosecutor General, that is distinct from that of Attorney General.

[48] These facts are derived from the decision of the Tribunal in the first 'referral' matter. See Footnote 40 above.

[49] SADC (T) 03/2009 (decided on 5 June 2009).

[50] Para 4 of the Tribunal judgment in SADC (T) 03/2009. See Footnote 49 above. It should be pointed out that other than being clearly contemptuous and disdainful of the Tribunal, the attitude of the Deputy Attorney General raises another fundamental concern: In terms of the then Constitution of Zimbabwe, specifically Sect. 76(4) & (4a), when exercising

The other piece of evidence that the Tribunal relied on was the speech by the Deputy Chief Justice of Zimbabwe, Mr Justice Luke Malaba, when he opened the 2009 legal year in Bulawayo. Justice Malaba had indicated in his speech that the Tribunal lacked jurisdiction to hear and determine the *Campbell* case.[51] The Tribunal also considered the statement by President Robert Mugabe during his birthday celebrations where he attacked the Tribunal's decision, labeling it nonsensical and of no consequence. The Tribunal also took into account the fact that all these statements were followed by the invasion of the lands of applicants and their intimidation and prosecution.

By this time, Zimbabwe had started challenging the legality of the Tribunal mainly on the basis of non-ratification of the Tribunal Protocol. Needless to say, the legal arguments advanced by Zimbabwe have quite clearly been demonstrated to be unsound mainly because the 2001 Agreement Amending the Treaty of SADC, itself based on a procedure acceptable at international law, made the Tribunal Protocol an integral party of the SADC Treaty.[52] In any event, not only did Zimbabwe participate in the amendment of the Treaty, it also, among other things, participated in the setting up of the Tribunal and actually seconded one of its judges to be a member of the Tribunal.[53]

Since the government of Zimbabwe was clearly not willing to abide by the *Campbell* decision on the merits, some of the applicants in *Campbell* had to resort to the domestic law of Zimbabwe on enforcement of foreign judgments in terms of article 32 of the SADC Tribunal Protocol.[54] While

his prosecutorial powers, the Attorney General was not supposed to be under the direction or control of any person or authority. Quite clearly, in this case, the Attorney General was pandering to the political whims of the government of Zimbabwe and thus failed to act independently in the discharge of his constitutional prosecutorial duties.

[51] The Tribunal judgment however does not state the name the Deputy Chief Justice.

[52] See generally the reasoning of Justice Patel in *Gramara (Private) Limited and Another v the Republic of Zimbabwe* HC 5483/2009.

[53] As above. See also E. de Wet 'The rise and fall of the Tribunal of the Southern African Development Community: Implications for dispute settlement in Southern Africa' (2013) 28 # 1 *ICSID* Review 54–56; Nathan (Footnote 27 above) 127–128.

[54] *Gramara* case (Footnote 52 above). As noted by H.S. Adjolohoun in 'Giving effect to the human rights jurisprudence of the Court of Justice of the Economic Community of West African States: Compliance and influence' unpublished LLD thesis, University of Pretoria, 2013; the problem with this procedure is that it treats the SADC Tribunal judgments as judgments of foreign courts instead of making them directly enforceable in Member States as if they were domestic judgments. The latter is in fact the case in EAC and ECOWAS where

the High Court of Zimbabwe boldly dismissed the argument of the government of Zimbabwe on the legality of the Tribunal, it refused to register the judgment on the basis of public policy, to *wit*, that the registration of the Tribunal judgment would conflict with the constitutional provisions in Zimbabwe.

Diplomatic machinations by Zimbabwe, made possible by the SADC Member States' general disregard of the rule of law, triumphed over law.[55] The Summit reacted by initially 'suspending' the Tribunal and subsequently effectively disbanding it in August 2012.[56] Thus, a body that should have exercised judicial control over the other institutions and organs of SADC, found itself being disbanded by the Summit without any meaningful inter-institutional conversation within SADC and without any regard to the rule of law. In fact, the SADC Summit, by failing to act on Zimbabwe's contempt of the Tribunal and instead suspending and disbanding the Tribunal, violated article 6(6) of the SADC Treaty which obligates Member States 'to co-operate with and assist institutions of SADC in the performance of their duties.'

In his address to the South African Constitutional Court's Alumni Association, Justice Ariranga Govindasamy Pillay, former president of the SADC Tribunal, observed that the actions of the heads of state or government of SADC were 'high handed and imperious' and akin to those of

the only formality for purposes of execution is the verification of the fact that the judgment emanates from the respective regional court. See pp. 109–111 and 125. A similar argument is made by de Wet (Footnote 53 above) 55. See also the reference thereunder.

[55] F. Cowell 'The death of the Southern African Development Community Tribunal's human rights jurisdiction' (2013) *Human Rights Law Review* (advance access March 12 2013) 9, 12 http://hrlr.oxfordjournals.org/ (accessed 26 April 2013).

[56] See also De Wet (Footnote 53 above) 58. Of the Summit's series of decisions on the Tribunal beginning August 2010 [these included the decision not to reappoint judges whose term of office would expire in August 2010 for another five years pending the review of the role, responsibilities, and terms of reference of the Tribunal by the Committee of Ministers of Justice/Attorneys General as mandated by the Summit; and that the members of the Tribunal would remain in office pending the said review but that the Tribunal should not entertain new cases until such time that an extraordinary meeting of the Summit would have decided on the legal status and roles and responsibilities of the Tribunal (See paras 9.3–9.5 of the minutes of Summit meeting of 16–17 August 2010, Windhoek. The minutes are available in the SADC library, Gaborone, accessed 10 March 2014)] the last and most decisive was the one taken at the August 2012 Maputo Summit. Per para 24 of its Maputo resolutions, where the Summit 'resolved that a new Protocol on the Tribunal should be negotiated and that its mandate should be confined to interpretation of the SADC Treaty and Protocols related to disputes between Member States.'

'kings and potentates who can do no wrong and who are not accountable for their actions.'[57] The actions of the Summit indeed raise a fundamental constitutional question: can an executive arm of an international organisation like SADC dissolve, in the absence of an amendment to the treaty, an integral treaty institution of the organisation, especially the very judiciary arm of the organisation that has the exclusive mandate to interpret the treaty, give advisory opinions, and adjudicate on internal labour disputes?[58] There can be no convincing answer to the above question other than the one in the negative.[59] A view may be expressed that this argument is academic since the Summit could have amended the Treaty and the Tribunal Protocol to achieve the same end since there is no legal requirement for ratification. However, at least there would have been some semblance of adherence to the rule of law had the Summit taken the route of treaty amendment.[60] But more importantly, the SADC Treaty (and Tribunal Protocol) amendment procedure has some safeguards since three quarters of the Summit should positively support the amendment. This is unlike the consensus-based general decision-making procedure which has less procedural safeguards.

The reasoning of the SADC Tribunal in the main *Campbell* matter is legally sound, even in the absence of an explicit grant of human rights jurisdiction by the SADC Treaty.[61] Indeed, the SADC Treaty does not

[57] Mail and Guardian http://www.mg.co.za/article/2011-08-19-killed-off-by-kings-and-potentates (accessed 1 October 2013).

[58] A similar question is posed by Ebobrah (Footnote 27 above) 109. See particularly footnote 35 on that page. There is a difference though since Ebobrah's question is simply whether one institution of SADC can exercise powers to suspend the operations of another. He does not extend his question to include the question of legality. Indeed the Summit can legally suspend or even dissolve any institution of SADC, including the Summit itself, through Treaty amendment. On the other hand, the Tribunal itself can (or could) suspend or nullify the existence of another institution or organ of SADC on the grounds that the institution or organ in question was not procedurally brought into existence.

[59] See also A. Saurombe 'The role of SADC institutions in implementing SADC Treaty provisions dealing with regional integration' (2012) 15 # 2 *Potchefstroom Electronic Law Journal* 471 https://doi.org/10.4314/pelj.v15i2.16 (last accessed 15 October 2014).

[60] This was in fact also pointed out by the members of the Tribunal in their letter addressed to the SADC executive secretary in the aftermath of the initial suspension of the Tribunal in 2010. See L. Nathan 'The disbanding of the SADC Tribunal: A cautionary tale' (2013) 35 # 4 *Human Rights Quarterly* 878–879 and the reference thereunder.

[61] Some scholars are not in total agreement though. See, for example, M.J. Nkhata 'The role of regional economic communities in protecting and promoting human rights in Africa: Reflecting on the human rights mandate of the Tribunal of the Southern African Development

proscribe human rights jurisdiction as is the case with, for example, in the EAC.[62] And over and above this, the general jurisdictional powers of the Tribunal are broad enough to support the Tribunal's reasoning.[63] Unfortunately, the SADC heads of state or government, with a history that is generally unsympathetic to democracy, human rights, and the rule of law, could not stand a regional court ready to take a stand in defence of these normative values. In the final analysis, it would be naive to think that it was only Zimbabwe's diplomatic push that resulted in the SADC 'kings and potentates' 'killing off the Tribunal.' The arguments advanced by Zimbabwe's political leaders simply found a market (in regional leadership) that is generally not yet ready to embrace democracy and all that go with it.[64]

With regards to Zimbabwe, it is very much probable that Mr Mugabe and members of his inner-political circle were more worried about possible future legal developments than just the SADC Tribunal's handling of the land question. Mr Mugabe and his long-time political colleagues stand accused of gross and massive human rights violations that took place for close to a decade in the period immediately after independence. The crimes they stand accused of range from the murder of an estimated 20,000 unarmed civilians, torture and rape among others.[65] With no possibility of seeking legal redress in Zimbabwe largely because of the reality

Community' (2012) *African Journal of International and Comparative Law* 100. Nkhata is convinced that the Tribunal did not do a good job in establishing its human rights jurisdiction. Although he does not dispute that the Tribunal has (had) a human rights mandate, he believes the SADC Treaty provisions relied upon by the Tribunal are not adequate to justify the Tribunal's jurisdiction.

[62] The institutions of the EAC are discussed in Chap. 6, Sect. 6.2.

[63] This is quite contrary to the observation on the similarity of the EAC Treaty provisions and those of the SADC Treaty and the (then) SADC Tribunal Protocol by S.T. Ebobrah in 'Litigating human rights before sub-regional courts in Africa: Prospects and challenges' (2009) 17 *African Journal of International and Comparative Law* (p. 84), at least in as far as the actual provisions of the relevant instruments are concerned. To his credit, Ebobrah later on concedes (at p. 91) that indeed there is a distinction between the EAC and the (then) SADC regimes.

[64] Mr Jakaya Kikwete (former president of the Republic of Tanzania) is said to have remarked at the time of the establishment of the Tribunal (he was then Minister of Foreign Affairs) that SADC was creating 'a monster that would devour us all.' See Mail & Guardian (Footnote 57 above).

[65] For a discussion of the nature of the crimes and the difficulties faced by victims and survivors of victims in seeking legal accountability in Zimbabwe and elsewhere, see generally M. Killander & M. Nyathi 'Accountability for the *Gukurahundi* atrocities in Zimbabwe

that most of the perpetrators still occupy high political, military, and intelligence offices in Zimbabwe; and the various legal hurdles including legal immunity and prescription, the possibility of victims and victims' survivors approaching the SADC Tribunal for redress was more than a theoretical possibility that might have scared Mr Mugabe and some in the government of Zimbabwe, thus spurring them into action to stop the SADC Tribunal in its tracks.

Some have argued that the SADC Tribunal could have survived had it not been asked to deal with such difficult human rights cases, the argument being that the Tribunal should have been allowed to deal first with less controversial cases until it had developed adequate legitimacy.[66] In that way, so the argument goes, it would have survived political machinations if in future it made determinations in the area of human rights. Other than being counterfactual, this argument seems to negate the fundamental role of a court of law in a democracy—to do justice between the parties before it on the basis of the law and the facts before it. This is what a judicial oath of office, or a solemn declaration, like the one in the SADC Tribunal Protocol is all about.[67] Also, it would be too much to expect that litigants, such as the ones in the *Campbell* case, who had suffered such violations of their rights and where judicial redress was clearly impossible at the national level, would worry about academically abstract survival considerations on behalf of the SADC Tribunal, instead of the need to have their cases determined. Also, no one would have imagined that the Summit would act in the manner that it subsequently did with regard to the SADC Tribunal. Granted, democracy may still not be deeply

thirty years on: prospects and challenges' (2015) 48 # 3 *Comparative and International Law Journal of Southern Africa* 463.

[66] De Wet (Footnote 53 above) 62. See also D. Wincott 'The Court of Justice and the European policy process' in J. Richardson (ed.) *European Union: Power and policy making* (1996) 195. Wincott, dealing with a similar argument in the context of the EU, criticises the view by one analyst who presented the CJEU's 'common tactic' as gradual introduction of a new doctrine, building a lot of qualifications around it and in due course, if there were not 'too many protests' the court would get rid of the initial qualifications and reveal the full extent of the doctrine. Wincott attacks this kind of analysis on the basis that although it 'gives a nice flavor of the tactics of the Court … it may attribute too much foresight to it.'

[67] Art 5 of the Tribunal Protocol, as read with rule 3 sub rule 1 and Annex 1 of the Tribunal Rules of Procedure.

entrenched in the SADC region, but the reaction of the Summit far exceeded the limit of arbitrariness.[68] The suspension and disbandment of the SADC Tribunal was challenged before the African Commission on Human and Peoples' Rights (the African Commission). The African Commission has since found, in the matter of *Luke Munyandu Tembani & Another v Angola and 13 Others* (Communication 409/12),[69] that article 7(1)(a) of the African Charter gives the right of individuals to access courts at the national level within the domestic legal systems of state parties to the African Charter, as opposed to intergovernmental or supranational judicial organs[70]; and that accordingly article 7(1)(a) of the African Charter does not impose an international legal obligation on SADC Member States to ensure access to the SADC Tribunal and that therefore there was no violation of article 7(1)(a) of the African Charter.[71] A similar reasoning was adopted by the African Commission with regard to article 26 of the African Charter which imposes on AU Member States an obligation to ensure the independence of the courts.[72] In addition to the above, the Commission held that it has no authority to supervise the application and implementation of other international treaties such as the SADC Treaty.[73]

The African Commission gave the issue of the relationship of the African Charter to institutions of African sub-regional economic communities a rather short shrift. The commission read too much into references to 'nation' in the African Charter and failed to appreciate the historical context of same. The African Charter was adopted in 1981. At that time, the development of regional economic communities on the African continent

---

[68] For a discussion of the state of democracy in Southern Africa with reference to the dissolution of the SADC Tribunal, see generally Nathan (Footnote 27 above) 123–137. One of the observations made by Nathan (at p. 133) is that in view of the general state of democracy in the SADC region, '...it is not possible for the SADC states to be bound—either in the sense of being united or in the sense of being constrained—by democratic principles.' According to Nathan, SADC legal instruments—the Treaty and protocols, are viewed by the SADC political elite as merely 'rhetorical rather than substantive and legally binding.'

[69] Banjul, Gambia, 54th Ordinary Session of the African Commission on Human and Peoples' Rights, 22 October to November 2013.

[70] Para 138 of the finding.

[71] Para 142 of the finding.

[72] Paras 143–145 of the finding.

[73] Para 131 of the finding.

was still in its infancy.[74] At the time of the adoption of the African Charter, upon which the judicial and quasi-judicial AU bodies are based; protection of human and peoples' rights at the level of the then OAU Member States, failing which at the continental level, was the only logical way of designing the then African human rights system.

The African Union (AU) has since evolved over time and the African nation state is no longer the sole building block of the envisaged continental union. In fact, article 3(1) of the AU Constitutive Act specifically mentions as one of the objectives of the AU the coordination and harmonisation of the policies between the existing and future RECs for the gradual attainment of the objectives of the Union.[75] Implicit in article 3(1) of the AU Constitutive Act objective is the realisation of the growing role and influence of regional economic communities in the organic development of the AU. Part of the reality of these sub-regional groupings is that member states of some of these organisations may surrender in whole or in part some of their sovereignty on matters that have hitherto been subject to the individual sovereignty of the AU Member States, thus giving rise to integrated regional, or for that matter supranational approach to common issues. Human rights protection is but one example. This gives the African human rights protection system a new paradigm that involves sub-regional economic communities, in addition to the African nation state and the continental institutions as initially envisaged at the time of the drafting of the African Charter. It is also significant that the preamble to the SADC Treaty itself seeks to associate SADC with continental processes and institutions such as the Lagos Plan of Action and the Final Act of Lagos of April 1980; the Treaty establishing the African Economic Community; and the Constitutive Act of the AU. There has thus developed a new form of a hierarchical and integrated human rights protection within the African human rights protection system that was not anticipated at the time of the adoption of the African Charter.

It also needs pointing out that in arriving at its finding, the African Commission also relied on the jurisprudence of the European Court of

---

[74] ECOWAS had been established barely six years back in 1975 and SADC became a treaty organisation in 1992.

[75] On the relationship between some of the institutions of the AU and African RECs, see S.T. Ebobrah 'Legitimacy and feasibility of human rights realisation through regional economic communities in Africa: The case of the Economic Community of West African States' unpublished LLD thesis, University of Pretoria (2009) 58, 81.

Human Rights, specifically the cases of *Maksimov v Russia*[76] and *Golha v The Czech Republic*.[77] Surprisingly, none of these two cases is of any relevance since they both involve violation of applicants' rights at the level of the Member States of the European Convention on Human Rights. No other level of protection, as in the case of SADC, was implicated.

The African Commission certainly missed an opportunity to develop meaningful jurisprudence that would have harmonised the national, subregional, and continental human rights protection systems rather than leaving them in a fragmented state. Arguably, one of the dangers inherent in the finding of the Commission is that it gives rise to the possibility (even if in theory) of member states of some of the RECs surrendering human rights protection to regional supranational institutions, secure in the knowledge that at that level they can afford to make do without such principles as judicial independence and the rule of law, while at the same time being untouchable by the continental judicial and quasi-judicial bodies. In the absence of a clearly defined relationship between the national, subregional, and the continental systems, the finding also leaves victims of human rights abuses in a quagmire when it comes to choice of forum for redress.[78]

On 18 August 2014, the SADC Summit adopted a new protocol for the SADC Tribunal—the 'Protocol on the Tribunal in the Southern African Development Community.' It is different from the previous Tribunal Protocol in several respects. However, three of these differences particularly stand out and their direct relevance to this study justifies a relatively detailed discussion. The Tribunal has been reduced to an interstate dispute resolution forum for contentious matters, with no access to individuals.[79] As indicated by the then Tribunal Registrar, the new Tribunal is likely to be a white elephant since from experience, Member States have never been known for taking each other to court.[80] Indeed, in practice

---

[76](2010) ECtHR 43233/028 March 2010 (Final 18 June 2010).

[77](2011) ECtHR 7051/0626 May 2011 (Final 26 August 2011).

[78]For a discussion on the relationship between national, sub-regional, regional, and international human rights systems (with particular reference to ECOWAS) see Ebobrah (Footnote 75 above) 139-140.

[79]Art 33.

[80]Mankhambira Mkandawire, presenting at a stakeholder roundtable discussion on the SADC Tribunal at the Centre for Human Rights, Faculty of Law, University of Pretoria held on 28 and 29 August 2014. The author was a participant and facilitator at that roundtable discussion.

exclusive use of regional judicial bodies by individuals appears to be the case with the other African RECs discussed in this study—the EAC and ECOWAS.[81] To compound matters, when it comes to non-contentious jurisdiction, specifically advisory opinions, only the Summit and the CoM have the competence to seek an advisory opinion.[82] All other institutions are excluded from this process. A clear implication of the advisory opinion procedure is that it leaves the interpretation of the SADC Treaty and subsidiary instruments at the mercy of the Summit and the CoM. No matter how compelling the need for an advisory opinion may be, this may not matter if the Summit and the CoM decide not to refer the matter to the Tribunal.

Therefore, while the right to seek an advisory opinion indeed exists, the nature of the current institutional configuration of the SADC institutions and the jettisoning of the right of individual access to the Tribunal can only lead one to conclude that this is a procedure that would never be put to use. As noted above, the interpretation of the SADC Treaty and other instruments would now be largely a political as opposed to judicial exercise thus practically extinguishing the need for the advisory opinion procedure.

The reduction of the new Tribunal's jurisdictional competence has not been compensated in any way, for example, through giving domestic courts in Member States the right to refer matters concerning the interpretation of the SADC Treaty to the Tribunal for a preliminary ruling, something that would have assisted in the harmonisation of SADC norms within Member States through consistent interpretation by the Tribunal.

The other difference brought by the new protocol is that unlike under the 'previous' dispensation where the Tribunal Protocol was an integral part of the SADC Treaty and was subject to the same amendment procedures as the Treaty, this is no longer the position. The new protocol is now like any other protocol and is subject to ratification and will come into force after deposit of instruments of ratification by two-thirds of Member States.[83] Also, only state parties to the new Protocol would participate in

---

[81] Presentation by Mr Yusuf Danmadami, Senior Recorder at the ECOWAS Court of Justice; and Professor John Ruhangisa, Registrar at the EACJ respectively, at the stakeholder roundtable discussion referred to in Footnote 80 above.

[82] Art 34. See also art 16 (4) of the SADC Treaty above.

[83] Arts 52 and 53.

its amendment.[84] Thus, before the deposit of instruments of ratification by two-thirds of the Member States, it is likely that in practice, there will continue to be a judicial vacuum in SADC except maybe for administrative matters (see footnote 89 below). This is so because while in terms of article 48 of the new protocol the 'old' Tribunal Protocol shall remain in force until the entry into force of the new protocol, de facto, there is currently no Tribunal to talk about.

The third difference is the law to be applied by the new Tribunal. This is now limited to 'the SADC Treaty and the applicable SADC Protocol.'[85] This is a significant departure from the previous dispensation where the SADC Tribunal was allowed to interpret the SADC Treaty; the SADC Protocols; all subsidiary instruments adopted by the Summit, the CoM or by any other institution or organ of the Community pursuant to the Treaty; and was also allowed to develop its own Community jurisprudence having regard to applicable treaties, general principles and rules of public international law, and any rules and principles of the laws of Member States. Needless to say, this reduction in the sources of the law to be applied by the Tribunal is clearly meant to arrest the growth of Community jurisprudence since it was through the expansive interpretation of the SADC Treaty and the SADC Tribunal's broad and liberal jurisdictional powers that the old Tribunal was able to develop its progressive jurisprudence.

Other notable differences include: the judges of the Tribunal would now be so called instead of being referred to as 'members'[86]; and unlike previously where the judges would elect one of their own as president, the new president would now be appointed by the Summit.[87]

Assuming that all efforts to reinstate the Tribunal in its previous form fail,[88] there is also the theoretical possibility of a challenge to the legality of the 'new' tribunal and that the new tribunal might be asked to pronounce itself on the legality of the Summit decisions on its predecessor.

---

[84] It should be noted that this is not provided for in the new protocol but is in terms of the SADC Treaty amendment of 17 August 2007.

[85] Art 35.

[86] See art 2(1), as read with art 3(1).

[87] Art 5(1).

[88] A number of civil society organisations in SADC are working on multipronged litigation and advocacy strategies for the reinstatement of the Tribunal in its previous form. This came out of some of the plenary discussions at a stakeholder roundtable discussion on the SADC Tribunal referred to in Footnote 80 above.

Whatever the 'new' tribunal's attitude would be (assuming that a 'new' tribunal will eventually come into being), what remains to be said is that SADC remains worse off in the absence of a judicial institution and shall remain so even after the operationalisation of the 'new' tribunal, since the new protocol does not give it much power. Indeed, impunity and abuse of discretion breed well in the absence of especially judicial checks. As noted by Schermers and Blokker, 'uncontrolled powers lead to dangerous bureaucracy, technocracy or autocracy.'[89]

4.3   THE SADC NATIONAL COMMITTEES

The SADC National Committees (SNCs) came into being through the 2001 amendment of the SADC Treaty. Their composition and functions are set out in article 16A. The Treaty mandates each Member State to create an SNC.[90] The SNCs are supposed to meet at least four times a year.[91]

It should be recalled that the pre-2001 SADC Treaty regime had an institution that was located at national level, the Sector Coordinating Units. Some have observed that with the demise of the decentralised sectoral approach and the jettisoning of the Sector Coordinating Units, the SNCs were established to fill the vacuum created by the demise of the former and the new institution was meant to be an avenue for broader participation by SADC citizens at the national level in SADC decision-making processes.[92]

Some scholars see a lot of potential in locating SNCs within the SADC Member States, with civil society and other non-state actors as integral parts of the SADC governance framework.[93] There is also the view that

---

[89] Schermers & Blokker (Footnote 1 above) 407. With regards to employment disputes between SADC and its employees however, SADC Administrative Tribunal (SADCAT) has now been established by means of ordinary Summit decision. See para 27 of the communiqué of the 35th Summit of SADC Heads of State and Government, Gaborone 17–18 August 2015 https://www.sadc.int/files/7814/3997/3204/Final_35th_Summit_Communique_as_on_August_18_2015.pdf (last accessed 8 April 2016).

[90] Art 16A (1) of the SADC Treaty.

[91] Art 16A (12) of the SADC Treaty.

[92] Nzewi & Zakwe (Footnote 3 above) 7.

[93] See S. Ngwenya 'Regional integration in Africa,' in M. Mbeki (ed.) *Advocates for change, how to overcome Africa's challenges* (2009); B. Moyo 'Civil society organisations' engagement with regional economic communities in Africa, people friendly or people driven?' *Final report submitted to the UNDP Regional Service Centre for Eastern and Southern Africa, Johannesburg,* 2007.

participation by civil society organisations (CSOs) at all levels in the fulfilment of SADC's core objectives constitutes 'an entrenched legal
imperative.'[94] According to this view, the democratic deficit in SADC can
be addressed through participatory democracy by involving civil society
actors.[95]

The SNCs are supposed to consist of 'key' stakeholders who are identified as government; the private sector; civil society; NGOs; and workers'
and employers' organisations.[96] No framework is provided in the Treaty
on the modalities of the constitution of the SNCs, including procedures
and the number of participants per stakeholder, save for the broad provision that the composition of each SNC shall reflect the core areas of integration and coordination referred to in the Treaty.[97]

Four responsibilities of the SNCs are outlined in the Treaty and these
are

- to provide input at the national level in the formulation of SADC
  policies, strategies, and programmes of action
- to coordinate and oversee, at the national level, implementation of
  SADC programmes of action
- to initiate projects and issue papers as an input to the preparation of
  the Regional Indicative Strategic Development Plan, in accordance
  with the priority areas set out in the SADC Common Agenda
- to create a national steering committee, sub-committees, and technical committees[98]

On the face of it, the SNCs have a policy formulation and implementation mandate. Their location in this chapter is more to do with the legal
reality arising from the overall construction of the Treaty in terms of their

---

[94] Moyo (Footnote 93 above) 53. It should be noted that participation by civil society
actors is not only provided for in the provisions dealing with the SNCs. Art 23(1) of the
Treaty commits SADC to 'involve fully, the peoples of the Region and key stakeholders in the
process of regional integration.' Unfortunately no peremptory framework of 'full involvement' is set out in the Treaty.

[95] See generally, D. Motsamai 'SADC's review of its Principles and Guidelines Governing
Democratic Elections: Need for civil society inputs?' *Institute for Global Dialogue* (October
2013) Issue # 102.

[96] Art 16A (1) as read with art 16A (13) (a)–(e).

[97] Art 16A (3).

[98] Art 16A (4) (a)–(d).

composition, functions, and linkages with other SADC institutions. Notwithstanding their stated and rather superficial responsibilities, the provisions of the Treaty on their exact position in the SADC institutional family are not clear. Certainly, the Treaty does not envisage real norm setting on the part of the SNCs, but rather the making of 'inputs' (from the outside) into norm setting by the relevant institutions of SADC. A holistic reading of the Treaty provisions on the functions and composition of SNCs, alongside the provisions on the institutions discussed in Chap. 3 above, reveal an intention to create no more than a consultative forum for both policy formulation and implementation issues, and arguably also a 'soft' oversight role over implementation, than a norm-setting institution.

On their structure, each consists of a chairperson and chairpersons of sub-committees.[99] These sub-committees (and technical committees) are constituted at ministerial and official levels.[100] There is also a national steering committee whose responsibility is to ensure rapid implementation of programmes.[101]

Quite curiously, article 16A (8) provides that 'sub-committees and technical committees shall endeavour to involve key stakeholders in their operations.' One would assume that by clearly stipulating that SNCs shall consist of key stakeholders, said stakeholders would be part of the SNCs' operations anyway, including those of the sub-committees and technical committees. The couching of article 16A (8) implies that when it comes to sub-committees and technical committees, the key stakeholders suddenly become outside stakeholders whose participation is left to the discretion of these committees.[102] Quite clearly then, participation by CSOs in SNCs and other SADC affairs, just like that of other key stakeholders, is not an entrenched legal position.[103]

---

[99] Art 16A (5).

[100] Article 16 A (6). Just like the sub-committees, the technical committees are not properly introduced, constituted, and given functions.

[101] Art 16A (7).

[102] Although the use of 'shall' implies a peremptory obligation, the subsequent employment of 'endeavour' clearly means participation of key stakeholders in these committees is merely directory.

[103] This is contrary to the conclusion reached by Moyo (Footnote 93 above). Indeed even the reference to the involvement of the peoples of the region and key stakeholders in the process of regional integration in art 23 could be said to be merely directory as it does not spell out a peremptory framework of engagement.

Another institution created by article 16A is the national secretariat to be created by each Member State whose remit is the facilitation of the operation of the SADC National Committee. Although falling under the rubric of SNCs, it would appear that the national secretariat was not intended to be a sub-organ of SNC. On reporting, each national secretariat is, in terms of article 16A (10) obligated to produce and submit a report to the SADC Secretariat at 'specified' intervals. The intervals are not specified in the Treaty. Also, nothing is said in the Treaty of what should happen to these reports upon their receipt by the Secretariat or for that matter, whether there are any sanctions to be suffered in the event of non-submission of these reports.

Then there is the issue of funding of SNCs. This is not as straightforward as some researchers suggest.[104] In fact, the Treaty is silent on the issue of funding of SNCs. The only mention of funding is with regard to the national secretariats. The funding of national secretariats is not a SADC supranational obligation but is an obligation imposed on Member States at the domestic level.[105] Since the SADC Treaty specifically imposes the obligation to fund national secretariats on Member States, one might reason that it follows that the same may not be the case with SNCs since the specific mention of national secretariats quite clearly excludes the former. This line of interpretation, however, leads to an absurdity that might not have been contemplated by the framers of the Treaty—there is no effort made by the SADC Treaty to harmonise the structure, particularly the size, of this institution which makes funding by SADC problematic largely because of the possibility of staffing disparities in Member States (among many other variables) which would most likely result in inequitable treatment of Member States. In any case, the SADC Treaty clearly delegates the responsibility to create SNCs to Member States.[106] The implication of this is that the role of a Member State does not end with the creation of this institution, but permeates its entire life, including its funding.

While the general lackadaisical attitude of SADC leaders on the establishment of regional institutions, especially their apparent reluctance to embrace institutional formalism, has been criticised elsewhere in this book,

---

[104] For example, Nzewi and Zakwe (Footnote 3 above) believe that the SADC Treaty categorically provides that SNCs should be funded by their respective Member States.

[105] Art 16A (11) of the SADC Treaty.

[106] Art 16A (1).

no plausible defence can be made on behalf of the rationale for establishing SNCs. It appears the SNCs were only established to give the appearance of stakeholder involvement.[107] Lack of a clear institutional framework
for SNCs is a clear indication that this is an institution that was never
designed to succeed.

For a broader perspective, it may be important at this stage to set out
the broader legal aspect of stakeholder involvement in SADC both in general terms and in the context of SNCs. There is the general article 23(1)
provision which provides for the full involvement of the people of SADC
and key stakeholders in the process of regional integration. There is also
the specific 'key stakeholder' involvement in the context of SNCs. The
involvement of key stakeholders in SNCs should be interpreted not as
substitute of the general right accorded to SADC citizens (and key stakeholders) within SADC to be fully involved in SADC processes. Rather, this
should be seen as an additional and specific institutionalised framework of
participation.

However, SADC institutions, particularly the CoM and the Secretariat
seem to have truncated the article 23(1) provision in practice. In its meeting of 11–16 August 2011 in Luanda, CoM noted that

> [T]he SADC Treaty recognizes key stakeholders as important partners in
> the implementation of the SADC Programme of Action. Article 23 of the
> SADC Treaty lays the foundation for key stakeholder participation and
> defines them as private sector, civil society, Non Governmnetal Organisation
> (NGOs), workers and employers' organisations.[108]

To the extent that the above leaves out the 'peoples of SADC,' it amounts
to a misrepresentation of the legal position. The key stakeholders mentioned in article 23(1) are in addition to the peoples of SADC, not as

---

[107] As noted by C. Ng'ongo'la in 'The framework for regional integration in the Southern
African Development Community' (2008) *University of Botswana Law Journal* at pp. 27–28,
the participation of stakeholders in the SADC integration project is deferred to this peripheral institution and is not accommodated in the core institutions of SADC which remain
intergovernmental in character. This view may not be entirely correct since, as pointed out
elsewhere in this section, the framework of involvement in art 23(1) is of a general character
as opposed to the specific one with regard to SNCs. However, even the art 23(1) framework
is, as argued below, not sufficient to guarantee effective stakeholder participation in the
SADC integration project.

[108] Item 4.5.4.1 (i) of extract of minutes of the said meeting. The minutes are available in
the SADC Library, Gaborone (accessed 10 March 2014).

representatives of same. The unfortunate result of this is that the SADC Secretariat might have put this misinterpretation of the legal position into practice through signing memoranda of understanding with those stakeholders that are deemed key including the SADC Council of NGOs, the Association of SADC Chambers of Commerce and Industry and the Southern Africa Trade Unions Coordination Council.[109] While these stakeholders have a regional character and are *prima facie* key as envisaged by article 23(1); and while it may not be wrong per se to enter into memoranda of understanding with them, the problem is that such relationships may, in the absence of another framework for the involvement of or participation by the generality of SADC citizens, be viewed as based on a truncated and accordingly faulty interpretation of article 23(1) of the SADC Treaty. This can possibly lead, deliberately or unwittingly, to the sidelining the generality of SADC citizens whose full involvement/ participation in the SADC integration processes is also specifically provided for in article 23(1).

However, with the demise of the SADC Tribunal and the new protocol's extinguishing of the right to access by individuals, stakeholder participation in SADC (both at the national and regional levels), at least from a legal perspective, is not guaranteed since citizens and key stakeholders alike have no regional judicial recourse to challenge either their exclusion in the SADC processes or to challenge the acts or omissions of SADC or any of its institutions.[110] The need for a clear, general, and justiciable stakeholder involvement framework cannot therefore be overemphasised.

Unsurprisingly, literature on SNCs paints a bleak picture of non-functionality; lack of technical capacity; resource constraints; and

---

[109] Item 4.5.4.1 (iii) of the minutes. See Footnote 108 above.

[110] Faced with a similar legal framework, the East African Court of Justice (EACJ) observed: 'However, neither Article 150 nor any other provision of the Treaty specifies the modality and extent of people's participation in cooperation activities in general and in the amendment of the Treaty in particular. Ideally, it would have been easier for this Court to uphold and apply the proposition that every amendment of the Treaty must involve prior consultation of the people, if the draftsman had provided the measure for determining such involvement or participation, as is done for example, in integration treaties that provide for consulting the people through referenda. Undoubtedly other forms of involving and consulting the people are also possible.' See *East African Law Society & 3 others v Attorney General of the Republic of Kenya & 4 others* (Reference 3 of 2007, decided on 1 September 2008), para 64. See Chap. 6, Sect. 6.2 for a detailed discussion of the EACJ.

coordination challenges.[111] If SNCs were meant to be sites of participation for civil society and other stakeholders in SADC policy formulation and implementation processes, this was not worth the effort. As noted by some, most of the SADC Member States do not view the matter of the establishment and functioning of the SNCs seriously.[112] It is as if the institution of SNC was an unwanted child of the SADC reform process. Real stakeholder participation in an organisation should be seen as going beyond merely creating entry points that only exist in appearance than substance, but should be guaranteed through the construction of a realistic and viable institutional framework that is also democratic, transparent, accountable, and effective.

With an institutional framework that adequately provides for checks and balances through, among other things, the creation of a parliamentary body with adequate legislative and oversight role; and a judiciary arm with significant powers of review, civil society and other stakeholders would certainly find a way of getting their voices heard and influencing policy, especially if that same framework creates a meaningful regime of access to information. As rightly observed by Peters, stakeholders such as NGOs and transnational corporations (and by extension of reason, local business) 'should be kept at a distance from the law making process … in order to fulfil their watchdog and opposition function.'[113]

4.4   THE SADC PARLIAMENTARY FORUM

While national parliaments can control policies at the international level through a variety of ways including, for example, ratification of treaties and control of financial contributions made by Member States to international organisations, these controls tend to be largely inefficient and

---

[111] See, for example, E.N. Tjønneland 'Making SADC work? Revisiting institutional reform' in Hansohm D. et al. (eds) *Monitoring regional integration in Southern Africa yearbook* (2005) 5, 171; Nzewi and Zakwe (Footnote 3 above) 9; L. Giuffrida & H. Müller-Godde 'Strengthening SADC institutional structures—capacity development is the key to SADC Secretariat's effectiveness' in Bösil, A. et al. (eds) *Monitoring regional integration in Southern Africa Yearbook* (2008); S. Zondi 'Governance and social policy in the SADC region: An issues analysis' (2009) Working Paper Series No. 2 *Planning Division, Development Bank of Southern Africa* 19.

[112] Zondi (Footnote 111 above) 19.

[113] A. Peters 'Membership in the global constitutional community' in J. Klabbers et al. (2009) *The Constitutionalization of international law* 156.

ineffective.[114] The solution to this, as Schermers and Blokker assert, 'is the establishment of international organs with the task of exercising political control over the executive.'[115]

The development of parliamentary bodies within or alongside regional organisations (some of these are based on inter-parliamentary agreements and have no formal status as institutions/organs of the respective organisations), while initially largely a European initiative (with all their varying statuses), is now a global phenomenon.[116]

From a global democratic theory perspective, specifically its cosmopolitan variant, the creation of regional parliaments in all parts of the world would lead to the development of a parliamentary culture and 'legitimate and independent sources of law' borne out of decisions of these regional parliaments. Such a development would, the proponents of the cosmopolitan democratic theory hope, constitute the building blocks for a global parliament in a constitutionalised global order.[117]

As has been noted by some scholars, international parliaments, whatever their nature and form, do have value and their effectiveness or contribution to the global international order (which is not usually visible immediately) should not be assessed only in positivist terms by merely looking at their formal powers, but also in terms of their 'norm entrepreneurship' agency—that is, the promotion of the acceptance of 'new norms and values.'[118]

---

[114] Schermers & Blokker (Footnote 1 above) 408–411.

[115] Schermers & Blokker (Footnote 1 above) 411.

[116] Schermers & Blokker (Footnote 1 above) 412–415. The examples given include the North Atlantic Assembly; the Parliamentary Assembly of the Council of Europe; the Parliamentary Assembly of the Organisation of Security and Cooperation in Europe; the Parliamentary Assembly of the Black Sea Economic Cooperation; the Parliamentary Assembly of ECOWAS; SADCPF; the Pan-African Parliament; the Latin American Parliament; and the Andean Parliament. For the challenges associated with attempting to categorise/classify international parliamentary institutions and for some of the attempts at their categorisation/classification, see O. Costa et al. 'Introduction' in O. Costa et al. (eds) *Parliamentary dimensions of regionalization and globalization: The role of inter-parliamentary institutions* (2013) 6–10.

[117] Z. Šabič 'International parliamentary institutions: A research agenda' in O. Costa et al. (eds) *Parliamentary dimensions of regionalization and globalization: The role of inter-parliamentary institutions* (2013) 25. Šabič makes reference to the works of David Held and Daniele Archibugi, proponents of the cosmopolitan democracy project. See Chap. 1 where reference to the cosmopolitan democratic model is also made, including an outline of a cosmopolitan global order that is envisioned by Held and Archibugi.

[118] Šabič (Footnote 117 above) 20–21.

Historically speaking, international parliaments proliferated post-World War II,[119] the push factor being the demand for transparency in decision-making at the international level.[120] This growth is thus directly linked to, among other things, the spread of globalisation and democratisation processes.[121] This trend also impacted the institutional character of regional integration processes in a number of regions in the world—Africa, Latin America, and Western Europe as these processes have from the late 1950 and late 1960s 'contained a parliamentary dimension.'[122] A further growth (including the 'renaming' and 'rebranding' of extant international parliamentary institutions) is recorded immediately after the end of the Cold War.[123] Generally speaking, therefore, the presence of international parliamentary institutions on the global scene, including in regional integration frameworks, can be directly linked to the need for and growth of democracy in governance beyond the state.[124]

The SADC Treaty establishes, in article 9(1), eight institutions.[125] The SADCPF is not one of the eight specifically mentioned institutions. In other words, the SADC Treaty neither establishes nor makes mention of the SADCPF or any parliamentary organ for that matter. Mention of this is important in order to understand the actual status of the SADCPF in the overall governance architecture of SADC.

The SADCPF was established in 1997 during the life of the old SADC Treaty whose article 9(1) was, save for the jettisoning of some institutions and the coming on board of new ones, substantially similar to the current

---

[119] The first international parliament, the Inter-Parliamentary Union was set up in 1889. See Costa et al (Footnote 116 above) 1.

[120] Costa et al (Footnote 116 above) 5. See also the reference thereunder.

[121] As above.

[122] As above.

[123] Costa et al. (Footnote 116 above) 6; M.A.M., Salih 'African regional parliaments: legislatures without legislative powers' in O. Costa et al. (eds) *Parliamentary dimensions of regionalization and globalization: The role of inter-parliamentary institutions* (2013) 152.

[124] Some scholars see the remarkable incremental growth of the European Parliament's powers within the EU project (discussed in detail in Chap. 6, Sect. 6.4) as a direct result of the influence of democracy as an ideology. See generally O. Costa & N. Brack 'The role of the European Parliament in Europe's integration and parliamentarization process' in O. Costa et al. (eds) *Parliamentary dimensions of regionalization and globalization: The role of inter-parliamentary institutions* (2013) 45–69.

[125] These are, as already discussed in detail so far: the Summit; the OPDS; the CoM; the SCMCs; the SCO; the Secretariat; the Tribunal; and SNCs.

article 9(1).[126] The current article 9(2) was also carried over from the old Treaty article 9(2) and it provides for the establishment of other institutions as may be necessary. It is in terms of article 9(2) that the SADCPF is often said to have been established.[127] There is also article 10(6) which gives the Summit the discretionary power to 'create committees, other institutions and organs as it may consider necessary.'

Article 3(2) of the SADCPF Constitution mentions article 9(2) of the SADC Treaty as one of the possible two bases for the establishment of the SADCPF. Article 3(2) provides that the 'SADC Parliamentary Forum is established in accordance with article 9(2) *or* article 10(6) of the Treaty' (own emphasis). Thus, it would appear that the framers of the SADCPF Constitution were themselves not sure which of the two mentioned articles is the basis of the establishment of the SADCPF. Had their attitude been that both of the two articles are the bases, they would have used the term 'as read with,' instead of casting it in the alternative.

There is a clear distinction in the wording of the two provisions. Article 9(2) does not state by which institution or organ of the Community the other institutions may be established. Read in the context of article 9(1) which creates what one may refer to as the core institutions of SADC, one would assume that the purpose of article 9(2) is to leave room for the establishment of other article 9 institutions that would form the core of SADC institutions. Interpreted this way, such institutions should be established by way of actual legislative act in the form of Treaty amendment.

On the other hand, article 10(6) specifically deals with the powers of the Summit. The committees and other institutions or organs that may be created under article 10(6) are those, it would appear, that are meant for the attainment of efficacious conduct of the affairs of SADC, not those that may result in a reconfiguration of inter-institutional relations within SADC. The establishment of article 10(6) institutions should thus be more of an exercise of subsidiary as opposed to primary legislative power. Interpreted this way, therefore, the establishment of an actual legislative body within SADC would fall under article 9(2).

---

[126] The date of establishment of the SADCPF is derived from the date of signing of its constitutive document, the SADC-PF Constitution, available at http://www.sadcpf.org (last accessed 9 September 2013).

[127] See, for example, the website of the SADCPF (Footnote 126 above, accessed 9 September 2013).

The establishment of the SADCPF was 'approved' by the Summit in the context of the above rather unclear legal position. An opportunity to settle this legal uncertainty presented itself in the case of *Bookie Monica Kethusegile-Juru and the Southern African Development Community Parliamentary Forum.*[128] In that case, applicant, Bookie Monica Kethusegile-Juru, approached the SADC Tribunal alleging that her contract of employment had been unlawfully terminated by respondent, the SADCPF. The SADCPF raised three points *in limine*. Only one of those preliminary objections is of relevance to this study. The SADCPF argued that the Tribunal did not have the jurisdiction to entertain the matter:

> in that it only has power to interpret the Southern African Development Community Treaty (the SADC Treaty), Protocols, Subsidiary Instruments and acts and Institutions of the Community and such other matters as may specifically be provided for in any agreements that Member States may conclude among themselves or within the Community, and which confer jurisdiction on the Tribunal.[129]

Therefore, since the SADCPF was not an institution of SADC, the SADCPF argued, the Tribunal had no jurisdiction to entertain the matter.

To its credit, the Tribunal reasoned that this was the 'crucial question'[130] for determination. Unfortunately, this is as far as the credit goes. The Tribunal then went on to state what it deemed to be the factual and legal background in the following terms:

> Article 9(1) of the SADC Treaty stipulates six institutions as having been established (sic). Under paragraph (2) the Community may establish other institutions '...as necessary.' On or about September 8, 1997, the Summit, held in Blantyre in the Republic of Malawi, established the Respondent as follows:
>> '7.8 The Summit *approved* the establishment of the SADC Parliamentary Forum as an autonomous institution of SADC, in accordance with Article 9(2) of the SADC Treaty.' (Own emphasis)[131]

---

[128] See Footnote 35 above.
[129] Para 2 of the ruling.
[130] Para 4 of the ruling.
[131] Para 5 of the ruling.

Having set out what it deemed to be a solid factual and legal background to the establishment of the SADCPF, the Tribunal determined that there was 'no doubt' that the SADCPF is an institution of SADC.[132] This is certainly one case in which the Tribunal should have *mero motu* sought the intervention of SADC, through the Secretariat. The matter involved two apparently distinct institutions and the least the Tribunal could have done was to afford the SADC Secretariat, as an interested party, an opportunity to present its side of the case.

However, for all intents and purposes, and notwithstanding the decision of the SADC Tribunal, the SADCPF is not a member of the SADC institutional family. Indeed, it is quite telling that the SADCPF also identifies itself as an autonomous institution of SADC.[133] But over and above this, it is significant that the SADCPF itself, in its submission to the SADC Tribunal *in casu*, plainly refused to be identified as an institution of SADC. Even the 'We,' referring to the 'founders' of the SADCPF in the preamble to the SADCPF Constitution, refers to members of the parliaments in SADC Member States, not the Summit.

It is also important to note that even the internal documents of SADC do not acknowledge the SADCPF as forming part of the institutional architecture of SADC. For example, a SADC publication, *Major achievements and challenges: 25th anniversary 1980–2005*, only mentions the institutions specifically listed under article 9(1) of the SADC Treaty as constituting SADC's institutional family.[134]

To further buttress the attitude of the SADC institutions that the SADCPF is not one of them, the final communiqué of the 28th Summit of Heads of State or Government held at Sandton, Johannesburg, from 16 to 17 August 2008, lists a number of organisations that were represented at the Summit: the African Union Commission (AUC); the United Nations Economic Commission for Africa (UNECA); the Common Market for Eastern and Southern Africa (COMESA); the EAC; the Southern African Customs Union (SACU); ECOWAS; the New Economic Partnership for Africa's Development (NEPAD); and the SADCPF.[135]

---

[132] Para 6 of the ruling.
[133] SADCPF website (Footnote 126 above).
[134] The document is available in the SADC library, Gaborone (accessed 10 March 2014).
[135] Para 6 of the communiqué of the Summit held at Sandton, Johannesburg, available in the SADC library, Gaborone (accessed 10 March 2014). It should also be noted that while the SADC website lists the SADCPF under the 'SADC Institutions,' the website goes on to state that the SADCPF 'does not have a reporting relationship to Summit and other SADC

Further, when it comes to observation of elections in the SADC region, the SADCPF has so far been sending its own election observer missions that are distinct from the official SADC Election Observer Missions (SEOM), and whose findings have at times contradicted those of SEOM leading to political tensions between the two organisations. For example, concerning the 2002 and 2008 Zimbabwean elections, the SADCPF election observation mission differed significantly with the SEOM and condemned the polls.[136] This is said to have strained the relations between SADC and SADCPF to such an extent that the SADCPF was sidelined from SADC activities by SADC.[137]

Any doubt about the status of the SADCPF in the SADC scheme of things should be laid to rest by recourse to the minutes of the Summit proceedings of 8 September 1997 held in Blantyre—the same minutes that are ironically the basis of the SADC Tribunal's judgment in the *Kethusegile-Juru* matter.[138] On the issue of SADCPF, the minutes read, in full:

7. SADC Parliamentary Forum

7.1. The Summit considered the Note (SADC/SM/1/97/7), on the SADC Parliamentary Forum, presented by the Secretariat.
7.2. The Summit recalled that at its meeting in Johannesburg, in August 1995, it *noted* (own emphasis) the establishment of the SADC Parliamentary Forum.
7.3. The SADC Parliamentary Forum is a grouping of twelve (12) National Parliaments in the region. The Forum has adopted a constitution which has been approved and ratified by nine (9) of the twelve (12) Member Parliaments.
7.4. The main objective of the Forum is to constitute a Parliamentary Consultative Assembly. The ultimate goal of the Forum is to

---

Institutions but works together with them on matters of common interest.' See http://www.sadc.int/about-sadc/sadc-institutions/sadc-parliamentarian-forum/ (last accessed 25 April 2015).

[136] For a relatively detailed discussion of the stance taken by the SADCPF on the 2002 Zimbabwe presidential elections, see J. Isaksen 'Restructuring SADC—progress and problems' *Development Studies and Human Rights*, Chr Michelsen Institute Report R 2002: 15: Norway at p. 33 www.cmi.no (accessed 12 December 2013).

[137] Nzewi and Zakwe (Footnote 3 above) 8.

[138] SADC library, Gaborone (accessed 10 March 2014).

establish a regional Parliamentary Framework for dialogue on issues of regional interest and concern.

7.5. The Summit noted that the Forum is governed by the following principles:

(a) The destiny of all our peoples is inextricably interlinked, and that regional development is imperative;

(b) Strengthening the implementation capacity of the Southern African Development Community must involve the active participation of the elected representatives of the SADC Member States;

(c) Some of the decisions taken by the Southern African Development Community may require the passage of the legislation by National Parliaments (sic);

(d) The Parliaments, as elected bodies of our peoples, are the appropriate stakeholders in this process.

7.6. The Summit noted the copy of the Constitution of the SADC Parliamentary Forum and in particular that the SADC Parliamentary Forum would amend certain provisions of the Constitution in order to align them to the provisions of the SADC Treaty.

7.7. The Summit also noted that the Parliamentary Forum would be sustained by contributions of the [M]ember States' national Parliaments.

7.8. The Summit approved the establishment of the SADC Parliamentary Forum as an autonomous institution of SADC, in accordance with Article 9 (2) of the Treaty.[139]

Clearly then, the coming into being of the SADCPF was a matter that was done outside the SADC Treaty framework and the SADCPF was brought to the Summit by its founders, the national parliaments of SADC Member States, merely for noting or endorsement. However, maybe the outcome

---

[139] However, art 1 of the SADCPF Constitution states, among other things, that 'The Constitution shall come into force upon the approval of the creation of the SADC Parliamentary Forum by the Summit of Heads of State or Government in accordance with *Article 10(6)* of the Treaty of the Southern African Development Community.' (Own emphasis).

of *Kethusegile-Juru* case served only to give the SADCPF legal and political legitimacy and a sense of belonging. But that can only remain within
the realm of speculation.

However, even post *Kethusegile-Juru*, there does not appear to have
been any review of the relationship between SADC and the SADCPF. The
'outsider' status of the SADCPF is still evident in the language of some of
the official documents of some of the institutions of SADC. For instance,
a portion of the CoM minutes of the 11–16 August 2011 in Luanda reads:

> 4.5.6.3 Council further recalled that, at its meeting held in Windhoek,
> Namibia, in March 2011, it noted that the relationship between the SADC
> Structures and the SADC Parliamentary Forum need to be reviewed.[140]

The reference not to *other SADC structures* but to *SADC structures* seems
to be deliberate and to leave no doubt that the SADCPF is not one of the
SADC structures. An argument could be made that just like in *Campbell*,
the Summit is refusing to take into account the decision of the Tribunal
regarding the status of the SADCPF. However, the establishment of a
regional parliament with both norm-setting and oversight roles should
rest on a solid treaty basis,[141] rather than on a tenuous judicial decision
which in any case was made during the course of a labour dispute, rather
than in a 'constitutional' case where a declaration on the status of the
SADCPF within SADC was being sought.

In terms of typology, the SADCPF clearly belongs to those organisations of parliamentarians identified by Schermers and Blokker as 'groupings of parliamentarians of members of some organizations (who) have
structured their consultations on the work of the organization without

---

[140] Available in the SADC library, Gaborone (accessed on 10 March 2014).

[141] The observation by Justice Mkandawire, former registrar of the SADC Tribunal is apposite:
'For as long as the SADC PF remains outside the mainstream SADC institutions actually men-
tioned in the SADC Treaty, it will continue to have negligible impact … in policy making in the
SADC.' See C. Mkandawire 'Perspective on the parliamentary transformation agenda' *Regional
Parliamentary Seminar on 'Africa's Regional Parliaments: State of Development, Cooperation
and Potential'* 6 Southern Sun Hotel, Johannesburg, South Africa, 17–18 May 2012 http://
www.awepa.org/wp-content/uploads/2012/05/3__Hon__Justice_Mkandawire_
Perspectives_on_The_Parliamentary_Transformation_Agenda.pdf (accessed 12 September
2014). See also T. Musavengana *The proposed SADC parliament: Old wine in new bottles or an
ideal whose time has come?* (2011) who, at p. 50 emphatically observes that SADCPF is not
considered a formal SADC structure.

being an organ of the organization ...'[142] Schermers and Blokker then go on to give as examples the Parliamentary Network on the World Bank (and the International Monetary Fund) and the Consultative Assembly of Parliamentarians for the International Criminal Court and the Rule of Law. The above discussion on the status of the SADCPF in SADC may appear to be unnecessarily exhaustive, especially since the Tribunal had made a final 'binding' decision on the matter. However, other than the need for a full discussion of this complex matter, there is another more important reason for the fullest possible enquiry—this is a matter that may still be far from being settled. With SADCAT having now been established,[143] there is more than a theoretical possibility of yet another labour dispute between the SADCPF and one or more of its employees. In such an event, SADCAT might be asked to revisit the matter. This calls for a detailed academic enquiry which might assist in any future judicial consideration of the matter.

The Constitution of the SADCPF provides that the headquarters of the organisation shall be in Windhoek. The double irony of the choice of headquarters is that it is far removed from the mainstream SADC institutions in Gaborone; yet close enough to the now disbanded SADC Tribunal. The SADCPF accords itself the status of an international organisation. In terms of article 4 (1), it has the capacity and power to enter into contract, acquire, own, or dispose of property and to sue and to be sued. Article 4(1)(i) states that in the territory of each Member State, the SADCPF shall have such legal capacity as is necessary for the proper exercise of its functions. The Constitution also gives the SADCPF's representatives and officials the usual parliamentary privileges.[144] Needless to emphasise, these provisions that give the SADCPF a legal personality that is distinct from that of SADC are a further manifestation of the fact that it is not part of the SADC institutional family.[145]

---

[142] Schermers & Blokker (Footnote 1 above) 413.

[143] See Footnote 89 above.

[144] Art 4(2).

[145] The legal status of SADC is set out in art 3 of the SADC Treaty. Para 1 provides that 'SADC shall be an international organisation and shall have legal personality with capacity and power to enter into contract, acquire, own or dispose of movable or immovable property and to sue and to be sued.' In terms of para 2, '[i]n the territory of each member state, SADC shall, pursuant to para 1[...], have such legal capacity as is necessary for the proper exercise of its functions.'

It now remains to discuss the role of the SADCPF in SADC. The intent of the framers of the SADCPF Constitution was not to create a legislative body, not even a nominal one. They made it clear that the body they were creating was not to be mistaken for a legislature of any sort. They were creating, as the preamble puts it, a 'Consultative Assembly' which could in the future be developed into 'a regional Parliamentary structure.' The expressed intent is the 'strengthening of the Southern African Development Community by involving [p]arliamentarians of Member States in its activities.'

The objectives listed in the Constitution include strengthening the implementation capacity of SADC by involving (SADC) parliamentarians in SADC activities; and facilitating the effective implementation of SADC policies and projects.[146] The SADCPF is therefore nothing more than an advocacy forum. Indeed, with regard to SADC policy input, the SADCPF is limited to making recommendations to relevant institutions of SADC and promotional work.[147]

On membership and composition, the SADCPF Constitution states that membership is open to national parliaments whose countries are members of SADC. It consists of presiding officers of national parliaments and up to five representatives per each national parliament elected on the basis of gender and political party equity.

The organs of the SADCPF, whose discussion falls outside the scope of this study, are the Plenary Assembly; the Executive Committee; the Office of the Secretary General; and the Standing Committees.[148] The Constitution gives the Plenary Assembly the power to approve the estab-lishment of other organs.[149] The desire of the SADCPF is that its Plenary Assembly should in future be transformed into a formal regional parliament.[150]

The discussion of the SADCPF under the rubric of oversight institu-tions of SADC is unavoidable especially in light of the decision in

---

[146] Among the many other objectives of the SADCPF [set out in art 5(a)–(o)] are to pro-mote the principles of human rights, gender equality and democracy within the SADC region; and to familiarise the people of the SADC countries with the aims and objectives of SADC.

[147] See generally art 8 of the SADCPF Constitution.

[148] Art 7(1).

[149] Art 7(2).

[150] Art 8(3) (b) of the SADCPF Constitution.

Kethusegile-Juru. This is not to validate the reasoning of the SADC Tribunal in that case, but rather to provide a holistic discussion.

The role of the SADCPF in influencing policy in SADC may be difficult to measure but it should not be dismissed merely because it does not belong to the formal SADC institutional family. However, in the absence of a legally enforceable right to contribute to norm setting in SADC and to play an oversight role over policymaking and implementation, the power of influence that may be possessed by the SADCPF remains limited. The disbandment of the SADC Tribunal and the new protocol's limitation of the right to access have all but extinguished any realistic chance of judicial review thereby limiting the influence of SADCPF and other stakeholders. Thus, while there may be a 'binding' decision of the Tribunal, that decision does not create an institutional framework that could make the SADCPF a meaningful player in influencing norm formation and implementation in SADC.

What the future holds for the SADCPF is uncertain. As recent as August 2011, the CoM, taking a cue from a Summit decision of 2004, opined that it was still 'premature to establish a Regional Parliament at this early stage of integration.'[151] On its part, the SADCPF tries to be as involved as much as possible in SADC affairs: it has been playing a crucial advocacy role in pushing for the operationalisation of the SNCs and its own formalisation into a regional parliament[152]; it gets involved in the observation of elections in SADC Member States; it attends CoM meetings; and it collaborates 'on harmonization of policies and regulatory frameworks concerning HIV and AIDS matters.'[153]However, as has been rightly observed, while the activities of the SADCPF such as the development of the Norms and Standards for Elections in the SADC Region and the Model Law on HIV and AIDS in Southern Africa are significant, these are largely ignored and their impact remains minimal, and they cannot even be considered as SADC soft law since they were not created by those institutions of SADC with a treaty mandate to do so.[154]

---

[151] Item 4.5.6.6 of minutes of meeting of CoM of 11–16 August 2011, Luanda, available in the SADC library, Gaborone (accessed 10 March 2014).

[152] Moyo (Footnote 93 above) 52.

[153] Item 4.5.6.5 of minutes of meeting of CoM of 11–16 August 2011 (Footnote 140 above).

[154] Mkandawire (Footnote 141 above) 4, 6, 7; Musavengana (Footnote 141 above) 23, 24. In fact, Mkandawire was making reference to the latter.

4.5   Conclusion

The role of oversight institutions in international organisations cannot be underestimated. Properly designed, they not only can exercise control over the other institutions, but can be part of the norm-setting machinery as well. However, as has been seen in this chapter, in order for oversight institutions to be effective, there is need for clear and detailed legal provisions that not only create the oversight institutions, but provide for their effective contribution in the affairs of the organisation.

Unfortunately, there is currently no judicial organ in SADC and it is not known when the recently adopted protocol will come into force. And if and when the new protocol does come into force, it will certainly result in the establishment of an ineffective interstate judicial forum with watered-down jurisdictional powers that would most likely not be put to any meaningful use. In the absence of judicial oversight, there is, in all probability, no guarantee that there would be any respect for the rule of law and the principles of good governance by the executive institutions of SADC. What compounds matters is the absence of a regional parliament with a wide range of powers in the areas of policy formulation and oversight. While increased participation by the SADCPF in SADC activities is welcome, it would however be doing so not as an 'equal' institutional partner since its membership of the SADC institutional family is, at best, tenuous. What is critical is the establishment of a regional parliament that is a SADC Treaty institution with a peremptory say in the regional integration project.

A good case for the reform of the whole institutional architecture of SADC in order to reflect the normative values of democracy and the rule of law has been made. Since it has already been indicated in Chap. 1 that an alternative model of governance will be proposed for SADC in this study, the next chapter discusses the elements of the concept of shared governance and how this model has been employed in different organisational settings.

CHAPTER 5

Shared Governance in International Institutional Law

5.1   Introduction

If there should be an alternative SADC institutional framework, on what theory should such a framework be based? Is there any general theoretical governance framework for public international organisations such as regional economic communities? Is it possible to propose an institutional reform agenda for SADC that resonates with the normative values of separation of powers and the rule of law? These are the questions that this chapter seeks to address.

So far, this study has demonstrated the nature and extent of the democratic deficit inherent in the SADC governance framework. What remains to be discussed is how this democratic deficit can be addressed. As already indicated, the reform proposal carried in this study is anchored in the concept of shared governance. This chapter discusses the concept of shared governance and its application in international organisations. It traces the development of this concept as an organisational theory in general so that its normative elements are clearly set out.

However, since there appears to have been no previous attempt in literature to explore the applicability of the concept of shared governance to international organisations as conceptualised in this study, it is necessary to start by discussing participatory democracy, a somewhat related concept that has been sufficiently dealt with in literature both in the context of domestic constitutional law and also at international law. The similarity between the two lies in the sense that they both serve to broaden the

© The Author(s) 2019
M. Nyathi, *The Southern African Development Community and Law*, https://doi.org/10.1007/978-3-319-76511-2_5

scope of participation in decision-making in a polity. However, as shall be shown later in this study, one is 'outward' looking, and the other is 'inward' looking. Discussing participatory democracy first is important so that a distinction between shared governance and participatory democracy is clearly established.

Political space and participation in that space by non-traditional actors both at national and international levels continue to be created and to expand. Whilst the classical position at the national level under the separation of powers doctrine views three distinct organs—the legislature, the executive, and the judiciary, as responsible for the governance of the state, new institutions now participate in the formulation and implementation of policies at the national level. It is not only public institutions that are implicated in this continuing evolution of the 'new' state. Private players, including non-governmental organisations, continue to enter the hitherto 'closed' domain of domestic governance. At the international level on the other hand, governance of international organisations has traditionally been an intergovernmental affair dominated by the executives of member states. However, and especially in the area of regional economic integration, there has been a movement from the classical inter-governmentalism to new forms of international governance. As the theory of institutionalisation briefly described in Chap. 1 would illustrate (its general validity or otherwise aside), this evolution has seen the gradual growth of supranational institutions which now play significant roles in transnational affairs including those that were hitherto reserved for the institutions of member states. Over and above supranational institutions, various other players are implicated in the creation of international norms that are enforceable on the domestic plane. These include, for example, such organisations like the Codex Alimentarius Commission in the area of food safety and the Basel Committee on Banking Supervision.[1]

Non-traditional actors thus participate in norm setting at both the domestic and international levels either through being part of the actual process of coming up with norms or through actively influencing the content of the norms ultimately made by others, for example, their local representatives at the local level or parliamentarians at the national level on the one hand and their states at the international level on the other hand.

But because there are various players that may participate in the governance of a polity, including an international organisation like SADC, and

---

[1] N. Krisch *Beyond constitutionalism: The pluralist structure of postnational law* (2010) 9.

because there are different ways in which such participation may take place, it is important to clearly distinguish the shared governance model that is proposed in this study from other forms of participation. But that is not to say there are inherent tensions between the various methods of participation. In fact, as shall be shown in several instances below, the various methods of participation discussed in this study are not necessarily exclusive and can and do in fact complement each other.

A number of international organisations, in addition to setting up internal decision-making frameworks for use by their various institutions/organs, also have provisions in their treaties or other institutional frameworks specifically dealing with participation by 'external' stakeholders in their norm-setting processes. In SADC, for example, the preamble of the SADC Treaty proclaims the need for the involvement 'of the people of the region centrally in the process of development and integration, particularly through the guarantee of democratic rights, observance of human rights and the rule of law....'[2] Also, article 23(1) of the Treaty provides that '[i]n pursuance of the objectives of this Treaty, SADC shall seek to involve fully, the people of the [r]egion and key stakeholders in the process of regional integration.' See also generally Sect. 4.3 which deals with SNCs in Chap. 4 above.

Also, in the EU, notwithstanding the fact that the EU's institutional balance legislative framework provides for elaborate and lengthy processes designed for, among other things, consensual decision-making involving multiple institutions, the European Commission has always wanted to see more participation by civil society actors in order to close the 'legitimacy gap' of European governance.[3]

---

[2] See the preamble of the SADC Treaty http://www.sadc.int/documents-publications/sadc-treaty (accessed 26 June 2013).

[3] See, for example, the European Commission's White Paper on Governance, under 'Involving civil society' http://www.europa.eu/legislation_summaries/institutional_affairs/.../110109_en.htm (accessed 14 June 2013), as commented on by M. Horeth 'The European Commission's White Paper on Governance: A 'tool-kit' for closing the legitimacy gap of EU policymaking? The paper was presented at the Workshop "Preparing Europe's Future. The Contribution of the Commission's White Book on Governance", Centre for European Integration Studies Bonn & Europe 2020, in cooperation with the Representation of the North Rhine Westphalia to the European Union in Brussels, November 2001 https://www.zei.uni-bonn.de/dateien/discussion-paper/dp_c94_hoereth.pdf (accessed 14 June 2013). A more detailed discussion of the EU institutional framework is found in Chap. 6, Sect. 6.4.

Participation in policymaking in international organisations has two dimensions—the internal and the external. The internal dimension encompasses the internal norm-setting framework—the individual and collective roles of the internal units or components of the organisation in policy formulation or lawmaking. The internal dimension is more often than not a rules-based game with clear and peremptory obligations imposed on the individual institutions of the organisation.

The external dimension, on the other hand, involves participation by externals—the 'stakeholders,' for example, CSOs and individuals. Stakeholder participation, like in the example of SADC given above, is usually provided for in vague and directory terms. This book focuses on the internal dimension of decision-making in SADC—how the different institutions of SADC contribute to the formulation and shaping of SADC norms and policies. This study does not focus on closing the 'legitimacy gap' through involving such 'external' stakeholders like regional citizens, CSOs, and the business community per se. However, as shall be shown in Chap. 7, democratising the internal dimension of norm setting in SADC has the 'default' effect of opening up participation sites for the external stakeholder as well, hence the complementarity of the shared governance model (as proposed here) with the participatory democracy one.

The discussion of the theories of participatory democracy and shared governance in this chapter is thus meant not only to distill their applicability in the governance of international organisations, but also, as has already been stated, to clearly distinguish shared governance from participatory democracy. In this study, the terms participatory democracy and participatory law formation are deliberately used interchangeably.

Before moving to the international sphere, it is important to first discuss the relevance of these concepts in the context of the governance of nation states and also as organisational theories in general. The following two sections deal with participatory democracy as a concept applicable in a domestic polity and also as a concept obtaining at international law. The discussion is limited to those aspects of the theory that are contextually congruent with the focus of the study. The next two sections discuss shared governance as organisational theory in general and its applicability in international law.

5.2   PARTICIPATORY DEMOCRACY IN THE CONTEXT OF CLASSICAL CONSTITUTIONAL LAW

Participatory democracy is distinct from representative democracy. As noted by Ochoa:

> Under a system of representative democracy, citizen participation is limited to voting for the individuals who will (at least in the idealized version) represent their interests [...] Representative democracy does not require representatives to acquire direct authorization from the people who they represent before making each political decision to act. They do not act as people's proxies. Rather, they are endowed with the power to act as they believe will best serve their constituents....[4]

On the other hand, participatory democracy envisages participation by the constituents beyond and in spite of the polls. In a participatory democracy, political constituents do not sit back after the polls and hope that their interests will be taken care of by their elected representatives. The constituents in participatory law formation 'engage one another directly and through organizations'[5] thereby leading 'to the development of norms and laws in an area that was not drawing the attention of legislative bodies.'[6]

Hildreth outlines the elements of participatory democracy as maximum participation by citizens in self-governance; this participation must be in all sectors of society; the participation must lead to transformation of the citizen into an active citizen through the experience gained from participation; and ultimately, the participation by citizens must lead to social transformation.[7]

The modern version of the concept of participatory democracy appears to have developed in the 1960s as a counterargument to the ideas of

---

[4] C. Ochoa 'The relationship of participatory democracy to participatory law formation' (2008) 15(1) *Indiana Journal of Global Legal Studies* 9. See also J.L. Ozanne et al. 'The philosophy and methods of deliberative democracy: Implications for public policy and marketing' (2009) 28(1) *Journal of Public Policy & Marketing*, who, at p. 30 observe that 'for many poor citizens, the political process ends with the vote at the polls' and 'they lack the immediate power to influence policies that will affect their lives.'

[5] Ochoa (Footnote 4 above) 16.

[6] Ochoa (as above).

[7] R.W. Hildreth 'Word and deed: A Deweyan integration of deliberative and participatory democracy' (2012) 32# 1 *New Political Science* 299–300.

democratic elitism and neo-liberalism.[8] The latter 'consign the participation of all citizens in public life to a peripheral and restricted role'[9] while 'participatory democracy [...] considers participation to be the central aspect of political practice.'[10] Thus, in a sense, participatory democracy aims at transforming thin democratic practice (confined to representative professional politicians) into one based on active citizen participation.[11]

The concept of participatory law formation is not without critics. The major criticism is that it is 'non-transparent, non-accountable and non-democratic.'[12] This democratic deficit is said to be borne out of the fact that participatory norm/law makers do not carry a direct mandate from the people on whose behalf they purport to be legislating. It is thus seen as elitist and its processes viewed as secretive.[13] On the other hand, 'state centred lawmaking ... typically results in public disclosure of the law and policies in place as well as the process by which they were adopted....'[14] However, some counter this argument by pointing out that a representative democratic model has its own legitimacy crisis as well. They point out, for example, the distance between the representatives and their constituents and lack of transparency, publicity, and accountability by authorities.[15]

However, the democratic deficit in participatory law formation can be mitigated by encouraging 'transparency ... including disclosure of the identity of participants, (and) the source of funds used in the law formation process....'[16] Also important is the availability of information on political and institutional processes and procedures to ensure that those involved in participatory law formation are accountable; and to improve access for minority views and other interested parties.[17]

It should be noted, however, that representative democracy and participatory democracy do not necessarily occupy opposing poles in the

[8] D. Vitale 'Between deliberative and participatory democracy' (2006) 32 # 6 *Philosophy & Social Criticism* 749.
[9] As above.
[10] As above).
[11] Vitale (Footnote 8 above) 750.
[12] Ochoa (Footnote 4 above) 13.
[13] Ochoa (Footnote 4 above) 16.
[14] Ochoa (Footnote 4 above) 17.
[15] Vitale (Footnote 8 above) 750.
[16] Ochoa (Footnote 4 above) 17.
[17] As above.

democracy spectrum, but in fact complement each other.[18] In the context
of the European Union, for instance, specifically under the concept of
multi-level governance, European citizenship and European governance
are said to be built and based on participation and that this has two dimensions namely: 'representative democracy, which is its foundation, and participatory democracy, which enhances it.'[19]

It is probably important at this stage to discuss the related concept of
deliberative democracy, which many scholars view as distinct from participatory democracy. Again, for an apt definition of the deliberative democratic theory, due deference is given to Hildreth, according to whom
deliberative democracy is about the expansion of the quality and quantity
of deliberation (not in all sectors of society but in selected ones) thereby
leading to the legitimation of deliberative outcomes.[20]

Understood in its broad sense, deliberative democracy is a process that
brings together various players—citizens, government, and private actors
(e.g. business) to discuss and shape public policy.[21] Deliberative democracy is thus discursive or dialogical in nature and it provides a platform
where stakeholders engage in (usually) face-to-face debate, and is said to
be based on such traditional forms of civic participation as town hall
meetings.[22]

Democracy is said to be realised through the deliberative model because
different free and equal groups (stakeholders) are able to share their reasoned viewpoints in an environment that is non-coercive, thereby leading
to legitimate political decision-making and self-government.[23] Various
methods of deliberative democracy have been applied in different settings.
These include deliberative focus groups; deliberative polls; citizens' juries;
consensus conferences; and scenario workshops.[24] The structural details,

---

[18] See Vitale (Footnote 8 above) at p. 750, who notes the representative democracy-
enhancing nature of participatory democracy through the creation of new spheres of discussion and political deliberation.

[19] Committee of the Regions' White Paper on Multi-level Governance, 80th plenary session (17 and 18 June 2009) 9, L. Van den Brande & M. Delebarre (Rapporteurs) http://
www.cor.europa.eu (accessed 28 May 2013).

[20] Hildreth (Footnote 7 above) 302.

[21] J.L. Ozanne et al. (Footnote 4 above) 29.

[22] As above.

[23] As above; J.J. Worley 'Deliberative constitutionalism' (2009) *Brigham Young University
Law Review* 441.

[24] Ozanne et al. (Footnote 4 above) 33–35.

theoretical underpinnings, and the empirical evidence of the efficacy of these methods are however outside the scope of this book.

Two major challenges of deliberative democracy have been pointed out: it is difficult to establish in societies that are not democratic, hence the need for a pre-existing democratic tradition; and marginalised groups may not fairly compete with the privileged.[25]

Deliberative democracy has also been said to be applicable to international organisations, or 'to the regimes of governance established by global regulators.'[26] The value of deliberative democracy at the international level is said to lie in the legitimation of the resultant decisions, since 'directives issued by a global regulator that does not enjoy [legitimate] authority cannot be regarded as international law norms (properly so called).'[27]

Thus, participatory democracy and deliberative democracy have usually been seen as two distinct theories. Participatory democratic theory (and its practice) is said by some to have flourished in the 1960s and 1970s, was on the wane in the 1980s, and was superseded by deliberative democracy and other democratic theories in the 1990s and to this day, only remains in the literature of a few political scientists who want to revive this dying or otherwise dead model of democracy.[28] And yet, some of the very scholars who appear to have written off participatory democracy in the current era concede that there is a link between deliberation and political participation.[29] Vitale, while viewing the two as distinct and independent, regards them 'as two key elements in the process of collective decision making.'[30] Also, Hildreth believes participatory and deliberative models can be combined into a coherent family of practices, through his harmonising concept of 'cooperative inquiry,' which sees the two as different phases of democratic action which sometimes overlap since, in his view, 'action gives rise to deliberation, and ... deliberation leads to subsequent action.'[31]

Without in any way suggesting that there is something inherently wrong with treating the theories (and practices) of participatory democracy

---

[25] As above.
[26] S. Wheatley, (2010) *The democratic legitimacy of international law* 312.
[27] Wheatley (Footnote 26 above) 332–333.
[28] J.D. Hilmer 'The state of participatory democratic theory' (2010) 32(1) *New Political Science* 43–49. See also Ozanne et al. (Footnote 4 above) 29, who makes a similar view. See also Vitale (Footnote 8 above) 740.
[29] Hilmer (Footnote 28 above) 50.
[30] Vitale (Footnote 8 above) 759.
[31] Hildreth (Footnote 7 above) 317–318.

and deliberative democracy as distinct concepts, in this study, at least for purposes of coherence and economy, 'participatory democracy' is the preferred term for the reason that it is intuitively broader in scope and thus encompasses the related and neighbouring (if not sub) concept of deliberative democracy. It is indeed difficult to maintain a realistic distinction between participatory democracy and deliberative democracy as such distinction is not substantive but rather results from the different modes and methods of participation.[32] Both clearly share the same ultimate goal of expanding 'citizen participation in public life.'[33]

5.3   Participatory Democracy in International Organisations

While instances of participatory democracy by citizens at the national level are well documented and backed by sound empirical evidence, participatory democracy by citizens in international law has largely remained an idealised position. However, this is not to say participatory democracy is non-existent at international law.

At international law, or rather in international relations, the dominant player has historically been the state.[34] Just like citizens in a domestic representative democracy, the citizens of a nation state 'are deemed to be represented by their state's participation in the international institutions that promulgate treaties and set policies....'[35] Thus, the classical position does not envisage the participation by citizens, as individuals or collectively, in the conduct of international relations and in the formulation of international law. Likewise, national parliamentary control did not extend to foreign affairs since the prevailing view was that 'these relations had no direct implication for the citizen, being the exclusive concern of the government.'[36]

Membership of and participation in international organisations have thus generally been understood to be an exercise of the sovereign will,

---

[32] Hildreth (Footnote 7 above) 298.

[33] Hildreth (Footnote 7 above) 299. See also R. Marchetti (2008) *Global democracy: For and against: Ethical theory, institutional design and social struggles* 10. Marchetti also acknowledges that the two theories overlap on a number of points.

[34] H.G. Schermers & N.M. Blokker *International institutional law: Unity within diversity* (2011) 3.

[35] Ochoa (Footnote 4 above) 9.

[36] Schermers & Blokker (Footnote 34 above) 408.

which will is located in the government of the day, specifically the executive arm. It has been held that 'the transposition of representative democracy … onto governance at the international level has not been entirely successful.'[37] However, within governments of member states, it is no longer the executive arms of government that still hold sway in the formulation of international norms. In a good number of constitutional democracies, as will be shown in Chap. 6, domestic parliaments now play a significant role in the ratification and domestication of treaties negotiated and entered into by the executive. Thus, through (generally) their parliaments, citizens are able, at least in theory, to shape international law. However, in the area of international relations, the executive has managed to retain considerable, if not dominant, influence.[38]

Instances of participatory democracy have been identified, for example, in such international organisations like the International Monetary Fund and the World Bank. These two institutions were initially perceived as following a 'top down' approach in their processes, but had to reform, to some extent, in order to accommodate participation by those most affected by their processes and programmes after significant civil society pressure.[39]

In the EU, there is a continuing debate on the deeper involvement of civil society in the EU lawmaking processes, particularly in the formulation of secondary or implementation legislation. The European Commission prefers a governance framework that expands its role (while taking on board participation by civil society actors) in the formulation of detailed implementation legislation. The Commission has been more in favour of a system that confines the legislative roles of the Council and the European Parliament (EP) to primary legislation on essential elements, and the reduction of state involvement in the shaping of detailed implementation legislation through Comitology Committees and the Committee of Permanent Representatives (COREPER) as this has resulted in 'time consuming and cumbersome' consensual decision-making

---

[37] Ochoa (Footnote 4 above) 10.

[38] In the United States of America, for example, while Congress has influence in the shaping of foreign policy, for example, through its powers to regulate foreign commerce; to raise and maintain armies; and to declare war, due deference is usually given to the president when it comes to foreign policy. See J.A. Barron &C.T. Dienes *Constitutional law in a nutshell* (2013) 183–189.

[39] G. de Búrca 'Developing democracy beyond the state' (2008) *Columbia Journal of Transnational Law* 221.

processes that result from the need to accommodate the individual interests of Member States.[40]

As indicated in the introductory part of this chapter, lawmaking at the international level has and continues to move from state-centred spaces to private spaces. In addition to 'non state' influence on the content of norms created by governments-led international organisations, there is also norm creation on the international plane by 'private actors' in the form of '[B]usiness entities, non-governmental organisations (NGOs), broader civil society and individuals'[41] with the end product being 'norms, soft law, regulation, or governance dealing with international matters.'[42]

5.4   SHARED GOVERNANCE AS ORGANISATIONAL THEORY

The model of shared governance as proposed in this study (or at least the core elements of this model) is borrowed from the application of this organisational model in the fields of university and college administration and in nursing professional practice particularly in the United States of America. In the context of universities and colleges, shared governance has been understood to mean that there must be 'shared responsibility and cooperative action' within an organisation.[43] For a clear and detailed understanding of what this entails in institutional terms, a look at the 1966 joint statement by the American Association of University Professors (AAUP), the American Council on Education (ACE) and the Association of Governing Boards of Universities and Colleges may be a good starting point.[44] The statement calls for 'shared responsibility and cooperative action among the components of the academic institution.'[45] The expressed hope was, and still is, that the principles expounded in the

---

[40] Committee of the Regions' White Paper on Multi-level Governance (Footnote 19 above).

[41] Ochoa (Footnote 4 above) 8.

[42] As above.

[43] R.J. Hexter [President, New England Association of Schools and Colleges (NEASC)] 'Recommendations on shared governance'. Available at http://www.hampshire.edu/offices/9812.htm 25 September 2008 (accessed 30 September 2011).

[44] Available at http://www.aaup.org/report/1966-statement-government-colleges-and-universities (last accessed 22 March 2014). The statement's title is 'Statement on government of colleges and universities.' However, it is generally recognised as a statement on shared governance. See http://www.aaup.org/issues/governance-colleges-universities (last accessed 28 March 2014).

[45] Para 1 of the preface to the statement.

statement would 'lead to the correction of existing weaknesses and assist in the establishment of sound structures and procedures.'[46]

What is important to note is the narrow focus of the statement: it does not seek to cover outside stakeholders like the government, government institutions, and agencies.[47] This exclusion should be viewed in the context of the need to concentrate on the internal stakeholder, rather than ignoring outsider interests. That this is so is clearly borne out of the statement itself: 'However, it is hoped that the statement will be helpful to those agencies in their consideration of educational matters.'[48] The statement's introduction speaks to the need to accommodate and integrate outside stakeholder interventions through a generally unified view' and emphasises the awareness by components of a college or a university of their 'independence'; 'usefulness of communication among themselves'; and of the force of 'joint action' which will enjoy increased capacity to solve educational problems.

The statement defines joint effort in 'areas of action' as involving, in part, the 'initiating capacity' and 'decision-making participation of all the institutional components....'[49] The statement further prescribes the need for certainty—the need for procedures (for review) to be clearly set out in the regulations.

Conversation before the 'final' decision is reached is one of the central concerns of shared governance. In the 'stakeholder version' of shared governance in a university setting, for example:

> shared governance is used to convey the idea that a lot of conversation ought to take place within and among various campus groups—board, administration, faculty, staff, students, etc.—before the people in power make the final decision ... All the stakeholders should have a place at the table; everybody, within reason, should be consulted. Once people have talked things over, those in charge make the final decision, presumably after having given serious consideration to the full range of opinions and recommendations. Because 'input' is sought and wide communication takes place, governance is said to be shared.[50]

---

[46] Para 2 of the preface to the statement.
[47] Para 2 of the preface to the statement.
[48] Para 2 of the preface to the statement.
[49] Sect. 2 (a) para 2 on joint effort.
[50] 'What is Shared Governance' (June 2007) http://www.uiowa.edu/~aaupweb/shared_gov.pdf (last accessed 18 September 20014).

However, shared governance goes beyond mere 'stakeholder' involvement in institutional decision-making. Again, in an academic setting, there is also emphasis on faculty autonomy in a number of areas:

> [Faculty] possess 'primary responsibility'—or authority—for reaching decisions in their areas of expertise, namely, 'curriculum, subject matter and methods of instruction, research, faculty status, and those aspects of student life which relate to educational process.'[51]

Rather than being seen as distinct conceptions of shared governance, the 'stakeholder' and 'autonomy' versions are in fact complementary when it comes to decision-making in an organisational setting: the same stakeholder involvement would be expected to permeate, to the extent possible, the 'autonomous' faculty decision-making process as well.

Access to information is key in the whole scheme of shared governance: 'Effective planning demands that the broadest exchange of information and opinion should be the rule for communication among the components….'[52] This centrality of access to information is also recognised in healthcare organisational setting, specifically in the nursing profession. As noted by Hess, '…one of the most distinguishing characteristics of a shared governance environment is that nurses feel they have access to the information necessary to make effective governance decisions.'[53]

In a professional organisational setting, therefore, shared governance represents a shift from the traditional bureaucratic and centralised decision-making model to one 'where independent authority is vested in the professional, thereby resulting in partnership, accountability, equity and ownership.'[54] As noted by Anthony (writing in the context of the application

---

[51] As above.

[52] Sect. 2 (c) para 2 of the 1966 Statement (Footnote 44 above).

[53] R.G. Hess 'From bedside to boardroom – nursing shared governance' (2004) 9 # 1 *Online Journal in Nursing.* http://gm6.nursingworld.org/MainMenuCategories/ ANAMarketplace/ANAPeriodicals/OJIN/TableofContents/Volume92004/No1Jan04/ FromBedsidetoBoardroom.html (last accessed 22 July 2014).

[54] M.K. Anthony 'Shared governance models: The theory, practice, and evidence' (2004) 9 *Online Journal of Issues in Nursing.* http://www.nursingworld.org/MainMenuCategories/ ANAMarketplace/ANAPeriodicals/OJIN/TableofContents/Volume92004/No1Jan04/ SharedGovernanceModels.aspx (last accessed 13 June 2013). In fact, while most recent writings and commentaries on shared governance emanate from the fields of university and college administration and nursing, Anthony traces the 'foundation' of the shared governance model to the 'human resources era of organizational theories,' mainly geared towards invest-

of shared governance in nursing professional practice), while there are different models of shared governance and differences in the 'depth' and 'scope' of the concept's definition, there are common characteristics that stand out: 'autonomy,' 'independence,' 'accountability,' 'empowerment,' 'participation,' and 'collaboration' in decision-making.[55] Even in the absence of sound empirical evidence of its benefits,[56] these are in themselves value-laden characteristics in any democratic polity that make shared governance a normatively sound alternative to a centralised and unaccountable bureaucracy.

Shared governance is therefore, in the final analysis, both a democracy-enhancing concept (and 'is certainly preferable to tyranny or dictatorship'[57]) and also an efficiency tool since decision-making is deferred to the appropriate site that is capable of making an informed decision in the relevant area. For example, as indicated above, in a university setting, there is a clear emphasis on decentralised autonomy in so far as academic and academic-related issues are concerned:

> By assigning primary authority in educational matters to the faculty, genuine shared governance, as articulated in the *Statement on Government*, promotes and sustains academic excellence. It doesn't take a doctorate in higher education to figure out why. In the plain words of one of the twentieth century's great university presidents, 'we get the best results in education and research if we leave their management to people who know something about them.' (Robert Maynard Hutchins, *Higher Learning in America*, Yale 1936, p. 21)[58]

Also (and moving away from college and university administration and nursing practice), the principle of the rule of law is easily accommodated in the concept of shared governance in that by assigning judicial authority to an independent, autonomous judiciary with specialised powers of adjudication including judicial review, it makes such an independent judiciary part of the inter-institutional conversation matrix of a polity.

ment in employee motivation and growth through such practices such as 'autonomy, empowerment, involvement, and participation in decision-making.'

[55] As above.

[56] For a discussion of the shortcomings of some of the research methodologies used in some of the research carried out in the field of nursing to establish the benefits of employing shared governance, see Anthony (Footnote 54 above).

[57] 'What is shared governance' (Footnote 50 above).

[58] As above.

Shared governance is distinguishable from participatory democracy in two significant respects: as already indicated above, the participants envisaged in the shared governance theory are the internal constituents of an organisation, as opposed to the 'outside' stakeholder in the participatory democratic model; and other than concerning itself with the sectors (the participatory democratic theory, as has been shown, envisages participation across all sectors while its 'sister' model, deliberative democracy, focuses on one chosen sector) shared governance's concern is the participation of the internal constituents in an organisation in the formulation of decisions that affect the organisation generally, while giving due deference and autonomy to those best suited to make certain decisions, for example, faculty in academic matters in a university/college setting.

Over and above these distinguishing characteristics that set shared governance apart from participatory democracy, shared governance goes on to provide the elements of independence, accountability, broadest possible exchange of information, empowerment, participation, and collaboration in decision-making. Not all these elements are unique to the shared governance model though. Some of them are very much embedded in the usual democratic discourse. Autonomy and independence, for example, resonates with the principle of separation of powers; and accountability falls within the broader purview of constitutionalism, specifically the obligation to state reasons and the right to review.

Also, empowerment and collaboration in decision-making are the elements of the shared governance theory that are similar to participatory democracy, and yet lacking in the usual constitutionalist language. The constitutionalist language, through especially the separation of powers doctrine, seems to value tension between arms of state as a guarantee against abuse of power. This deliberate institutional tension is best captured by Kommers, who, writing in the context the German Basic Law, notes that German constitutional scholars 'often see separation of powers in terms of creative tension between parliament and government, a view anchored in the Basic Law itself.'[59]

The classical constitutionalist doctrine is thus overly concerned about the abuse of political power and hence its emphasis on designing necessary and effective constraints to curtail abuse of power. As Kommers notes in

---

[59] D.P. Kommers *The constitutional jurisprudence of the Federal Republic of Germany* (1997) 116.

his discussion of the 'new constitutionalism' encapsulated in the German Basic Law:

> In content and style the Basic Law follows a pattern typical of constitutions adopted by other liberal democracies ... [I]t guarantees individual rights independent of the state, creates a political system of separated and divided powers, provides for an independent judiciary crowned by a high court of constitutional review, and establishes the Constitution as the supreme law of the land.[60]

On the other hand, shared governance puts more emphasis on institutional empowerment, partnership (collaboration), and conversation. Shared governance is thus framed in positive language. However, this distinction is more apparent than real, since, even within the classical constitutionalist language, the values of empowerment, participation and, collaboration can be cultivated and nurtured.[61] There are thus quite clearly a number of similarities between the shared governance model and other democratic models including the major ones of constitutionalism, separation of powers, and the rule of law, themselves being interrelated and overlapping. Thus, like separation of powers and the rule of law, shared governance can be viewed as part of the 'constitutional' theory. The absence of shared governance theory from national and international democratic discourse has probably been due to its confinement to the fields of nursing practice and college and university governance. What sets these concepts and principles apart are not so much their normative

---

[60] Kommers (Footnote 59 above) 31.

[61] This is best illustrated in the budget control case (45 (BVerfGE 1 [1977]) where the German Constitutional Court took the liberty to impose on all constitutional organs the duty 'to cooperate in the timely enactment of the budget bill.' The Court also 'announced that constitutional organs are obliged to consider each other's interests in the exercise of their constitutional responsibilities.' In the same judgment, the court emphasised the duty to 'communicate and consult' as between the executive and the legislative organs. See Kommers (Footnote 59 above) 123. See also J. Klabbers 'Setting the scene' in J. Klabbers et al. *The constitutionalization of international law* (2009) 9. Klabbers sees the empowerment of political institutions as part of constitutionalism. Cooperation/collaboration is also a feature of the EU institutional design: Art 13(2) of the consolidated version of the Treaty on European Union http://eur-lex.europa.eu/LexUriServ/LexUriServ.do?uri=OJ:C:2010:083:0013:00 46:en:PDF (accessed 10 October 2013) constrains all the EU institutions to act within the limits of the powers conferred on that particular institution by the Treaties and to conform to procedures, conditions, and objectives set out in the Treaties and to practice mutual sincere cooperation.

elements, but rather their different emphasis within the democratic discourse.

Therefore, while it may be easy to draw the outer boundary of democracy (itself ever increasing in its scope), it is difficult, if not impossible, to draw its internal boundaries separating constitutionalism, the rule of law, accountability, separation of powers, and shared governance. In fact, it may not even be necessary to do so since all these concepts and principles, among others, are cross-cutting and enrich one another.

5.5   THE RELEVANCE OF THE SHARED GOVERNANCE THEORY IN INTERNATIONAL ORGANISATIONS

There is not much literature on shared governance as a full-fledged theory in the context of international organisations. The closest one comes to the applicability of at least some of the elements of shared governance in international organisations are the principles of subsidiarity and multi-level governance in the context of the EU. In short, the two principles deal with the relationship between the European Union and its Member States as opposed to among the various institutions of the EU.[62]

In the EU, there is a remarkable preoccupation with the delimitation and delineation of the roles of the EU institutions and the Member States. There are some areas where the EU institutions have exclusive competence and others where competence is shared with Member States. Shared governance within the EU integration model is thus mainly expressed in vertical terms, a movement from 'state-centric' to 'multi-level' governance.[63] The effect of this 'shared' governance is that state executives no longer have monopoly in the integration process since decision-making competences are shared by different actors in this vertical stratum.[64]

The development of the concept of exclusive competence appears to have initially resulted from the case law of the European Court of Justice (ECJ), now Court of Justice of the European Union (CJEU). The CJEU sometimes disallowed some legislative measures or conclusion of treaties

[62] A more detailed discussion of the EU governance framework is found in Chap. 6, Sect. 6.4.

[63] G. Marks et al. 'European integration from the 1980s: State centric v multi-level governance' (1996) 34 #3 *Journal of Common Market Studies* 341, 342 & 346. See also P. Craig 'Integration, democracy and legitimacy' in P. Craig & G. De Búrca (eds) *The evolution of EU law* (2011) 22.

[64] Craig, as above and the references thereunder. See also Marks (Footnote 63 above) 346.

independently by Member States because of the exclusive power of the EC.[65] Yet, on the other hand, the Court held that certain competencies were not exclusive to EC institutions, thus not preventing the Member States from acting.[66]

The principles of shared and exclusive competence have since been made part of the EU treaty law through the principle of subsidiarity, which came into being through the 1992 Treaty of Maastricht.[67] Subsidiarity means that:

> in areas which do not fall within its exclusive competence, the Union shall only act if and in so far as the objectives of the proposed action cannot be sufficiently achieved by the Member States, either at the central level or at the regional or local level, but can rather, by reason of scale or effects of the proposed action, be better achieved at Union level.[68]

Multi-level governance, on the other hand, is expressed in somewhat different terms. The European Union Committee of the Regions' White Paper on Multi-level Governance defines this concept as:

> Coordinated action by the European Union, the Member States and local and regional authorities, based on partnership and aimed at drawing up and implementing EU policies. It leads to responsibility being shared between the different tiers of government concerned and is underpinned by all sources of democratic legitimacy and the representative nature of the different players involved.[69]

The recommendations carried in the White Paper include support for participatory democracy and reinforcing the partnership practice (both

[65] R. Leal-Arcas 'Exclusive or shared competence in the common commercial policy: From Amsterdam to Nice' (2003) 30 (1) *Legal Issues of Economic Integration* 5.

[66] Leal-Arcas (as above).

[67] The Treaty of Maastricht was signed on 7 February 1992 and entered into force on 1 November 1993 and is available at http://www.eurotreaties.com/maastrichtec.pdf (accessed 14 June 2013). This Treaty has since been superseded by the Treaty of Lisbon. For a more detailed discussion of the latter, especially with regards to the relationship between the EU institutions, see Chap. 6, Sect. 6.4.

[68] Art 5(3) of the Consolidated Version of the Treaty on European Union http://eur-lex.europa.eu/legal-content/EN/TXT/?uri=uriserv:OJ.C_.2012.326.01.0001.01.ENG#C_2012326EN.01001301 (accessed 7 August 2014).

[69] Preamble to the EU Committee of the Regions' White Paper on Multi-level Governance (Footnote 19 above).

vertically between local and regional authorities on the one hand and national government and the EU on the other; and horizontally between local and regional authorities on the one hand and civil society on the other). Thus, within the EU, 'shared' governance finds expression in the context of multi-level governance involving the EU institutions, Member States, and subnational authorities. In a sense, putting aside the recommendations for the horizontal partnership between local and regional authorities and civil society at the domestic level (in a sense the participatory democracy dimension), the multi-level concept is basically a vertical partnership involving the different tiers in the EU governance stratum.[70]

It is perhaps not surprising that shared governance in the EU has been expressed as a multi-level phenomenon rather than being viewed an intra EU inter-institutional governance phenomenon. The so-called institutional balance design of the governance architecture of the EU, as shall be seen in Chap. 6 (Sect. 6.4), already provides for, to some significant degree, conversation and participation by all the major institutions in the lawmaking processes of the organisation, thereby ensuring, among other things, transparency and checks and balances.

However, this is not to say that within the EU shared governance (or at least some elements of this concept) cannot be seen in inter-institutional terms. For example, Neyer, while writing on deliberation within the EU multi-level framework, draws an interesting parallel between the 'sharing of competencies between the Commission and the Member States in the implementation of rules' and the legislative competencies shared among the Commission, the Council, and the European Parliament.[71] Within the context of the EU, therefore, both multi-level governance and 'shared' governance seek to establish openness, participation, responsibility, effectiveness, and coherence. These principles, at least in the context of the EU, underpin good governance.[72]

---

[70] For an interesting discussion of 'shared' governance through the pooling together by the Member States of the EU of their sovereignties, see J. Neyer 'Discourse and order in the EU: A deliberative approach to multi-level governance' in E.O. Eriksen et al. (eds) *European governance, deliberation and the quest for democratization* (2003) 243 http://www.arena. uio.no. (accessed 16 April 2014). This work is also available as a paper in Volume 41 of the *Journal of Common Market Studies*, 2003.

[71] Neyer (Footnote 70 above) 244.

[72] European Commission White Paper on European Governance 2001-europa doc http:// www.europa.eu/legislation_summaries/institutional_affairs/.../110109_en.htm. (accessed 21 February 2014).

The convergence of these different principles appears to be inescapable. The implementation of multi-level governance, for example, is said to depend on respect for the principle of subsidiarity.[73] The principle of subsidiarity is understood as aimed at guaranteeing 'that policies are conceived and applied at the most appropriate level.'[74] Thus, the two are said to be 'indissociable' with subsidiarity demarcating the responsibilities of the different tiers of the overall EU governance stratum on the one hand and multi-level governance '[emphasising] their interaction.'[75]

With its theoretical grounding largely in relatively small organisational settings, and its application at the international level seen through a different conceptual lens, of what relevance then is shared governance to large international organisations? And with the discourse on the consitutionalisation of international organisations gaining momentum, why not embed the shared governance model in the broader constitutionalisation debate, rather than proffer it as an alternative model for SADC? These may indeed be fair questions that this study should address.

First and foremost, there is yet to be developed a general and acceptable democratic model of governance of international organisations, or at least those that can be democratised, including RECs. The constitutionalisation debate has largely remained within the realm of an academic discourse that has yet to come up with a clearly articulated institutional model that can sustain an infrastructure of norm production and implementation and the control of such. As indicated elsewhere in this study, the EU's 'institutional balance' model has been held by some, and rightly so, to be 'too vague and indeterminate.'

The shared governance model is proffered not parallel to, but rather within the broader democratisation and constitutionalisation paradigm, with its advantage being that it has clearly articulated core elements upon which a general, rules-based, institutional framework can be constructed. As an institutional model, therefore, shared governance can easily accommodate the principles and objectives set out in the SADC Treaty including the respect and promotion of democracy and the rule of law.

As has already been indicated above, the practice of shared governance is certainly not new in international organisations. Shared governance, as

[73] Committee of the Regions' White Paper on Multi-level Governance (Footnote 19 above) 7.
[74] As above.
[75] As above.

shall be illustrated in detail in Chap. 6, permeates EU governance. Taking, for example, the election of the Commission President, the European Council is obligated to hold appropriate consultations before proposing a candidate to the EP.[76] Thus, the involvement of two institutions acting independently in their own autonomous spheres in the election of the Commission President clearly answers to some of the requirements of shared governance: diffusion of power among multiple actors in an organisation; collaboration; and the acknowledgment of the responsibilities and interdependencies of various stakeholders in an organisation.

Still on the EU, and without unnecessarily pre-empting a more detailed discussion of this organisation in the next chapter, while the Council of the European Union is not involved in the election of the Commission President, it nonetheless gets involved in the eventual makeup of the whole Commission since it adopts, by common accord with the Commission President-elect, the list of the proposed commissioners who would have been selected on the basis of the suggestions made by Member States, with the whole proposed lot then subjected to a vote of consent by the EP and then appointed by the European Council.[77]

By and large, shared governance is a practised, although unacknowledged mode of governance in regional economic communities.[78] In fact, some of the elements of the shared governance model are to a large extent 'borrowed' from the classical domestic model of governance in constitutional democracies. For example, while the tension-and-constraint based doctrine of separation of powers appears to be the cornerstone of the American Constitution, the three arms of state (but especially congress and the executive) remain in constant conversation over a broad array of policy matters from the budget process right up to declaration of war.[79]

Also, while both at the domestic and international levels the judiciary is not ordinarily in the dialogue arena in the strict sense since its involvement is predicated on litigants bringing matters before it, its value as an

---

[76] Art 17(7) of the Treaty on European Union http://eur-lex.europa.eu/legal-content/ EN/TXT/?uri=uriserv:OJ.C_.2012.326.01.0001.01.ENG#C_2012326EN.01001301 (last accessed 7 August 2014). (TEU Consolidated Version).

[77] As above.

[78] While the EU might provide more instances of the shared governance model, there is a growing tendency in other RECs to open up decision-making processes to more institutions/organs. See Chap. 6 for examples.

[79] For the workings of the United States of America's system of government, see generally Barron & Dienes (Footnote 38 above).

institution cannot be underestimated—it is an important player as it is the guardian of the norms of engagement (and substance) through its oversight role of judicial review. Even in the absence of litigation, its mere presence is enough to guarantee the constraint of those institutions and agents involved in the active formulation and implementation of organisational norms. But over and above its role as guardian of norms, it at times enters the conversational arena of policymaking, as was the case in the development of the doctrine of direct effect in European Union, to be discussed in detail in Chap. 6.

Thus, as indicated above, there is more to the separation of powers doctrine than mere tension and control, since the three parts, while working independently and autonomously, are drawn together to the duty of governance of a single polity. The destiny and fate of the polity do not lie in the hands of a single institution. It is a shared destiny maintained by constant conversation supported by availability of information.

5.6   CONCLUSION

This chapter has sought to demonstrate that democracy as a governance ideal at the international level has continued to receive not only just academic attention, but has also been infused, to varying degrees, into the processes of some of the international organisations, including the unlikely ones such as the IMF and the World Bank.[80]

This chapter has sketched out the core credentials of the shared governance model whose emphasis is on an organisation's internal inter-institutional relations. This model does not extend, at least as conceptualised and proposed in this study, to include participation of 'external' stakeholders (including individuals and CSOs) as is the case with participatory and, to the extent that they are different, deliberative forms of participation. However, as has already been indicated above and will be illustrated in Chap. 7, by adopting a shared governance framework, SADC will, by default, enhance participatory democracy. This shows the complementarity of the various democratic theories so far discussed in this study.

The next chapter discusses three RECs—the EAC, ECOWAS, and the EU. It seeks to demonstrate that in terms of objectives, there are a lot of similarities between these three RECs and SADC. As will be shown, the three RECs have, to varying degrees, transformed their institutional

---

[80] De Búrca (Footnote 39 above) 221–278.

frameworks over time, and in EAC and ECOWAS, there are expressed intentions (as provided for in their respective treaties) to continue doing so in future, in order to address their democratic deficits. They thus, again to varying degrees and in different areas, present good practices in REC governance and SADC can learn a lot of lessons from the three organisations in its future reform efforts.

CHAPTER 6

Institutional Design of Regional Economic Communities: A Comparative Analysis

6.1 INTRODUCTION

The first five chapters cover, among other things, the background to this study, the various institutions of SADC and the theoretical underpinning of the study. Having set out the SADC institutional architecture, it now remains to benchmark SADC against other regional economic integration arrangements. Three organisations have been chosen as comparators: the EAC, ECOWAS, and the EU. The centrality of the comparative tool of analysis is well recognised in legal scholarship.[1] Comparative analysis helps to determine 'whether solutions adopted elsewhere function or not.'[2] The use of the comparative analysis method is not only important when the organisations (or jurisdictions) compared have some similarities, but also where there are marked differences between the comparators, since it is from the differences that some lessons can be learnt.[3]

---

[1] See, for example, J.M. Smits 'Redefining normative legal science: Towards an argumentative discipline' in F. Coomans et al. (eds) *Methods of human rights research* (2009) 52, 54.

[2] Smits (Footnote 1 above) 52.

[3] Schermers & Blokker succinctly note, in their justification for their comparative study methodology, that '[a]lthough each (international) organization has its own legal order, institutional problems and rules of different organizations are often more or less the same and, in practice, an impressive body of institutional rules has developed.' See H.G. Schermers & N.M. Blokker *International institutional law: Unity within diversity* (2011) vi. The authors buttress this point at p. 27 by noting that '[i]nstitutional law does not differ dramatically from one organization to the next,' particularly with regards to institutional legal matters. At p. 30, they argue that even where there are clear differences in the institutional law

© The Author(s) 2019
M. Nyathi, *The Southern African Development Community and Law*, https://doi.org/10.1007/978-3-319-76511-2_6

The EAC and ECOWAS are particularly relevant because of their politi-cal and socio-economic similarities with SADC and the fact that in terms of institutional design, there are evident differences between the two sub-regional organisations and SADC. This study seeks to identify and critique the marked structural differences between the institutional makeup of these two organisations and SADC. The choice of the EU on the other hand, the different political and socio-economic underpinnings notwith-standing, is based on the fact that although the EU has evolved over time, and so far has the deepest regional integration framework the world over, it still remains a sub-regional economic community and thus a good choice for comparative analysis.[4] A notable feature of the three organisations is that they all accommodate, although to varying degrees, democracy and the rule of law in their constitutive legal instruments.[5]

The main reason for adopting the comparative analysis tool therefore is to compare the institutional designs of the three chosen comparators and the progress they have respectively made and also the challenges that they have faced in their respective integration journeys, especially with respect to the accommodation of democracy and the rule of law. The output of the comparative analysis will thus be: an assessment of whether there is best practice that can be derived from the EAC, ECOWAS, and the EU; and a finding of whether there may be any pitfalls on the road to deeper integration that should be avoided by SADC.

When discussing the three comparators, while the historical underpin-nings of each organisation cannot be ignored, what is paramount is focus-ing more on the products—the legal instruments of the various integration

---

of different organisations (e.g. some aspects of EU law are close to municipal law), a com-parative analysis 'may contain lessons for other organizations' or may 'indicate possible direc-tions for the future development of the law of these organizations.'

[4] See the observations by Schermers & Blokker in this regard (Footnote 3 above). See also J. Klabbers *An introduction to international institutional law* (2009) 13.

[5] See art 6 of the EAC Treaty; art 4 of the Revised Treaty of ECOWAS; Para 5 of the pre-amble to the Treaty on European Union and art 2 of same. These instruments are available at http://www.google.co.za/url?sa=t&rct=j&q=&esrc=s&source=web&cd=2&sqi=2&ved=0CCIQFjAB&url=http%3A%2F%2Fwww.eac.int%2Fnews%2Findex.php%3Foption%3Dcom_docman%26task%3Ddoc_download%26gid%3D11%26Itemid%3D70&ei=94HLVOfTL7Kv7AblroHIBQ&usg=AFQjCNErqCYJxlgaoiWJcd_G64cHz8Ft5w (last accessed 30 January 2015); http://www.comm.ecowas.int/sec/?id=treaty&lang=en (last accessed 30 January 2015); and http://eur-lex.europa.eu/legal-content/EN/TXT/?uri=uriserv:OJ.C_.2012.326.01.0001.01.ENG#C_2012326EN.01001301 (last accessed 7 August 2014) respectively.

models.[6] It should be noted that the discussion of each of the selected organisations is not meant to be an exhaustive treatise in relation to every aspect of its inter-institutional relations, but rather to provide a broad outline of each organisation's institutional framework particularly in relation to the principles of separation of powers and the rule of law.

It should be noted that while every international organisation, let alone a regional economic community, may be unique in terms of its background, membership, institutions, and challenges[7]; there are a number of similar institutional challenges faced by different international organisations and, in addition to these similar challenges, there are trends and normative values that now cut across international organisations and are now approaching near universality.[8] Thus, the uniqueness of each international organisation notwithstanding, international institutional law reflects, to a large extent, strong similarities between organisations.[9]

Some scholars have labelled the European Union an organisation *sui generis*, occupying the hitherto unoccupied space between municipal law (especially within a federal setup) and international law.[10] Habermas sees the EU as 'this new kind of transnational federal polity.'[11] The EU may

---

[6] For a discussion of the comparative approach of looking at regionalism, see L.V. Langenhove 'Why we need to "unpack" regions to compare them more effectively' in L. Fioramonti (ed) *Regionalism in a changing world: Comparative Perspectives in the new global order* (2013) 25. Langenhove refers to G. Morgan *The idea of a European superstate* (2005) Princeton University Press, New Jersey, who makes use of three distinct comparative tools: processes, projects, and products. In this context, processes include the historical development of a certain region; the projects include the visions behind the development of a region; the products are the treaties, institutions and practices of a region.

[7] For a similar remark on the uniqueness of international organisations, see Schermers & Blokker in the preface to their book (Footnote 3 above) v, para 2.

[8] Schermers & Blokker (Footnote 3 above) paras 3.

[9] Schermers & Blokker (Footnote 3 above) vi.

[10] See, for example, N. Krisch *Beyond constitutionalism: The pluralist structure of postnational law* (2010) 7 and the reference thereunder; H.P. Hestermeyer 'The implementation of European Union law,' an unpublished and unpaginated paper presented at the workshop *The Implementation of International Law in South Africa – Strengthening the Rule of Law by Following the German Model?* 16–17 May 2014, Faculty of Law, University of Pretoria, in cooperation with the Max Planck Institute for Comparative Public and International Law, the Konrad Adenauer Stiftung/Foundation & the Alexander von Humboldt Stiftung/Foundation.

[11] J. Habermas 'The crisis of the European Union in the light of a constitutionalization of international law (2012) 23 # 2 *The European Journal of International law* 342 http://www.ejil.org/pdfs/23/2/2211.pdf (accessed 16 July 2013).

thus be seen as not a good comparator in a study whose focus is SADC. Such a view ignores the fact that the EU has been evolving, and so has SADC, the EAC, and ECOWAS. Further transformations of these organisations may be on the minds of politicians and scholars alike. What the future holds, no one exactly knows.

Some writers locate the so-called uniqueness of the EU (and thus its unsuitability as a universal model of integration) in the historical and political landscape of Europe post World World II.[12] However, there has not been any compelling, clearly reasoned argument to disqualify the suitability of the EU model to any other regional polity of a similar nature. To overemphasise the historical underpinnings of institutions in one polity and to disqualify the suitability of those institutions in a different polity merely on the basis of the difference in historical and social background is akin to attacking the very basis of human advancement—transfer of knowledge. As stated above, what is important are the products of the various integration models—the legal instruments. The main enquiry should be directed at whether the instruments, whatever their historical underpinnings, are suitable for the attainment of the goal of integration.

The main aim of this chapter therefore is to illustrate that despite the different historical underpinnings of the three selected RECs, there are some similarities between them that clearly show the pervasiveness of separation of powers as a dominant feature in their respective institutional designs, alongside the desire, at the very least, to reflect the rule of law as one of their core organisational normative values. At the end of the day, what sets these different organisations apart are not their historical *raison d'etre* as such, but rather the degree of their accommodation of separation of powers and the rule of law (among other related concepts and values) and their different levels of integration. There is, in the final analysis, a lot to be learnt from other organisations falling within the same typology as SADC.

This chapter has three main sections, in addition to the introduction and the conclusion. The three sections discuss the EAC, ECOWAS, and the EU respectively. They each cover the brief history of each organisation,

---

[12] Kufuor is particularly scathing in his attack of the recommendations of the Committee of Eminent Persons (CEP) that was set up to review the 1975 ECOWAS Treaty. According to Kufuor, the CEP, in allowing itself to be also guided by the EU model, evidently did not come 'to grips with the dynamics of the European supranational process.' See K.O. Kufuor, in *The institutional evolution of the Economic Community of West African States* (2006) 59.

its current institutions, and the opportunities and challenges posed by its governance framework. Just like the treatment of SADC in Chaps. 3 and 4, the emphasis is on rule-making/norm-setting organs and oversight organs and how these interact within the overall governance scheme of each of the selected organisations.

6.2 THE EAST AFRICAN COMMUNITY

The EAC has a long and broken history.[13] Its evolution predates the attainment of independence by the three countries that initially comprised it: Kenya, Tanzania, and Uganda. The EAC gradually grew from the establishment of joint services in the form of railway lines, postal services, customs union, and common monetary services. The three territories were under British authority although each had a different status. Kenya was a colony and Uganda a protectorate. Tanganyika (present day Tanzania after uniting with the Republic of Zanzibar) was a mandate territory after World War I when Germany was dispossessed of its overseas territorial possessions by the 1919 Treaty of Versailles. Tanganyika's status later changed to that of a Trustee territory under the United Nations Trusteeship system at the conclusion of World War II.

The joint services management arrangement transformed into the East African Governors' Conference in 1926 and further evolved into the East African High Commission which was established in 1948 with the status of a body corporate whose remit was the administration of the common services.

Although the East African High Commission was not an international organisation (it being a creation of British law), its institutions were very much similar to those of a number of modern day international organisations: at the apex was the Commission comprising the three Governors of Kenya (chairing), Tanganyika, and Uganda; it had a Legislative Assembly with a token representation of Africans, Indians, and Arabs (one from each racial group). Interestingly, the Legislative Assembly had powers to make

---

[13] The historical material on the EAC below is largely derived from S.E.A. Mvungi 'Constitutional questions in the regional integration process: The case of the Southern African Development Community with reference to the EU' unpublished doctoral thesis, Hamburg University (1995) 108–119. Also, the preamble to the East African Treaty itself provides a detailed historical background of East African integration. The Treaty is available at http://www.afrimap.org/english/images/treaty/EACTreaty.pdf (accessed 4 October 2013).

laws (within its areas of competence as prescribed in the British Order in Council) that were directly applicable in the three territories.

With the independence of Tanganyika, the East African High Commission was transformed into the East African Common Services Organisation (EACSO) which comprised the president of the newly independent Tanganyika and the Governors of Kenya and Uganda. The latter two countries were yet to attain independence and were, on their attainment of independence, represented by their presidents.

The institutional structure of EACSO comprised the Authority (the three presidents); Ministerial Committees in various fields; an East African Court of Appeal which could hear appeals from the high courts of the three states; and the East African Legislative Assembly with slightly extended powers which included the determination of its procedures. There was some movement towards the establishment of the East African Federation which however suffered a still birth.

In 1967, the EACSO was transformed into the EAC by the Treaty for East African Co-operation. The institutions of the EAC included the East African Authority; the East African Legislative Assembly; the East African Ministers; the East African Community Council; the Common Market Tribunal; and the Court of Appeal of East Africa. The Court of Appeal decided appeals from Member States on the basis of the Member States' domestic legal systems. An interesting feature of the EAC was the institution of East African Ministers. These were not members or immediate past members of their countries' cabinets to ensure their supranational independence.

In the areas falling within the East African Community's competence, the Legislative Assembly enacted Bills. Each member of the Authority had to assent to a bill passed by the Legislative Assembly and in the event of the withholding of assent by any one of them for nine months, such bill would lapse. The laws passed by the East African Legislative Assembly were directly applicable in the domestic jurisdiction of the three countries.

Despite its success in the first three years of its existence, the EAC eventually collapsed and the Treaty was officially dissolved in 1977 owing to a number of challenges, among them the tensions caused by economic disparities in the Member States; the 1971 overthrow of the civilian government in Uganda; and the suspension of less profitable routes to Member States by the East African Airways and the establishment by Kenya of its own national airline and the grounding of the East African Airways leading to serious tensions culminating in closure of borders and freezing of Community assets.

The eventual collapse of the EAC notwithstanding, the organisation at least left some historical legacy in the area of international institutional law. In all its earlier forms, it was by far the most advanced regional integration model of its time.[14] This puts to rest the observation by some scholars that most integration arrangements in sub-Saharan Africa have strong European roots.[15] Even if an admission could made that the EAC model was engineered in Britain and hence it was in essence a European model, it still remains that it was an integration arrangement between African territories not informed by a similar arrangement existing in Europe at the relevant time. In any case, those who are quick to view regional integration as historically a European construct do so apparently with the EU as their reference point. However, the earlier forms of the EAC on which the current institutions are largely built cannot be said to have been inspired by the EU model whose genealogy is linked to the post-World War II Franco-German conception.

The present Treaty for the Establishment of the EAC was signed on 30 November 1999 and entered into force on 7 July 2000 following its ratification by Kenya, Tanzania, and Uganda, with Rwanda and Burundi acceding to the Treaty on 18 June 2007, and becoming full members of EAC with effect from 1 July 2007.[16] The preamble to the EAC Treaty states the eventual establishment of a political federation as one of the ultimate aims of the EAC.

The EAC Treaty is a lengthy document spanning some 117 pages and 153 articles. In addition to establishing EAC institutions, it covers in detail virtually all areas of integration and harmonisation. It includes in the body of the Treaty itself most of what in SADC would be in subsidiary protocols. On admission of new members into the EAC, the EAC Treaty

---

[14] Mvungi (Footnote 13 above) 113.

[15] This argument is advanced by, for example, P. Draper 'Breaking free from Europe: Why Africa needs another model of regional integration' (2012) 47 # 1 *The International Spectator: Italian Journal of International Affairs* 68. For an argument similar to the one made by Draper, See A. Acharya 'Comparative regionalism: A field whose time has come?' in L. Fioramonti (ed) *Regionalism in a changing world: Comparative perspectives in the new global order* (2013) 12. According to Acharya, regional integration is a 'distinctly Western European idea.'

[16] http://www.eac.int/index.php?option=com_content&view=article&id=1:welcome-to-eac&catid=34:body-text-area&Itemid=53 (last accessed 28 September 2013). South Sudan joined the EAC in 2016, bringing the current membership of the EAC to six countries.

sets out peremptory objective criteria.[17] This is unlike SADC where the matter is left to the absolute administrative discretion of the Summit, which makes it difficult for the Summit's decision to be reviewable.

Article 9(1) of the EAC Treaty establishes various organs of the EAC Community: the Summit; the Council; the Co-ordination Committee; the Sectoral Committees; the East African Court of Justice (EACJ); the East African Legislative Assembly (EALA), and the Secretariat. There is a distinction between organs and institutions. The latter are defined in article 9(2) as 'such bodies, departments and services as may be established by the Summit.'

The Summit consists of the heads of state or government of the Partner States who may be represented in a meeting of the Summit by a minister after consultation with other members.[18] The functions of the Summit include giving general directions and impetus as to the development of the objectives of the EAC; consideration of annual reports and such other reports submitted to it by the Council; review of the state of peace, security and good governance within the Community and the progress achieved towards the establishment of a political federation.[19]

The EAC Treaty provides for the delegation of the powers of the Summit. The Summit may, of its own volition, delegate the exercise of any of its functions to a member of the Summit, to the Council or to the Secretary General.[20] The other method of delegation is a statutory one: an Act of the Community may provide for the delegation of any of the powers, including legislative powers, conferred on the Summit (whether by the EAC Treaty or by an Act of the Community) to the Council or the Secretary General.[21] There are some powers that are non-delegable though. These include the giving of general directions and impetus; the appointment of Judges to the EACJ; the admission of new members and the granting of Observer Status to foreign countries; and assent to Bills.[22]

Below the Summit is the Council which consists of a minister responsible for EAC affairs of each Partner State; such other minister of a Partner State as may be determined by the latter; and the Attorney General of each

[17] Art 3(3) of the EAC Treaty.
[18] Art 10 paras 1 & 2 of the EAC Treaty respectively.
[19] Art 11 paras 1–3 of the EAC Treaty.
[20] Art 11(5) of the EAC Treaty.
[21] Art 11(6) of the EAC Treaty.
[22] Art 11(9) of the EAC Treaty.

Partner State.[23] The Council is said to be the 'policy organ' of the EAC.[24] Its specific functions include the promotion, monitoring, and constant review of the implementation of the programmes of the EAC and ensuring proper functioning and development of the EAC.[25]

The Council is empowered to, among other things,[26] initiate and submit Bills to the EALA; give directions to the Partner States and to all organs and institutions of the EAC other than the Summit, the Court and the EALA; make regulations, issue directives, take decisions, make recommendations, and give opinions in accordance with the provisions of the Treaty[27]; consider the budget of the Community; make staff rules and regulations of the Community; establish Sectoral Councils[28]; establish Sectoral Committees; and implement the decisions and directions of the Summit as may be addressed to it.[29] The Council is also authorised to request advisory opinions from the EACJ.[30]

The power vested in the Council to give directions to other organs or institutions of the EAC other than the Summit, the EACJ or the EALA is an interesting one to note. While clearly showing that the Council is subordinate to the Summit in the general policymaking hierarchy, with regard

---

[23] Art 13 of the EAC Treaty. In practice, the configuration of the Council is not static. Save for the ministers responsible for EAC affairs, each Partner State sends different ministers to Council meetings as informed by the agenda of the meetings. See *Mwatela v East African Community* (Application No.1 2006, decided on 1 October 2006), para 23. As observed by the EACJ in para 39 of the judgment, it is difficult to ascertain the total membership of the Council. The Court urged that a more transparent system of setting out the composition of Council should be put in place to avoid uncertainty which might lead to legal disputes. See a related argument in Chap. 2, Sect. 2.3 in relation to the SADC CoM.

[24] Art 14(1) of the EAC Treaty.

[25] Art 14(2) of the EAC Treaty.

[26] For the powers of the Council, see generally art 14 of the EAC Treaty.

[27] In terms of art 16 of the EAC Treaty, the regulations, directives, decisions and recommendations of the Council have a general binding effect on the Partner States in their domestic jurisdictions; on all organs and institutions of EAC (other than the Summit, the Court and the Assembly); and on those to whom they may be addressed.

[28] Art 14(3)(i) of the EAC Treaty. According to this provision, only members of the Council can sit on the Sectoral Council. This was affirmed by the EACJ in *Mwatela* (Footnote 23 above) in para 34. The Court reasoned that the rationale of this provision was to 'avoid distortion of the elaborate structural hierarchy of representation of the Partner States at different levels in the organizational framework of the Community ... (which might defeat the) objective of separation of functions' between the different organs. Also, in terms of the same provision, the decisions of the Sectoral Council are deemed to be those of the Council.

[29] Art 14(3)(k) of the EAC Treaty.

[30] Art14(4) of the Treaty.

to the other two institutions, it also indicates, although not expressly, the respect of the doctrine of separation of powers in the EAC.[31]

As is the case with the rules and orders made by the Summit [per article 11(8)], the Council is obligated, in terms of article 14(5), to cause all regulations and directions made or given by it to be published in the EAC Gazette, which regulations come into force on the date of their publication or as provided otherwise.

There is also the Co-ordination Committee which consists of Permanent Secretaries for East African Affairs in each Partner State and such other permanent secretaries of the Partner States as each Partner State may determine.[32] The functions of the Co-ordination Committee include submission of reports and recommendations on the implementation of the EAC Treaty to the Council either on own initiative or as requested by Council.

Sectoral Committees are established by article 20 of the EAC Treaty. The establishment of these committees, including their composition and functions, is dependent on the recommendation of the Co-ordination Committee which has the power to make the necessary recommendation to the Council if it feels the establishment of a Sectoral Committee is necessary for the achievement of the objectives of the EAC Treaty.[33]

The EAC is serviced by a Secretariat on a day-to-day basis. The Secretariat comprises of the Secretary General and his deputies, Counsel to the Community and other officers as may be deemed necessary by the Council.[34] Some of the functions of the Secretariat are transmission of Bills to the EALA; strategic planning, management and monitoring EAC programmes; dissemination of information on the EAC; general administration and financial management; resource mobilisation; submission of

---

[31] This position was affirmed by the EACJ in *Mwatela* (Footnote 23 above), although the Court did not specifically engage the separation of powers doctrine. The Court held that the 'decisions of the Council have no place in areas of jurisdictions of the Summit, the Court and the Assembly.' See para 54 of the *Mwatela* judgment.

[32] Art 17 of the EAC Treaty.

[33] Notwithstanding this broad deferral provision on the establishment of Sectoral Committees, art 21 of the EAC Treaty goes on to provide 'pre-determined' functions of the Sectoral Committees including preparation of a comprehensive implementation programme and setting out priorities for each sector.

[34] Art 66 of the EAC Treaty.

budget to the Council for the latter's consideration; and implementation of Summit and Council decisions.[35]

The composition and functions of the Secretariat are largely determined and influenced by the executive institutions: the Secretary General is appointed by the Summit upon nomination by the relevant Head of State under the principle of rotation[36]; the Deputy Secretaries General are appointed by the Summit on recommendation of the Council also on a rotational basis[37]; the Secretary General acts as the Secretary of the Summit[38]; and over and above the duties of the Secretary General specifically provided for in the Treaty, the Council may give to him or her other duties from time to time.[39]

There is also the East African Legislative Assembly. The EALA consists of nine members elected by each Partner State and *ex officio* members who include the minister responsible for East African Affairs (or in his absence the assistant or deputy of such minister), the Secretary General, and Counsel to the Community.[40] Generally modelled along national legislatures with a speaker, clerk, and other staff, and with the power to establish its committees and its rules of procedure (and those of its committees), EALA has several functions: it is the legislative organ of the EAC; it liaises with national assemblies of Partner States on matters relating to the EAC; it debates and approves the budget of the EAC; it receives reports on the activities of the EAC, annual audit reports of the Audit Commission and any other reports referred to it by the Council; it discusses matters pertaining to the EAC and makes recommendations to the Council as it may deem necessary for the implementation of the EAC Treaty; and it recommends the appointment of its clerk and other officers.[41]

The nine members elected by the national assemblies of each Partner State are not members of the national assemblies of Partner States. They should represent diverse interests, taking into account the various political

---

[35] Art 71(1) of the EAC Treaty. It is interesting to note that the Secretariat is also specifically obligated to establish 'practical working relations with the Court and the Assembly.' The spirit of the Treaty appears to be that of the development of the EAC by all organs in concert, their different roles and functions notwithstanding.

[36] Art 67(1) of the EAC Treaty.

[37] Art 68(2) of the EAC Treaty.

[38] Art 67(3)(d) of the EAC Treaty.

[39] Art 67(3)(d) of the EAC Treaty.

[40] Art 48(1) of the EAC Treaty.

[41] Art 49 of the EAC Treaty.

parties represented in the national assembly, shades of opinion, gender, and other special interest groups in that Partner State, in accordance with such procedure as the national assembly of each Partner State may determine.[42]

The EAC Treaty also has provisions dealing with tenure of office of elected members; determination of questions as to membership of EALA[43]; speaker of EALA; invitation of persons to assist the EALA; meetings of EALA; quorum and vacancies in EALA; voting in EALA; bills and motions; rules of procedure; and powers, privileges, and immunities of EALA and its members.

Article 62 of the EAC Treaty provides for the passing of legislative Bills by the EALA which, upon assent by the heads of state become Acts of the Community.[44] If, however, a Bill has not received an assent, it is sent back to the Assembly for reconsideration. If the bill is discussed and approved by the Assembly, it is sent back to the heads of state.[45] If, however, one of the heads of state withholds his or her assent to the resubmitted Bill, the Bill lapses.

Lawmaking in the EAC is thus a shared responsibility between the Assembly, the Council, and the Summit. But over and above that, the exchange of information between the EALA and the national assemblies of Partner States provided for in article 65 of the EAC Treaty (this article provides for a detailed information exchange regime including between the EALA and the national assemblies and also between the EALA and the Council) is likely to lead to (and is apparently designed for) participation by a wide spectrum of stakeholders in the EAC lawmaking process.

Article 23 of the EAC Treaty establishes the EACJ. The EACJ is mandated to 'ensure the adherence to law in the interpretation and application of and compliance with' the EAC Treaty. The EACJ has two divisions, the

---

[42] Art 50(1) of the EAC Treaty.

[43] Art 52 of the EAC Treaty.

[44] It would appear that the EALA's powers are not just paper powers. It has to date passed a number of community acts and approved EAC budgets for a number of financial years. See T. Musavengana *The proposed SADC parliament: Old wine in new bottles or an ideal whose time has come?* (2011) 49, 50. In *Mwatela* (Footnote 23 above), the EACJ affirmed the right of any member of the Assembly to introduce a Bill (except those specifically proscribed by the Treaty) and categorically held that 'Council does not have exclusive legislative initiative in the introduction (and withdrawal) of Bills in the Assembly.' See para 44 of the *Mwatela* judgment.

[45] The meaning of 'discussing and approving the Bill' is not clear. It could be interpreted to mean approving the Bill as initially passed or approving the Bill as amended.

First Instance Division and the Appellate Division. The qualifications of the judges include proven integrity, impartiality, and independence. The judges must be jurists of recognised competence who qualify to hold high judicial office in their respective states. It should be noted that unlike ECOWAS and SADC, the EAC Treaty does not simply defer matters to do with the EACJ to a protocol. All major issues are dealt with in the Treaty itself.

The judges are appointed by the Summit on the basis of recommendations made by the Partner States, provided that no more than two judges of the Court of First Instance Division and no more than one judge of the Appellate Division shall be appointed on the recommendation of the same Partner State.[46]

There is a measure of security of the judges' tenure of office.[47] They can only be removed from office on the basis of misconduct (which unfortunately is not qualified) or inability to perform judicial functions due to physical or mental infirmity. Although the Summit has the ultimate say on the removal of a Judge from office, this can only be on the basis of the recommendation of an ad hoc independent tribunal appointed by the Summit. However, for those judges also holding judicial or public office in a Partner State, disqualification or misconduct in a Partner State has similar implications at EAC level.[48]

The jurisdiction of the EACJ is provided for in article 27. The EAC Treaty gives the EACJ the jurisdiction to interpret and apply the EAC Treaty but only to the extent that the EAC Treaty does not confer such jurisdiction to interpret the Treaty upon organs of Partner States.[49] The Treaty also makes provision for expanded jurisdiction including original and appellate human rights jurisdiction and it tasks the Council to determine the nature and extent of such jurisdiction which has to be carried in a protocol to be concluded by the Partner States at a later date.[50]

In terms of article 28 of the EAC Treaty, a Partner State has a right to refer a matter to the EACJ for adjudication where such a Partner State

---

[46] Art 24 of the EAC Treaty.

[47] Art 26 of the EAC Treaty. This article also provides for suspension of judges under investigation and appointment of temporary judges, among other ancillary matters.

[48] This ground for suspension/removal from office was introduced by one of the several amendments to the EAC Treaty that came into effect in March 2007. A detailed discussion of these amendments is found towards the end of this section below.

[49] Art 27(1) of the EAC Treaty.

[50] Art 27(2) of the EAC Treaty.

considers that another Partner State or organ or institution of EAC has failed to fulfil an obligation under the EAC Treaty. A Partner State may also ask the EACJ to pronounce itself on the legality of any Act, regulation, directive, decision, or action on the ground that it is *ultra vires* or unlawful or it constitutes an infringement of the provisions of the EAC Treaty or any rule of law relating to its application or amounts to a misuse or abuse of power.

The Secretary General also has the power to refer a matter to the EACJ.[51] The referral by the Secretary General is subject to detailed procedures laid down in the EAC Treaty. The right of referral is also accorded to legal and natural persons,[52] but the EACJ has jurisdiction only if the impugned Act, regulation, directive, or decision has not been 'reserved by the EAC Treaty to an institution of a Partner State.'[53] There is a further curtailment of the EACJ's jurisdiction in that any proceedings instituted by natural or legal persons in terms of article 30(1) of the EAC Treaty must be instituted within two months of the cause of action or within two months of the day the complainant became aware of the cause of action.[54]

The EACJ also acts as a tribunal in the determination of disputes between the EAC and its employees and ancillary matters.[55] It may also act as an arbitral body under private international law where there is an arbitration clause in a contract or agreement where the EAC or any of its institutions is a party; or where Partner States involved in a dispute regarding the EAC Treaty agree to refer the matter to the EACJ; or where third parties have conferred jurisdiction on it.

It should be noted that the EACJ does not have exclusive jurisdiction over matters where the Community is a party. National courts of Partner States have concurrent jurisdiction as long as the Treaty does not specifically confer jurisdiction on the EACJ. However, decisions of the EACJ on the interpretation and application of the Treaty take precedence over those of national courts in similar matters.[56]

---

[51] Art 29 of the EAC Treaty.

[52] Art 30(1) of the EAC Treaty.

[53] Art 30(3) of the EAC Treaty. This para was also brought in by the amendments that came into force in March 2007 to be discussed in detail in below.

[54] Art 30(2) of the EAC Treaty. Just like art 30(3) above, this para was also brought in through the amendments that came into effect in March 2007, to be discussed in detail below.

[55] Art 31 of the EAC Treaty.

[56] Art 33 of the EAC Treaty.

The remainder of the EAC Treaty provisions on the EACJ deal with such matters as preliminary rulings on matters pending in the national courts of Partner States; judgments of the EACJ (which are generally given in open session); review of judgments of the EACJ; appeals; advisory opinions; right of appearance before the EACJ; acceptance of the judgments of the EACJ[57]; interim orders; intervention; proceedings; rules of the EACJ and oaths of office; immunity of the judges and the holding of other offices; execution of the judgments of the EACJ; Registrar of the EACJ and other staff; and the official language and Seat of the EACJ.

The protocol expanding the jurisdiction of the EACJ has been drafted and is being negotiated.[58] It would appear that expanding the jurisdiction of the EACJ has been unnecessarily delayed, and this has resulted in the EACJ expressing its displeasure over the delay and blaming the EAC Secretary General, among others, over the matter.[59] There is clearly mounting pressure for the express granting of human rights jurisdiction to the EACJ as evidenced by the EACJ's own pronouncement on the issue; the adoption by the EALA of a Bill of Rights; and the adoption by the Sectoral Council of a draft EAC Protocol on Good Governance.[60]

The absence of a protocol carrying the extended jurisdiction of the EACJ has not stopped the EACJ from entertaining matters with human rights content. While acknowledging that it cannot engage in full-fledged human rights jurisdiction, the EACJ has indicated that it will not shy away from exercising article the 27(1) interpretive jurisdiction merely because a matter before it includes allegations of human rights violations; nor will it recoil from exercising jurisdiction where there is an alleged breach of the

---

[57] In terms of art 38, any dispute concerning the interpretation or application of the EAC Treaty or any of the matters referred to the Court shall not be subjected to any method of settlement other than those provided for in the EAC Treaty. This article also prohibits conduct by Partner States which might be detrimental to the resolution of the dispute or might aggravate the dispute. It also obligates Partner States or the Council to take, without delay, measures required to implement a judgment of the Court.

[58] E.S. Nwauche 'The ECOWAS Community Court of Justice and the horizontal application of human rights' (2013) 13 *African Human Rights Law Journal* 55.

[59] See generally the EACJ's decision in *Sitenda Sebalu v Secretary General of EAC* (Reference 1 of 2010, decided on 30 June 2010); Nwauche (Footnote 58 above) where he makes reference to the EACJ's decision in *Sebalu*; H.S. Adjolohoun 'Giving effect to human rights jurisprudence of the Court of Justice of the Economic Community of West African States: Compliance and influence' unpublished LLD thesis, University of Pretoria (2013) 119.

[60] See above.

fundamental and operational principles of the EAC Treaty like good governance; democracy; the rule of law; accountability; transparency; social justice; equal opportunities; gender equality; and the universally accepted standards of human rights as provided for in articles 6(d) and 7(2) of the EAC Treaty.[61]

However, as has been held by the Appellate Division, there must be a 'legal linkage and basis' for the EACJ to exercise jurisdiction which is separate and distinct from human rights violation.[62] In the absence of legal nexus, therefore, the EACJ cannot exercise jurisdiction. This legal position, while progressive, is far from being satisfactory. While human rights jurisdiction remains 'proscribed,' there is need for the EACJ to clearly and narrowly define what constitutes human rights jurisdiction. This would enable prospective litigants to know in advance the extent of the EACJ's jurisdictional competence so that they may be able to appropriately frame their causes of action and the reliefs they are seeking. It has been suggested by some that the EACJ's 'derivative human rights competence' would provide 'a platform for future litigation of human rights before the Court, subject to proper wording of the claim and innovative advocacy on the part of lawyers.'[63]

This section on the institutions of the EAC would not be complete without a discussion of the amendments to the EAC Treaty that were adopted by the Summit in December 2006 and which came into effect in

---

[61] *Katabazi and Others v Secretary-General of the East African Community and another* (2007) AHRLR 119 (EACJ Reference 1 of 2007, decided on 1 November 2007) http://www1.chr.up.ac.za/index.php/browse-by-subject/485-uganda-katabazi-and-others-v-secretary-general-of-the-east-african-community-and-another-2007-ahrlr-119-eac-2007.html (accessed 17 December 2013); *Independent Medical Unit v Attorney General of Kenya* (Reference no 3 of 2010, decided on 29 June 2011) http://www.worldcourts.com/eacj/eng/decisions/2011.06.29_Independent_Medical_Unit_v_Attorney_General.pdf (last accessed 10 July 2014); *Attorney General of Kenya v Independent Medical Legal Unit* (Appeal 1 of 2011, decided on 15 March 2012) http://www.eacj.org/docs/judgements/Attorney-Gen-of-Kenya-v-IMLU-15-03-2012.pdf (accessed 17 December 2013); *Attorney General of the Republic of Rwanda v Rugumba* (Appeal 1 of 2012, decided on 4 July 2012); http://www.eacj.org/docs/judgements/Plaxeda-Rugumba-Vs-AG-Rwanda.doc (accessed 17 December 2013). For an interesting discussion of these cases in the context of horizontal application of human rights and the 'dual' jurisdictions of the EAC, ECOWAS, and SADC regional courts, see generally, Nwauche (Footnote 58 above).

[62] *Attorney General of Kenya v Independent Medical Legal Unit* (Footnote 61 above).

[63] S.T. Ebobrah 'Litigating human rights before sub-regional courts in Africa: Prospects and challenges' (2009) 17 *African Journal of International and Comparative Law* 82.

March 2007.[64] In a move reminiscent of the reaction of the SADC Summit to the various decisions of the SADC Tribunal that were made against Zimbabwe, the EAC Summit adopted hasty amendments to the EAC Treaty limiting the jurisdiction of the EAC and exposing some of the judges of the EACJ to an expanded and different scope of disciplinary measures and processes.[65]

These amendments are far-reaching and they include

- a scaled down jurisdiction of the EACJ (the EACJ no longer has power to entertain matters the jurisdiction over which has been conferred on or reserved to organs and institutions of Partner States),[66]
- a tightened time limitation on access to the EACJ (cases are now supposed to be lodged within two months of the cause of action or within two months of complainant's knowledge of the cause of action),[67]
- a broader disciplinary scope for those judges who hold judicial or public office in their home country. In addition to susceptibility to

[64] For a detailed and incisive discussion of the amendments, their background and implications, see generally H. Onoria 'Botched-up elections, treaty amendments and judicial independence in the East African Community' (2010) 54 # 1 *Journal of African Law* 74.

[65] The amendments were not only made in haste but also, as correctly held by the EACJ in para 61 of *East African Law Society & 3 others v Attorney General of the Republic of Kenya & 4 others* Reference no 3 of 2007 (decided on 9 September 2008), with no 'serious' and 'widespread' consultations with stakeholders in the Partner States. Within just a week of the Summit meeting that condemned the EACJ in *Prof Peter Anyang' Nyong'o & 10 others v Attorney General of Kenya & 2 others* (Reference 1 of 2006 decided on 30 March 2007), a ruling that triggered the amendments, the staff of the attorneys general of then Partner States and the EAC Secretariat had finalised the draft amendments. The draft carrying the amendments was approved by the attorneys general within two days of their finalisation by their respective staff and the EAC Secretariat and was adopted by the Council of Ministers a day after their approval by the attorneys general. This was followed by the submission of the proposed amendments by the Secretary General of the EAC to the Partner States and receipt of the replies by the latter (the replies were effectively those of the cabinets of the Partner States) by the former, after which the amendments were adopted by the Summit. The amendments were then ratified by Kenya within six weeks (early January 2007) of the EACJ's ruling in November the previous year, followed by the ratifications by Uganda and Tanzania in February and March 2007 respectively. See Onoria (Footnote 64 above) 90, 91. See also para 5 of *East African Law Society & 3 others v Attorney General of the Republic of Kenya & 4 others*. In fact, the EACJ, in setting out the background of the case, described the processes leading up to the adoption of the amendments as 'a flurry of activity.'

[66] Art 30(3) of the EAC Treaty.
[67] Art 30(2) of the EAC Treaty.

suspension and removal based on the original grounds of miscon-duct and inability to perform the functions of their office due to infirmity of mind or body, these judges are now susceptible to sus-pension and removal on expanded grounds of:

- removal from judicial or public office they hold in their respective Partner States for misconduct or due to inability to perform the functions of such office *for any* reason (own emphasis),
- *resignation* from the office they hold in their home state *following allegations* of misconduct or inability to perform the functions of the office *for any* reason (own emphasis),
- if such a judge is adjudged bankrupt under any law in force in a Partner State, or
- if such a judge is convicted of any offence involving dishonesty or fraud or moral turpitude under any law in force in a Partner State.

Needless to mention, removing a judge from office on the basis of his own voluntary resignation following allegations against him goes against one of the cardinal principles of law—the presumption of innocence until one is proven guilty. Indeed, voluntary resignation is at times a better option for a judge who faces spurious and scurrilous allegations meant to frustrate him or her out of office than facing an enquiry that is likely to lack independence and impartiality.

While the generality of these expanded grounds may appear to be objective on the face of it, they have the unfortunate implication of treat-ing the judges of the EACJ un-uniformly and thereby affecting the inde-pendence of the Court. As the EACJ rightly opined:

Article 26 of the Treaty established a mechanism for the removal of judges for misconduct and inability to function as determined by an independent tribunal appointed by the Summit, obviously applying uniform standards. When read together with Article 43 (2) [this article provides that a judge of the EACJ shall not hold any political or any office in the service of a Partner State or the community nor engage in any trade, vocation or profession that is likely to interfere or create a conflict of interest to his or her position] it becomes apparent that the objective of the Treaty is for judges of the Court to be independent of the Partner States they originate from. The introduc-tion of automatic removal and suspension on grounds raised or established in the home State, and applicable to only those in judicial or public office, makes possibilities of applying un-uniform standards to judges of the same court endanger the integrity of the Court as a regional court. Under the original mechanism such grounds could be submitted for consideration at the Community level.[68]

These amendments were made in reaction to the order of the EACJ in the *Prof Peter Anyang' Nyong'o* case[69] where the EACJ restrained the Clerk of the EALA and the Secretary General of the EAC from recognising the nine 'members' of the EALA from Kenya as duly elected by the National Assembly of Kenya to the Assembly.[70] The EACJ had held that the process that gave rise to the nine names that were forwarded to the Assembly did not constitute an election as envisaged by article 50 of the EAC Treaty. What followed thereafter was political condemnation of the EACJ by the Kenyan government [specifically its then President, Mr. Kibaki and its minister for East African and Regional Co-operation who accused the EACJ of bias (linked to the Kenyan members of the EACJ)][71]; a legal challenge to the EACJ impartiality based on the perceived bias on the part of the Kenyan members of the EACJ bench [the two were being accused of not disclosing that they had been suspended from their judicial duties in Kenya pending an inquiry into judicial misconduct (in fact one of the judges had actually been cleared of any wrongdoing in Kenya) and that they were likely to be biased against the government of Kenya]; and their intimidation (the Kenyan Solicitor General and his team visited them in their chambers in the absence of the other parties to the case, contrary to the usual practice in applications for recusal) with a view to ensure their recusal.[72]

The amendments were clearly linked to the developments post *Prof Peter Anyang' Nyong'o*. They were clearly meant to clip the wings of the EACJ through the curtailment of its jurisdiction (no longer would the EACJ have jurisdiction over similar matters); time limitation of access to it; and making the suspension and removal of some of its judges procedurally easy by expanding the scope of disciplinary grounds and giving such power to individual Partner States. To compound matters, article 26(2A)

---

[68] *East African Law Society & 3 others v Attorney General of the Republic of Kenya & 4 others* (Footnote 65 above) 45. See also Onoria (Footnote 64 above) 83–86.

[69] Onoria (Footnote 64 above). See Footnote 65 above for the citation of the *Prof Peter Anyang' Nyong'o* case.

[70] *East African Law Society* case (Footnote 65 above) 2. See also generally the *Prof Peter Anyang' Nyong'o* case (Footnote 65 above).

[71] Onoria (Footnote 64 above) 80. See also the reference thereunder.

[72] See Onoria (Footnote 64 above) 80, 81.

(this article provides that for a judge suspended under the expanded disciplinary regime, the home state of such a judge shall propose his temporary replacement) raises a real risk that Partner States would recommend pliant judges.[73] Also, the new two-tier court system was apparently meant to outflank the then EACJ bench, since it gave rise to the possibility of appealing the decision to a newly constituted (and perhaps pliant) Appellate Division, since the then existing court was rendered the First Instance Division.[74]

The timing of the 2007 amendments to the EAC Treaty raise a lot of questions about the commitment of the (then) Partner States to the rule of law, especially the respect of the independence and impartiality of judicial organs. What is even more worrying is the possibility of a cross-pollination effect of this 'successful' disregard of the rule of law on other international organisations like SADC, especially since Tanzania is a member of both organisations.[75]

However, the 2007 amendments to the EAC Treaty notwithstanding, there are some lessons that can be learnt from the EAC governance framework. The EAC Treaty is a detailed document that attempts to exhaustively deal with all the institutions and integration processes within the body of the treaty itself. No integral organ is deferred to a subsidiary legal instrument as is the case with SADC and, as will be seen in the following section, ECOWAS. The EAC framework also provides a measure of separation of powers between the different organs, although admittedly, more could be done in this area especially with regards to the too much power bestowed on the Summit and the relatively weak Secretariat.[76] The lawmaking

---

[73] See also Onoria (Footnote 64 above) 85, 86.

[74] Onoria (Footnote 64 above) 84. Onoria does not attack the principle of a two-tier system though. He views the new system, without elaboration, as 'laudable.' His concern is the timing of its creation, which he calls 'suspect.'

[75] The participation of (now former) President Kikwete of Tanzania in the two discredited processes of the EAC 2007 amendments and in the dissolution of the SADC Tribunal (with regards to the latter, President Kikwete is said to have called the SADC Tribunal a 'monster that will devour us all' at the time of its creation when he was still Tanzania's minister of Foreign Affairs [http://www.mg.co.za/article/2011-08-19-killed-off-by-kings-and-potentates (accessed 1 October 2013)]) is something that should not be taken lightly, especially in view of the fact that in both these processes, it was the judicial organ that was crudely dealt with politically.

[76] However, according to Professor John Ruhangisa (Registrar of the EACJ) in his presentation at a stakeholder roundtable discussion on the SADC Tribunal that was convened by the Centre for Human Rights, Faculty of Law, University of Pretoria (28–29 August 2014),

framework, if it is backed by progressive political will, would most likely lead to expedited integration and harmonisation processes. There is need, therefore, to strengthen the other organs (in addition to the Secretariat) especially the EACJ through a robust guarantee of its independence and impartiality and also the expansion of its jurisdictional competence.

6.3   THE ECONOMIC COMMUNITY OF WEST AFRICAN STATES

Some writers trace the history of West African integration from the nineteenth-century ideas of Africanus Beale Horton and Edward Wilmont Blyden, a Sierra Leonean and a Liberian respectively.[77] A somewhat formalised attempt at integration was the formation of the National Congress of British West Africa (NCBWA).[78] The NCBWA went as far as establishing a constitution with such structures as the Executive Council, the Legislative Council, and the House of Assembly.[79] Largely perceived as an elitist organisation not interested in confronting the continued existence of colonialism, preferring instead to see the infusion of democracy into the colonial system, the NCBWA eventually collapsed in the 1940s.[80]

The early post-colonial period of the late 1950s and early 1960s saw several unsuccessful bilateral (and trilateral) attempts at integration through the formation of federal states: the Mali Federation (merger of Mali and Senegal); the Ghana-Guinea Union; and the Ghana-Guinea-Mali Union.[81] A similar attempt at integration through federalism was made in 1982 through the creation of the Senegambia Confederation which eventually collapsed in 1989.[82] There had also been a 1959 integration scheme by the former French colonies. This was through the

---

(and notwithstanding the limited powers bestowed on the EAC secretariat including the Secretary General), the EAC Secretary General (the incumbent at the time of the above roundtable discussion) has been able to exact pressure on some of the Partner States like Burundi to address concerns of good governance and the rule of law. The author was a participant and facilitator at that roundtable discussion.

[77] Kufuor (Footnote 12 above) 20.
[78] As above.
[79] As above.
[80] As above.
[81] Kufuor (Footnote 12 above) 21.
[82] As above.

establishment, by way of a convention, of the West African Customs Union.[83]

The Treaty establishing the Economic Community of West African States (ECOWAS) was signed on 28 May 1975 and revised on 24 July 1993.[84] The review of the Treaty followed the establishment in 1992 of the Committee of Eminent Persons whose remit was the review of the 1975 ECOWAS Treaty.[85] Some of the findings of that Committee were that the powers of the Authority of Heads of State or Government were vague and ambiguous; the Council of Ministers' powers were restricted as it had no original or delegated powers; there were no clearly defined voting procedures to be followed by treaty organs; there was no role for the Executive Secretariat in decision-making and thus on the overall integration process; and there were no provisions allowing for national interests groups to participate in norm setting at community level.[86] In a sense, these findings were critical of not only the lack of a 'cooperative' framework of decision-making among the institutions of the old ECOWAS but also lack of a participatory democratic framework.

The ECOWAS Treaty provides that ECOWAS 'shall ultimately be the sole economic community in the region for the purpose of economic integration and the realisation of the objectives of the African Economic Community.'[87] Just like in the case of SADC, as discussed in Chap. 4 in the context of the finding by the African Commission in the communication on the suspension of the SADC Tribunal, the reference to the African Economic Community in the ECOWAS Treaty creates a sense of a hierarchical framework of integration in Africa.

The institutions of ECOWAS are the Authority of Heads of State or Government (the ECOWAS Authority); the Council of Ministers (ECOWAS Council); the Community Parliament (ECOWAS Parliament); the Economic and Social Council (ECOWAS ECOSOC); the Community Court of Justice (ECCJ)); the ECOWAS Commission; the Fund for

---

[83] S.T. Ebobrah 'Legitimacy and feasibility of human rights realisation through regional economic communities in Africa: The case of the Economic Community of West African States' unpublished LLD thesis, University of Pretoria (2009) 2.

[84] http://www.comm.ecowas.int/sec/index.php?id=treaty&lang=en (last accessed 29 September 2013).

[85] Kufuor (Footnote 12 above) 29.

[86] This condensed (and rephrased) summary of the findings of the Committee of Eminent Persons is derived from Kufuor (Footnote 12 above) 29–32.

[87] Art 2(1) of the ECOWAS Treaty.

Co-operation, Compensation and Development (ECOWAS Fund); Specialised Technical Commissions; and any other institutions that may be established by the Authority.[88]

The highest decision-making body of ECOWAS is the Authority of Heads of State or Government. The powers of the ECOWAS Authority are largely similar to those of the SADC Summit.[89] In addition to the power to seek an advisory opinion from the ECCJ on legal matters, the ECOWAS Treaty authorises the ECOWAS Authority to refer any matter to the ECCJ in the event of unlawful acts or omission by Member States and ECOWAS institutions.[90] On decision-making modalities, the ECOWAS Treaty provides three ways of taking decisions by the Authority, depending on the subject matter under consideration: unanimity, consensus, or two-thirds majority.[91]

The ECOWAS Council comprises two ministers from each Member State—a minister responsible for ECOWAS affairs and an additional minister. Its powers are also similar to those of the SADC Council of Ministers and it reports to the ECOWAS Authority.

With regard to the ECOWAS Parliament; the ECOWAS ECOSOC; the ECCJ; and the Arbitration Tribunal, the Treaty merely creates these but their composition and functions are deferred to the relevant protocols.[92]

The ECOWAS Commission was initially established as a Secretariat by article 17 of the revised Treaty. The Secretariat was headed by the Executive Secretary who had Deputy Executive Secretaries below him. On qualifications, the Executive Secretary was supposed to have 'proven competence and integrity, with a global vision of political and economic problems and regional integration.'

The Executive Secretary was responsible for, among other things, the execution of the decisions of the ECOWAS Authority and those of the ECOWAS Council, preparation of draft budgets and programmes of

---

[88] Art 6 of the ECOWAS Treaty.

[89] Art 7 of the ECOWAS Treaty.

[90] Art 7 (3) (g) of the ECOWAS Treaty.

[91] Art 9(2) of the ECOWAS Treaty. These methods of decision-making were deferred to a protocol pending which the ECOWAS Authority would take all its decisions by consensus. See para 3 of art 9 of the ECOWAS Treaty. A similar provision is applicable to the regulations adopted by the ECOWAS Council [art 12(3)]. Decisions of the ECOWAS Authority and the regulations made by the ECOWAS Council are supposed to be published in the official journal of the Community. This is similar to what obtains in the EAC.

[92] Arts 13–16 of the ECOWAS Treaty. Curiously, the Arbitration Tribunal is not specifically mentioned as one of the institutions of ECOWAS in art 6 of the ECOWAS Treaty.

activity of ECOWAS, submission of reports to the meetings of the ECOWAS Authority and ECOWAS Council and appointment of low-level ECOWAS staff.

The Secretariat was transformed into the ECOWAS Commission in 2006. The Commission has enhanced powers and Commissioners are each in charge of smaller and clearly defined sectors.[93]The Revised ECOWAS Treaty also established Technical Commissions (now Technical Committees).[94] These cover the areas of food and agriculture; industry, science, technology, and energy; environment and natural resources; transport, communications, and tourism; trade, customs, taxation, statistics, money, and payments; political, judicial, and legal affairs, regional security and immigration; human resources, information, social and cultural affairs; and administration and finance. However, the ECOWAS Authority has the power to restructure the committees and to create new ones.[95]

The functions of the Technical Committees include preparation of projects and programmes for consideration by the ECOWAS Council[96]; ensure the harmonisation and coordination of projects and programmes of ECOWAS; monitor and facilitate the application of the ECOWAS Treaty and protocols relevant to the particular Committee; and carry out other functions assigned to the relevant Committee by the ECOWAS Treaty.[97]

The Technical Committees are to some extent similar to the SADC National Committees and the Sectoral Committees of the EAC. Their powers are not only broadly couched but have already been, like in the latter RECs, given to other institutions or organs. Just as is the case with the SADC National Committees as stated in Chap. 4, it is as if the creation of this institution was meant to give the appearance of broader participation by citizens of Member States without any concern over the effectiveness of that participation.

Articles 26–34 provide for cooperation in a number of areas: industry; science and technology; energy; environment; hazardous and toxic wastes; natural resources; transport and communications; posts and telecommuni-

---

[93] http://www.comm.ecowas.int/ (accessed 10 October 2013).
[94] Art 22(1) of the ECOWAS Treaty.
[95] Art 22(1) of the ECOWAS Treaty.
[96] Art 23(a) of the ECOWAS Treaty.
[97] Art 23 paras (a)–(d).

cations; and tourism. However, these provisions are lean on detail and are largely broad undertakings without any clearly articulated implementation framework. Also, it is not clear how they are linked to the Technical Committees.

The ECOWAS Treaty seeks to involve civil society, specifically NGOs and voluntary development organisations 'in order to encourage the involvement of the peoples of the region in the process of economic integration and mobilise their technical, material and financial support.'[98] There are no details in the Treaty on how this should be done, save to only state that ECOWAS 'shall set up a mechanism for consultation with such organisations.' This provision is similar to the one in article 23 of the SADC Treaty, the only significant difference being an implicit admission in the ECOWAS Treaty that such provision is not enough, hence the provision that calls for the setting up of a consultative framework later. It is difficult though to appreciate the need for this deferral. Admittedly though, in SADC, there is also an attempt in the SADC Treaty itself to involve CSOs and other stakeholders in the work of SADC through the dysfunctional SNCs. There is also a provision on ECOWAS' relations with regional socio-economic organisations and associations.[99]

The other important institution of ECOWAS is the ECOWAS Community Court of Justice (ECCJ). The ECCJ is as old as ECOWAS, as it was established by the original ECOWAS Treaty, although it was originally christened the 'Tribunal of the Community.'[100] The establishment of the ECCJ is provided for in article 15 of the Revised Treaty of ECOWAS. However, the Treaty defers further matters—status, composition, powers, and other issues concerning the Court to a Protocol. The Protocol was later adopted in July 1991.[101] The jurisdiction granted to the ECCJ was originally a limited one. The citizens of ECOWAS had no direct access to the Tribunal—it could only determine matters brought before it by Member States which could bring cases to the ECCJ on behalf of their citizens.[102] Indeed, in the *Afolabi* case, the first ever case that was brought before the ECCJ in its then almost three decades of existence, the ECCJ

---

[98] Art 81 of the ECOWAS Treaty.
[99] Art 82 of the ECOWAS Treaty.
[100] R. Robert 'The social dimension of regional integration in ECOWAS' (2004) *Working paper No. 49* Policy Integration Department, International Labour Office 12.
[101] The Protocol is available at http://caselaw.ihrda.org/1991_prot-eco/ (accessed 26 February 2014).
[102] Art 9(3) of the 1991 Protocol on the Community Court of Justice.

decided that it could not entertain the matter on the merits since private individuals and corporations had no direct access to the ECCJ.[103] That case was instituted by a businessperson whose complaint was that the closure by Nigeria of its border with Benin resulted in loss of revenues and was a violation by Nigeria of the ECOWAS Protocol on the Free Movement of Goods and Persons.[104]

This limited jurisdiction led the then President of the ECCJ, Justice Hansine Donli to engage in diplomacy and urge the Member States of ECOWAS to reconsider the question of standing and to grant individuals direct access to the ECCJ.[105] Following the decision in *Afolabi*, ECOWAS adopted, in 2005, the Supplementary Protocol of the ECOWAS Community Court of Justice which, among other things, grants the ECCJ additional jurisdiction over cases of human rights violations that occur in Member States.[106]

Following the adoption of the Supplementary Protocol, the ECCJ has developed a sizable jurisprudence. Some of the legal developments have clearly been significant: ECOWAS Member States and community institutions can be sued before the ECCJ[107]; and individuals can approach the ECCJ where they allege violation of their human rights as enshrined in the African Charter on Human and Peoples' Rights (the African Charter).[108]

---

[103] See generally, *Olajide Afolabi v Federal Republic of Nigeria* 2004/EWC/CCJ/04 (decided on 27 April 2004) http://caselaw.ihrda.org/doc/ecw.ccj.jud.01.04/view/ (last accessed 12 September 2014). See also Robert (Footnote 100 above) 13.

[104] As above.

[105] Robert (Footnote 100 above) 13.

[106] Nwauche (Footnote 58 above) 40. The Supplementary Protocol is available at http://www.caselaw.ihrda.org/doc/2005_prot_eco/ (accessed 26 February 2014).

[107] Three cases that have been decided by the ECCJ are instructive and would suffice for the present purposes: *Peter David v Ambassador Ralph Uwechue* (ECW/CCJ/RUL/03/10); *The Registered Trustees of the Socio-Economic Rights and Accountability Project (SERAP) v The President of the Republic of Nigeria* (ECW/CCJ/APP/07/10, delivered on 10 December 2010 http://www.worldcourts.com/ecowasccj/eng/decisions/2010.12.10_SERAP_v_Nigeria.htm, last accessed 12 September 2014): and *Tandja v Djibo and Another* (ECW/CCJ/05/10, decided on 8 November 2010 http://www.courtecowas.org/site2012/pdf_files/decisions/judgements/2010/MONSIEUR_MAMADOU_TANDJA_v_S_E_GEN_SALOU_DJIBO_&_L_ETAT_DU_NIGER.pdf (accessed 12 September 2014). For a brief discussion of these cases see Nwauche (Footnote 58 above) 30–31.

[108] The application of the African Charter is based on art 4 of the ECOWAS Treaty and also on the Protocol on Democracy and Good Governance. For a detailed discussion on the

There have been further developments after the revised ECOWAS Treaty. Some of these developments are far-reaching and were effected through the Supplementary Protocol A/SP.1/06/06 Amending the Revised ECOWAS Treaty.[109] These include, as has already been indicated, the transformation of the ECOWAS Secretariat into a Commission. The Commission comprises a President, a Vice President, and seven other Commissioners and such other staff as may be required for the smooth functioning of the ECOWAS.[110] With the transformation of the Secretariat into a Commission, the technical Commissions established by the 1993 Revised Treaty were transformed into Technical Committees, discussed above.[111]

While the power to appoint the President of the Commission vests in the ECOWAS Authority, that of the Vice President, Commissioners, and statutory appointees in other institutions vests in the Council of Ministers acting on the recommendation of the relevant Ministerial Committee.[112] Limiting the role of the ECOWAS Authority to the appointment of the President of the Commission is a continuation of the 1993 dispensation where everyone under the Executive Secretary was appointed by the Council of Ministers on the recommendation of the relevant Ministerial Committee. This is different from the SADC position where the Summit is the ultimate appointing authority even for the Deputy Executive Secretaries. To some extent, decision-making in ECOWAS lies in different autonomous sites and the ECOWAS Authority does not, at least on paper, have overarching powers compared to those of the SADC Summit.

The powers of appointment apply *mutatis mutandis* to dismissals.[113] There is also provision for the dismissal of the Judges of the ECCJ. While this is a matter that ultimately is decided by the ECOWAS Authority, dismissal of a judge can only be done on the recommendation of a Community Judicial Council established by the Authority.[114]

---

applicability of the African Charter and other international human rights instruments see Nwauche (Footnote 58 above) 42–44.

[109] http://documentation.ecowas.int/download/en/legal_documents/protocols/ Supplementary%20Protocol%20Amending%20the%20Revised%20ECOWAS%20Treaty.pdf (accessed 24 May 2014).

[110] New art 17 of the Revised ECOWAS Treaty.

[111] New art 22 (1) (a).

[112] New art 18 (1) & (3) (a).

[113] New art 18 (3) (d).

[114] As above.

The ECOWAS Parliament, initially known as 'Community Parliament,' is another institution of ECOWAS. It was formally constituted through Protocol A/P2/8/94.[115] The role of the ECOWAS Parliament was, in terms of the 1994 Protocol, very insignificant. Per article 6 of this Protocol, it was limited to such things as consideration of some issues and the making of recommendations and the directory right to be consulted in some areas. This Protocol was later amended by the Supplementary Protocol A/SP.3/06/06 Amending Protocol A/P.2/8/94 Relating to the Community Parliament 2006. Other than establishing new institutions of the Parliament and dealing with such other matters including the rules of procedure, the Supplementary Protocol did not introduce any significant new powers of the Parliament, save for the directory right, per article 4(3), to be consulted in specified areas ranging from communication links to respect for human rights and fundamental freedoms 'in all their plenitude.' In terms of article 4(2) as read with article 4(3), there is an intention to progressively enhance the powers of the ECOWAS Parliament 'from advisory to co-decision making and subsequently to a law making role in areas to be defined by the Authority,' once the parliamentarians, it would appear, are elected by direct universal suffrage. Why the increase of powers should await direct universal suffrage, to the extent that these are linked, or why such form of representation is necessary in the first place, is not clear.[116]

---

[115] http://documentation.ecowas.int/download/en/legal_documents/protocols/Protocol%20Relating%20to%20the%20Community%20Parliament.pdf (accessed 24 May 2014).

[116] The wording of the second and third paras of art 4 is not very clear. Art 4(2) states that '[t]he powers of the ECOWAS Parliament shall be progressively enhanced from advisory to co-decision making (co-decision making is itself not defined) and subsequently to a law making role in areas to be defined by the Authority.' Art 4 (3) provides that pending direct universal suffrage, 'the ECOWAS Parliament may be consulted for its opinion on matters concerning the Community.' Art 4 (3) goes on to specify some areas where it is peremptory to seek the ECOWAS Parliament's opinion. One way to interpret these two paras is to link the third to the second, thereby anchoring co-decision-making (whatever its meaning in the context of ECOWAS is) and lawmaking in universal suffrage. The other way to interpret the two paras would be to delink them. In terms of the latter construction, the ECOWAS Authority can enhance the powers of the ECOWAS Parliament in terms of art 4 (2), that is, by elevating the ECOWAS Parliament to the status of 'co-decision' maker, even in the absence of universal suffrage. Universal suffrage would then be confined only to art 4(3), the effect of which would be to make it peremptory to seek the opinion of the ECOWAS Parliament on every matter affecting the ECOWAS, over and above whatever additional powers it might then be having. Needless to say, the latter construction is a bit convoluted.

It would, however, appear that there is some limited organic growth in the powers of the ECOWAS Parliament. In practice, there seems to be a new requirement for the opinion of the ECOWAS Parliament to be sought before Community legislation is passed.[117] Indeed, since 2008, when adopting Supplementary Acts, the practice has been to include a statement to the effect that the ECOWAS Parliament was consulted and its opinion taken into account.[118] However, the formal role of the ECOWAS Parliament either as a contributor to norm setting or as an oversight institution remains largely superficial.

In addition to the above amendments, the Supplementary Protocol brought in a new regime of community lawmaking. This is found in the new article 9. The result was moving away from the lengthy protocol and convention-based lawmaking which are subject to parliamentary ratification by Member States to a system of lawmaking through Supplementary Acts, Regulations, Directives, Recommendations, and Opinions.

In terms of this new regime, lawmaking powers are 'shared' between three institutions: the ECOWAS Authority, the Council, and the Commission.[119] The ECOWAS Authority adopts supplementary acts which are annexed to the Treaty. The Council enacts regulations, issues directives, and takes decisions or formulates recommendations and opinions. The Commission's legislative powers are confined to secondary implementation legislation—the adoption of rules meant for the execution of acts enacted by the Council, with such rules having the same legal force as acts adopted by Council the execution of which the rules are adopted. The Commission also has the power to formulate recommendations and opinions.

The legal effects of these various instruments are set out in sub-articles 3–8 of the new article 9 as follows:

3. Supplementary Acts adopted by the Authority shall be binding on the Community institutions and Member States, where they shall be directly applicable without prejudice to the provisions of Article 15 of the revised Treaty.[120]

---

[117] Ebobrah (Footnote 83 above) 135.
[118] Ebobrah (Footnote 83 above) 167.
[119] There is no mention of the ECOWAS Parliament.
[120] Art 15 is the article that establishes the ECCJ. Art 15 (4) provides that 'Judgments of the Court of Justice shall be binding on the Member States, the Institutions of the Community and on individuals and corporate bodies.'

4. Regulations shall have general application. The provisions of Regulations shall be binding and directly applicable in Member States. They shall equally be binding on the Community institutions.
5. Directives shall be binding on all Member States in terms of the objectives to be realized. However, Member States shall be free to adopt modalities they deem appropriate for the realization of such objectives.
6. Decisions shall be binding on all those designated therein.
7. Recommendations and opinions are not enforceable.
8. Unless otherwise provided in this Supplementary Protocol, Community Acts under consideration shall be adopted by unanimity, consensus, or by a two-thirds majority of the Member States.

With a superficial regional parliament whose powers are still confined to making non-binding advisory opinions, there is still some long way for ECOWAS to go in terms of creating a democratic decision-making architecture underpinned by separation of powers and a multiplicity of voices in the integration process. The idea that the ECOWAS Parliament can only play an expanded role once modalities of direct elections of its members have been operationalised is, to the extent that this is the interpretation intended by article 4(3) of the Supplementary Protocol A/SP.3/06/06, superfluous, since[121] there does not appear to be any logical link between direct representation/universal suffrage and an expanded legislative role of the ECOWAS Parliament.

However, there does appear to be some political will within ECOWAS to continue to enhance the powers of the ECOWAS Parliament, and thus reconfigure inter-institutional relations and the balance of power within the ECOWAS governance framework. A Supplementary Act on the Enhancement of Powers of the Parliament was adopted by the ECOWAS Authority during the 14–15 December 2014 Summit and is now awaiting signature.[122]

---

[121] See Footnote 116 above.

[122] See 'Constituents relations and outreach: Experience of the ECOWAS Parliament under reduced mandate and transition to legislative powers' a presentation by Simon Odei-Mensah, fourth Deputy Speaker of ECOWAS Parliament. The presentation was made at Mount Meru Hotel, Arusha, Tanzania at a Parliamentary Exchange Workshop on the Institutional Strengthening of International Parliamentary Bodies. The workshop was held on 10–11 February 2015. Available at http://www.awepa.org/wp-content/

While the current position (before the coming into force of the Supplementary Act) is that representatives (members of the ECOWAS Parliament) are selected from among members of national assemblies of Member States, under the Supplementary Act, representatives would be elected from among citizens by national assemblies acting as electoral colleges.[123] With regard to decision-making powers, the current position, as already indicated, is that the ECOWAS Parliament gives only non-binding advisory opinions in limited areas. Under the Supplementary Act, the ECOWAS Parliament would be able to give simple opinions, mandatory assent, and would also have co-decision and co-legislative powers.

The other notable development is that ECOWAS Parliament would now have the power to exercise co-decision-making, together with the Council of Ministers, over the adoption of the budget. The Supplementary Act also confers on the ECOWAS Parliament some oversight functions, including the power (which it would exercise through the office of Parliamentary Ombudsman) to confirm statutory appointees. The Parliament would also play a legally entrenched diplomatic role in the area of conflict prevention and management, something that is not formally provided for in the current legal framework. The Parliament would participate in the meetings of the Mediation and Security Council as an observer and may also request the President of the ECOWAS Commission to activate a conflict management mechanism.

Another formal enhancement of powers which is meant to catch up with what is already happening in practice is the Parliament's participation in election-monitoring. The ECOWAS Parliament would now have the legal right to nominate a number of representatives to participate in election-monitoring missions.

However, as some analysts have observed, whilst the enhancement of the powers of the ECOWAS Parliament has meant some dilution of the executive-dominated ECOWAS governance infrastructure, the powers that have been accorded ECOWAS Parliament remain largely modest.[124]

uploads/2015/03/Hon-Osei-Mensah_ECOWAS-P-Outreach-and-Representation1.pdf (accessed 7 October 2015).

[123] For the analysis of this development, including an outline of the changes carried in this and the next two paragraphs, see generally L. Boré & F. Henkel 'Disturbing a cosy balance? The ECOWAS Parliament's rocky road to co-decision' International Policy Analysis, Friedrich Ebert Stiftung, January 2015 available at http://library.fes.de/pdf-files/iez/11185.pdf (last accessed 16 April 2016).

[124] See generally, Boré & Henkel (Footnote 123 above).

However, the lack of an effective role for the ECOWAS Parliament and the related executivism in ECOWAS notwithstanding, there are some things that can be learnt from ECOWAS: To some extent, there is space for the sharing of responsibility in the area of lawmaking between the Commission and the political institutions; and ECOWAS has also been able to establish, although admittedly over time and not without significant challenges, a relatively strong judicial arm with a relatively busy docket especially in the area of human rights.[125] With regard to the latter, there is, however, a need to build additional safeguards especially with regard to enforcement/implementation of court decisions.[126]

6.4   The European Union

What is most remarkable about the EU is that it has never been shy of transforming itself. With its foundation being the post-World War II European Coal and Steel Community (established in 1951), later evolving into the 1957 Rome Treaties establishing the European Economic Community (EEC) and the European Atomic Energy Community, with a number of transformations in between, both organic and treaty based (including the 1986 Single European Act), the European Union was formally established through the Treaty of Maastricht which entered into force on 1 November 1993.[127]

The EU has been able to radically redefine its institutional framework, with some of the transformation happening within a decade of the previous one. From the Single European Act of 1986 to the 1993 Treaty of Maastricht, the EU, as it is known today, has undergone significant reconfiguration of its inter-institutional relations and intra-institutional decision-making procedures.[128] The most recent transformation was in 2007,

---

[125] For a glimpse of the ECCJ's judicial activity, see S.T. Ebobrah 'Human rights developments in African sub-regional economic communities during 2012' (2013) 13 # 1 *African Human Rights Law Journal* 191–213.

[126] Enforcement/implementation of the decisions of the ECJ still remains a significant challenge. See H.S. Adjolohoun (Footnote 59 above) 164–185.

[127] D.M. Curtin & I.F. Dekker 'The European Union from Maastricht to Lisbon: Institutional and legal unity out of the shadows' in P. Craig and G. De Búrca (eds) *The evolution of EU law* (2011) 155–185; P. Craig 'Integration, democracy, and legitimacy' in P. Craig and G. De Búrca (eds) *The evolution of EU law* (2011) 13; H.P. Hestermeyer (Footnote 10 above).

[128] See G. Marks et al. 'European integration from the 1980s: State centric v. multi-level governance' 1996 (34) # 3 *Journal of Common Market Studies* 342. Marks et al. point out

through the Treaty of Lisbon, some of whose provisions are the subjects of this section.

As has been noted by Curtin and Dekker, most of these formal constitutional changes, especially those brought about by the most recent Lisbon Treaty, did not establish anything new, as they are a reflection of 'institutional realities that had evolved and ripened to such an extent that the formal provisions of the Treaty of Lisbon caught up with "living" and sedimentary practices.'[129]

These 'institutional realities' that had 'evolved and ripened' over time are, to some extent, a clear sign that there have been many players that have shaped the development of EU, chief among which has been the Court of Justice of the European Union (CJEU) (to be discussed in detail below) which has been credited with 'developing the "living" constitution over time.'[130] The most clear and undisputed example of the role of the CJEU in the development of norms in the EU is the development, in the absence of explicit bases in the relevant treaties at the time, of the direct effect and primacy doctrines in the 1960s.[131]

The institutions of the European Union are set out in article 13(1) of the consolidated version of the Treaty on European Union (TEU).[132] These are the European Parliament (EP); the European Council; the Council of the European Union (the Council); the European Commission (the Commission); the CJEU; the European Central Bank; and the Court of Auditors. Just like in the case of the ECOWAS Fund, this study does not discuss the European Central Bank and the Court of Auditors because of their specialised and technical nature and also because they do not,

the introduction of qualified decision-making in the Council and the increase of the powers of the EP as some of the major developments in EU evolution leading to an increase in the 'scope and depth of policy-making.'

[129] Curtin & Dekker (Footnote 127 above) 156.

[130] As above.

[131] Direct effect, in the context of the EU is 'the capacity of a norm to be applied in domestic court proceedings' whereas the related doctrine of primacy means 'the capacity of the norm of Union law to overrule inconsistent norms of national law in domestic court proceedings.' See B. de Witte 'Direct effect, primacy, and the nature of the legal order' in P. Craig & G. de Búrca (eds) *The evolution of EU law* (2011) 323, 324. A brief discussion of the introduction of the doctrine of direct effect into EU law is found below where the CJEU is discussed.

[132] http://eur-lex.europa.eu/LexUriServ/LexUriServ.do?uri=OJ:C:2010:083:0013:0046:en:PDF (accessed 10 October 2013).

strictly speaking, form part of the general norm-setting governance architecture of their respective organisations.

Quite significantly, article 13(2) of the Treaty constrains all the EU institutions to act within the limits of the powers conferred on that particular institution by the Treaties (as to what constitutes 'the Treaties,' see note 179 below) and to conform to procedures, conditions, and objectives set out in the Treaties and to practice mutual sincere cooperation.

The powers of the EP are set out in article 14(1). The EP is the legislative arm of the EU. However, the EP shares the legislative power with the Council. This joint exercise of power extends to the budget adoption process as well. The EP also exercises the functions of political control and consultation. The EP elects the President of the European Commission.

The members of the EP are directly elected at EU Member State level on the basis of proportional representation, with minimum and maximum threshold of 6 members and 96 members per Member State.[133] The actual composition of the EP is a matter unanimously decided by the Council, but on the initiative of, and with the consent of the EP.[134]

The European Council consists of Heads of State or Government of EU Member States, the President of the European Council, and the President of the Commission.[135] The responsibility of the European Council is to 'provide the Union with the necessary impetus for its development ... and [to] define [its] general political directions and priorities....'[136] The European Council is specifically prohibited from exercising any legislative functions.[137]

The President of the European Council is elected by the European Council by a qualified majority and serves two and a half years' term, renewable once, and may be removed from office by the European Council by the same majority in the event of an impediment or serious misconduct.[138] The composition of the European Council is relatively unique when compared to similar institutions in other RECs. It is headed by

[133] Art 14(2) of TEU (Consolidated Version).
[134] As above.
[135] Art 15(2) of TEU (Consolidated Version).
[136] Art 15(1) of TEU (Consolidated Version). As if by design, there is a marked difference in institutional sequencing in the EAC, ECOWAS, and SADC Treaties on the one hand and the EU Treaty on the other. The former starts with the 'all-important organ/institution' of the heads of state or government and the latter starts with the parliamentary institution.
[137] As above.
[138] Art 15(5) of TEU (Consolidated Version).

someone who is not a head of state or government.[139] The President of the European Commission (the executive institution of the EU discussed below) is, as stated above, also a member of the European Council; and the High Representative for Foreign Affairs and Security Policy (an institution discussed below) takes part in the work of the European Council.[140] Headship by a person with no taxing domestic political functions is likely to be a source of effectiveness, while the inclusion of the President of the Commission (not just presence in the European Council meetings or playing the role of secretary as is the case with the Secretary General of the EAC and the Executive Secretary of SADC), is bound to lead to robust dialogue.

In addition to his or her other functions, which include chairing the European Council meetings and driving forward the work of the European Council, the President of the European Council is obligated to present a report to the EP after each of the meetings of the European Council,[141] another example of the 'cooperative' nature of the EU institutional framework, allowing for among other things, continuous exchange of information between different institutions.

There is also the Council. In addition to the joint exercise of legislative and budgetary functions with the EP, the Council carries out policymaking and coordinating functions as provided in the Treaties.[142] In any of its various configurations, the Council consists of a representative of each Member State at ministerial level, who may commit their government and cast its vote.[143] There is a General Affairs Council that is tasked with

---

[139] The system of having a permanent President of the European Council was introduced by the Lisbon Treaty which came into force on 1 December 2009. Prior to that, the President of the European Council (then an informal institution within the EU) was held, subject to a six-month system of rotation, by the head of state or government of the EU Member State that held the Presidency of the Council of the EU. See http://www.european-council.europa.eu/the-president/the-presidents-role; http://europa.eu/legislation_summaries/institutional_affairs/treaties/lisbon_treaty/ai0007_en.htm (both accessed 8 October 2014).

[140] Art 15(2) of TEU (Consolidated Version). In terms of art 235(1) of the TFEU, if the European Council takes decision by a vote, the President of the European Council and the President of the Commission do not take part in the vote.

[141] Art 15(6)(d) of TEU (Consolidated Version).

[142] Art 16(1) of TEU (Consolidated Version).

[143] Arts 16(2) & 16(6) of TEU (Consolidated Version). The wording of this provision appears to deliberately cast the decisions of the Council within the strict intergovernmental realm.

ensuring consistency in the work of the different configurations of the Council.[144] The General Affairs Council prepares and ensures follow-up to meetings of the European Council in liaison with the President of the European Council and the Commission.[145]

The role of the Commission is to 'ensure the application of the Treaties, and of measures adopted by the institutions pursuant to them.'[146] The Commission oversees the application of EU law, subject to the control of the Court of Justice.[147] Other functions of the Commission include execution of the budget and management of programmes; exercise of coordination, executive and management functions; and ensuring the EU's external representation (except in those matters specifically provided for in the Treaties, for example, the Common Foreign and Security Policy).

EU legislative acts, except otherwise provided in the Treaties, may only be adopted on the basis of a Commission proposal. Where the Treaties so provide, this right of initiation can be peremptory, rather than merely directory.[148] Within the EU, the Commission is thus a truly 'executive' institution. This is very much unlike in SADC where formally the Secretariat is largely an administrative organ that provides secretarial services to the political executive institutions of SADC and acts as directed by the decisions of especially the Summit and the CoM. In the EU, the Council has its own administrative structure in the form of its General Secretariat.[149] This clearly shows that the Commission is not subordinated to the Council, as would be the implication were the Commission to provide administrative services to the Council.

Holding office for five years, members of the Commission must possess general competence and European commitment, and their independence should be beyond doubt.[150] Up to 31 October 2014, the Commission

---

[144] Art 16(6) of TEU (Consolidated version).

[145] As above. Also specifically mentioned in the same article is the Foreign Affairs Council whose mandate is to 'elaborate the Union's external action on the basis of strategic guidelines laid down by the European Council to ensure that the Union's action is consistent.'

[146] Art 17(1) of TEU (Consolidated Version).

[147] As above.

[148] Art 17(2) of TEU (Consolidated Version).

[149] Art 240 of the TFEU. This is the same body that services the European Council (art 235 of the TEU).

[150] Art 17(2) of TEU (Consolidated Version). On the question of independence, article 17(3) specifically provides that in carrying out its responsibilities, the Commission shall be completely independent and its members shall not seek or 'take instructions from any Government or other institution, body, office or entity.'

consisted (and still does) of a representative from each EU Member State, the President of the Commission and the High Representative of the Union for Foreign Affairs and Security Policy who is also one of the Vice Presidents of the Commission.[151] In terms of article 17(5), with effect from 1 November 2014, the Commission will consist of its President, the EU's High Representative for Foreign Affairs and Security Policy and a number of members corresponding to two-thirds of the number of Member States, unless the European Council unanimously decides to alter this number. The European Council has in fact already taken a decision not to reduce, for the being, the number of Commissioners and is likely to make its 'final' decision in 2019.[152]

The European Council, acting by a qualified majority, proposes a candidate for President of Commission to the EP. The European Council should take into account the elections to the EP and it has to hold 'appropriate consultations' before coming up with a candidate.[153] The

---

[151] Art 17(4) of TEU (Consolidated Version).

[152] The maintenance of the *status quo* was apparently an act of appeasement to the Irish who had initially rejected the Lisbon Treaty in the first referendum in 2008. One of their areas of concern was the reduction of the size of the Commission which would have meant that larger countries would have maintained permanent seats on the Commission with the remaining seats being rotated among the smaller countries. See 'EU Summit: Current Commission size extended to 2019: EU leaders vote to overrule Lisbon Treaty's plan for reduction in the number of Commissioners' *European Voice*, 22 May 2013 as updated on 23 April 2014 http://www.politico.eu/article/eu-summit-current-commission-size-extended-to-2019/ (accessed 26 April 2015). It should be noted though that the European Council did not overrule the Lisbon Treaty as alleged by this report since it acted within the discretionary powers bestowed upon it by the Treaty itself.

[153] Art 17(7) of TEU (Consolidated Version). While this provision suggests that the election of the Commission President should be a matter of consultation between the European Council and the EP, which consultation should be informed by the democratic outcome of the EP elections, it would appear that some EU heads of state have been of a different view and believe that the election of Commission President is a matter of European Council high politics. This is illustrated by the battle between the EP and some of the leading EU heads of state like Mrs. Angela Merkel, the German Chancellor and Mr. David Cameron, the British Prime Minster after the 2014 EP elections. While the majority coalition in the EP was in favour of Jean-Claude Juncker to be the next Commission President, some leaders including the German Chancellor, the British Prime Minister and the Swedish Prime Minister were prepared to ignore the views of the EP. See Spiegel Online International 'The democratic deficit: Europeans vote, Merkel decides' 2 June 2014 http://www.spiegel.de/international/germany/power-struggle-europts-between-european-parliament-and-eu-leaders-a-972870.html (accessed 19 February 2015). Whatever the different views on this issue may be, at least it is a good illustration of inter-institutional conversation (even if tension filled) at work.

Commission President is elected by the EP by a majority of its component members.[154] If the candidate does not obtain the required majority, the European Council, again acting by a qualified majority, shall propose a new candidate within one month for election by the EP following the same procedure.[155]

The other members of the Commission are chosen on the basis of common accord between the Council and the Commission President-elect. The Council and the President-elect adopt a list of prospective members of the Commission, who are selected on the basis of suggestions made by Member States.[156] The whole lot, that is to say, the President-elect, the High Representative for Foreign Affairs and Security Policy and the other members, is then subjected to a vote of consent as a collective by the EP by a majority, after which the Commission is appointed by the European Council acting by qualified majority.[157]

Thus, like in ordinary legislation and budget adoption processes, we see several institutions of the EU having not just a nominal but a critical say in the choice of the Commission. No single institution holds a prerogative. There is space for intricate inter-institutional conversation which is enough to give some democratic legitimacy to this executive arm of the EU. Over and above this inter-institutional dialogue, there are also intra-institutional legitimating tools like the qualified majority vote of the European Council (including the mandatory appropriate consultations before nominating a candidate for President of the Commission) and the majority vote of the EP.

However, in addition to rule making/norm setting by the above Treaty institutions, there is an expanding site of influence in the form of independent agencies.[158] Examples of these agencies include the Aviation Safety Agency; the Agency for Safety and Health at Work; the Maritime Safety Agency; the Fisheries Control Agency; and the European Energy Agency

---

Indeed one could view it as a healthy democratic tension between indirect state-based legitimacy (represented by the European Council) and Europe-wide direct legitimacy (in the form of the EP).

[154] As above.
[155] As above.
[156] As above.
[157] As above.
[158] For a detailed discussion of the development and role of independent agencies in the EU, see M. Shapiro 'Independent agencies' in P. Craig & G. De Búrca (eds) *The evolution of EU law* (2011) 111–120.

(EEA).[159] These agencies are perceived to be independent in the sense that they do not fall within any of the Commission's directorates, but they are dependent on and report to the Commission as a whole, yet others are dependent not on the Commission, but on the Council.[160] The agencies were conceived as institutions of expertise 'designed to inject a high level of technological expertise into the EU-policy-making process.'[161] They are both supranational and intergovernmental in character, since they comprise 'technical experts designated by Member States but dedicated to objectively correct technical judgment.'[162] The usual structure and appointment procedure for these agencies has been summarised as follows:

> [T]ypically these agencies have a single head usually appointed by its executive board on nomination by the Commission—the executive board typically consisting of one member nominated by each of the Member States and expert in the relevant fields of knowledge, and a Commission representative and staff of technical experts who are members of the European Union civil service.[163]

While the roles of the first agencies were limited to such non-norm-setting tasks like the gathering, collation, and dissemination of information, some of them have gradually assumed significant policymaking powers. For example, the Aviation Safety Agency has a safety and environmental certification that is binding on the aviation industry and its 'rule-making is in the form of recommendations to the Commission and/or Member States.'[164]As noted by Shapiro:

> Over time, moreover, a number of the agencies have become major sources of Union soft law, issuing model sets of rules, procedures, standards, best practices, guidance documents, and consensus reports of coordination

---

[159] Shapiro (Footnote 158 above) 112, 115, & 119.

[160] Shapiro (Footnote 158 above) 112, 114.

[161] Shapiro (Footnote 158 above) 118.

[162] As above.

[163] Shapiro (Footnote 158 above) 111.

[164] Shapiro (Footnote 158 above) 112. See also the reference thereunder. The democratic legitimacy of the powers of the Aviation Safety Agency is apparently secured by stakeholder involvement, since (as Shapiro notes) it 'is one of the few agencies whose procedures provide for extensive participation by non-governmental parties similar to US "notice and comment" rule-making.'

meetings … [S]ome of the agencies, particularly those engaged with trans-
portation matters, come close to full regulatory powers. Others issue
European-wide marketing authorizations that amount to the creation of
legally enforceable intellectual property rights comparable to patents or
copyrights.[165]

In addition to agencies, there are also committees that assist the
Commission in discharging its implementation powers.[166] These committees, consisting of Member States representatives and chaired by the
Commission, operate through the so-called comitology procedure and
their dialogical nature assist the Commission to ensure 'that (implementation) measures reflect as far as possible the situation in each of the countries concerned.'[167]

The Court of Justice of the European Union, comprising the Court of
Justice, the General Court and the specialised courts, is established by
article 19.[168] The Court of Justice consists of one judge from each Member
State, while the General Court includes at least one judge per Member
State.[169] The independence of the judges of the Court of Justice and its
Advocates-General and the judges of the General Court should be beyond
doubt.[170] They are appointed by common accord of the governments of
Member States.[171]

The jurisdiction of the CJEU includes ruling on actions brought by
Member States, institutions, or natural or legal persons; giving preliminary
rulings, when requested to do so by courts or tribunals of Member States

---

[165] Shapiro (Footnote 158 above) 112.

[166] http://europa.eu/legislation_summaries/glossary/comotology_en.htm (accessed 14
April 2014).

[167] As above.

[168] TEU (Consolidated Version).

[169] Art 19(2) of TEU (Consolidated Version). The Court of Justice is assisted by
Advocates-General.

[170] As above. The further conditions are provided for in arts 253 and 254 of the Treaty on
the Functioning of the European Union, including the requirement that the Judges and
Advocates-General should possess qualifications required for appointment to the highest
judicial offices in their respective countries or are jurisconsults of recognised competence
http://eur-lex.europa.eu/LexUriServ/LexUriServ.do?uri=OJ:C:2008:115:0047:0199:en:
PDF (accessed 12 October 2013).

[171] As above.

on the interpretation of EU law or the validity of acts adopted by the institutions; and ruling in other matters provided for in the Treaties.[172]

There is to some extent some similarity between the jurisprudential journeys of the CJEU and the SADC Tribunal. As has been noted in Chap. 4, the human rights jurisprudence in SADC was developed in the absence of an explicit conferral provision in the SADC Treaty.[173]A similar development took place in the EU. It suffices for the purposes of this study to make mention the development of the doctrine of direct effect in the latter organisation, a legal principle that was not explicitly provided for in the then treaties.

An opportunity arose in the *Van Gend & Loos* case, when a referral was made to the then ECJ by a court in the Netherlands, on the interpretation of article 12 of the then EEC Treaty, which proscribed customs duty increases in the trade between Member States.[174] Instead of following one of legal schools on the reception/application of international law in domestic jurisdictions—either monism or dualism—whereby national courts determine the applicability of an international legal norm in their jurisdiction, the CJEU stated that article 12 of the EEC Treaty was directly applicable in the territory of a Member State.[175] The decision of the CJEU was informed by what would, to a current scholar, appear like an obvious line of reasoning: by coming together under the aegis of the EEC, the Member States limited their sovereignty in specified fields and by so doing they came up with a new international legal order whose subjects were not just EEC Member States but nationals of the Member States as well.[176] Thus, the CJEU established a new supranational legal order whereby the EU (then EEC) would determine, by and of itself, when an EU law had a direct effect in Member States, and commanding protection by courts in Member States; and by consequence, the CJEU assumed for itself the

---

[172] Art 19(3) of TEU (Consolidated Version). However, art 24(1) of TEU (Consolidated Version) outs the jurisdiction of the Court in matters dealing with the Common Foreign and Security Policy.

[173] However, human rights jurisdiction was not proscribed either, as in the EAC.

[174] The *Van Gend & Loos* case, decided in 1963, is rarely absent in any scholarly article that discusses the role of the CJEU in the evolution of the EU. However, for a succinct summary of the background of the case, its salient facts and the reasoning of the (now) CJEU, see Hestermeyer (Footnote 10 above).

[175] Hestermeyer (Footnote 10 above).

[176] As above.

jurisprudential power of determining which Treaty provisions had direct effect.[177]

However, at the time of *Van Gend & Loos*, the classical position of the nation state in relation to international law was that only states could decide which international legal norms were applicable (and how) in their domestic jurisdictions. The implications of such a radical change were clearly evident in the level of contestation at the litigation stage of the case, and in the slender majority of the court that won the day.[178] The CJEU has thus been part of the process of the evolution of the EU—which process has not just been left to the other institutions through the usual way of norm creation at the international level—positive treaty law. However, as indicated in Chap. 1 and as illustrated elsewhere in this study, the primacy of treaty law has been clear in these historical developments. In the case of the EU, these 'sedimentary' developments have subsequently been accommodated (or clearly spelt out) in EU treaty law by subsequent treaty amendments.

The Treaty on the Functioning of the European Union (TFEU) carries provisions that organise in detail the functioning of the EU and 'determines the areas of, delimitation of, and arrangements for exercising its competences.'[179] By way of an example, and because of the importance of a budget in any organisational setup, it is important to highlight here the detailed framework of the adoption of the EU budget.[180] While the TEU vests the function of adoption of the EU budget in the Council and the EP, it is the TFEU that provides the detailed budgetary framework. This is provided for in article 314.[181] In terms of this article, the budget of the

---

[177] As above. Other legal doctrines that have directed the 'course of integration' that were developed by the CJEU include: primacy; conformity; state liability; and proportionality. See C. Baudenbacher & M.J. Clifton 'Courts of regional economic and political integration agreements' in C.P.R. Romano et al. (eds) *The Oxford handbook of international adjudication* (2013) 255.

[178] Hestermeyer (Footnote 10 above).

[179] Art 1(1) of the Treaty on the Functioning of the European Union (Consolidated Version 2012). Art 1(2) of the same Treaty provides that the two Treaties (TEU and TFEU) shall be referred to as 'the Treaties' and have the same legal value.

[180] The EU budget-making process has been singled out for a detailed discussion for a number of reasons including that the procedure is clear and very detailed; almost all EU institutions are involved in the initial budget formulation stage; all major EU institutions are significantly involved in the eventual adoption of the budget; and there are several ways of reaching a consensus in the event of inter-institutional differences.

[181] Paras 1–8 of art 314 of the TFEU.

EU is established by the EP and the Council acting in accordance with a special legislative procedure.

Each EU institution (with the exception of the European Central Bank) draws up, before a prescribed date, estimates of the expenditure for the following year. The Commission then consolidates these various estimates in a draft budget which may contain different estimates, after which it submits a proposal containing the draft budget, with estimates of revenue and expenditure, to the EP and the Council by a prescribed date.[182] The Council should adopt its position on the draft budget and forward it, together with full supporting reasons, to the EP, by a predetermined date. At that stage, the EP may approve the position of Council.

If the EP does not take a decision, the budget is deemed to have been adopted. In the event that the EP adopts amendments by a majority of its component members, the amended draft is forwarded to the Council and the Commission. At that stage, the President of the EP, in agreement with the President of the Council, shall immediately convene a meeting of the Conciliation Committee, which meeting would fall away if within a speci-fied period the Council informs the EP that it has approved all its amendments.

If the Conciliation Committee (comprising members of the Council or their representatives and an equal number of members representing the EP, with the Commission taking part in the proceedings and playing a conciliatory role) agrees on a joint text of the draft budget, the EP and the Council are given a period within which to approve the joint text. If how-ever, only one of these institutions approves the text and the other one does not, the budget is deemed to be approved in terms of the joint text. In the event that both the Council and the EP (in the case of the EP, the majority thereof) reject the text, or one of these institutions rejects the text while the other fails to take a decision, or the EP (the majority thereof) rejects the joint text while the Council approves it, a new draft budget shall be submitted by the Commission. The same would apply were the Conciliation Committee fail to agree on a joint text.

In the event that the EP approves the joint text and the Council rejects it, the EP may, within a prescribed period, decide, by majority and subject to a threshold of votes cast, to confirm all or some of the amendments it

---

[182] It should be noted that in terms of art 314(2), the Commission may amend the draft budget during the procedure until the appointment of the Conciliation Committee in the event of disagreement between the EP and the Council.

made earlier. Where an amendment is not confirmed, the position agreed in the Conciliation Committee on the budget heading which is the subject of the amendment shall be retained and the budget will be deemed adopted accordingly.

Article 314(9) vests the President of the EP with the power to declare that the budget has been definitively adopted when the article 314 procedure has been completed. Article 315 deals with allowable expenditure in the event that the budget has not been definitively adopted.

The EU governance framework can be described in several, and at times overlapping terms such as 'shared governance,' 'cooperative governance,' 'mutual dependence,' and so on. The following summary by Neyer effectively captures the overall modus of the EU institutional framework:

> The Council cannot act without a proposal on the part of the Commission, and also needs the Commission to manage its implementation. Similarly, the Commission must formulate its legislative proposals in a way that is likely to pass the scrutiny of both the Council and the Parliament, and must also secure Member State approval for its implementing measures. Furthermore, because the Commission has only limited capacities to enforce European law, it dedicates a great deal of effort to the safeguarding of broad political support for its proposal, consults as many interests groups as possible … [T]hus, successful political interaction in the [then] First Pillar of the EU is strongly characterized by a demand … for a shared and co-operative exercise of governance among the Member States and the European institutions.[183]

Despite the dense web of institutions in the EU that are meant to achieve 'institutional balance' and to close the democratic deficit in decision-making, there are strong arguments that the EU governance framework has democratic deficits. The list of these democratic deficits is a long one, and it includes the following: the EU voter does not have a say in the legislative process—while she can determine the composition of the EP, she cannot vote out, at the EU level at least, the other players in the legislative process; decision-making in the EU is dominated by the executive in the

---

[183] J. Neyer 'Discourse and order in the EU: A deliberative approach to multi-level governance' in EO Eriksen et al. (eds) *European governance, deliberation and the quest for democratization* (2003) 244 http://www.arena.uio.no (accessed 16 April 2014). See also the reference thereunder. This work is also available as a paper in Volume 41 of the *Journal of Common Market Studies* (2003).

form of the Council and the European Council and the EP does not have adequate power to constrain this executive dominance; there is lack of transparency in decision-making with much of the decision-making happening behind closed doors; the legislative procedures are complex and beyond the understanding of the ordinary EU citizen; and decision-making is centralised at Brussels, far away from the nation state which is closer to the citizen.[184]

However, as argued by Craig, most of the democratic deficit arguments are exaggerated.[185] So emphatic is Craig in his argument that he adds: '...[i]nsofar as there are problems within the EU these are no greater than in nation states, and that they would exist even if there were no EU.'[186] Indeed, De Búrca's democracy-striving approach is worth mentioning in this context, since it 'acknowledges the difficulty and complexity of democratizing transnational governance yet insists on its necessity, and identifies the act of continuous striving itself as the source of legitimation and accountability.'[187]

While the EU is touted by some as an organisation with 'unique geo-political foundations, complex governing institutions, elaborate co-ordination mechanism, and levels of internal economic integration that developing countries can only dream about,'[188] its institutional structures are largely informed by the doctrine of separation of powers so prevalent in modern constitutional democracies and are therefore not exactly a new innovation. In a sense, the EU has not reinvented the wheel. It has to a great extent adopted the governance tools that have been available in a number of domestic models. To a constitutional and administrative lawyer, the EU institutional architecture is familiar territory. There is thus nothing wrong with SADC emulating some of the elements of the EU model under the shared governance model proposed in this study.

As indicated in several parts this study, the EU is not a perfect model to be emulated wholesale by regional integration schemes in other parts of the world. Indeed it would not come as a surprise if in the not-so-distant

---

[184] Craig (Footnote 127 above) 30.
[185] Craig (Footnote 127 above) 29.
[186] Craig (Footnote 127 above) 30.
[187] G. de Búrca 'Developing democracy beyond the state' (2007–2008) 46 *Columbia Journal of Transnational Law* 234.
[188] P. Draper, 'Breaking free from Europe: Why Africa needs another model of regional integration' (2012) 47 # 1 *The International Spectator: Italian Journal of International Affairs* 80.

future other fundamental changes are introduced to address the democratic deficit in the EU, among other things. Some scholars have already started pointing out some areas they feel need institutional reform. Habermas, for example, would want to see a reconfiguration of power, including: equality of legislative powers between the Council and the European Parliament 'in all relevant political fields'; and also that the Commission be 'dependent equally on Parliament and Council and be answerable to both of them.'[189]

It should be emphasised though that although the current institutions of the EU have their own historical foundations, there has been a continuing transformation of the EU arising from new thinking not exactly tied to 'coal and steel' and 'the fear of another war.' They now reflect the broader democratic ethic that, probably more than in any other part of the world, has continued to grow in the EU. As noted by Baudenbacher and Clifton '…gradually the motivation for integration has shifted in favour of individual and later fundamental rights.'[190]

The EU model, while trend setting, is nothing out of the ordinary and does not need any special capacity, let alone historical foundations similar to those of the post-World War II Europe, to be built and sustained: its sustenance needs respect for a few basic things—democracy, the rule of law, and good governance principles and all that go with these normative values, including the adoption of a robust access to information regime.

6.5   CONCLUSION

As stated in Chap. 1, although international organisations may differ in terms of their objectives and the means of achieving same, they usually face similar institutional challenges. This is especially the case with RECs. There may also be a number of dissimilarities in the historical development and institutional makeup of SADC and the other three RECs that form part of the comparative analysis in this study. However, using these other RECs as comparators, it is possible to critically assess the institutional architecture of SADC, especially through the lens of democracy and the rule of law.

---

[189] J. Habermas 'The Crisis of the European Union in the light of a constitutionalization of international law (2012) 23 # 2 *The European Journal of International law* 345 http://www.ejil.org/pdfs/23/2/2211.pdf (accessed 16 July 2013).

[190] Baudenbacher & Clifton (Footnote 177 above) 272.

None of the selected RECs can be said to represent a perfect institutional model for the governance of RECs in every respect, but there is a lot that can be learnt from the collective comparative analysis. There appears to be a growing trend of adherence to the principle of separation of powers in the design of RECs, with the concomitant respect for the principle of the rule of law. The EU is clearly leading in this regard, although there are still concerns about the relatively weak position of the EP. The EAC's institutional makeup is also progressive. However, as noted in the conclusion of the section dealing with the EAC, a lot still needs to be done, especially with regard to increasing the jurisdictional powers of the EACJ. Also, in the area of policymaking, there is a need to broaden the space of participation by more institutions, especially through strengthening the regional bureaucracy—the Secretariat, since at present it is playing a largely subservient role to the executive institutions.

ECOWAS has also been able to transform itself over time. The ECCJ now has broader jurisdictional powers and the Secretariat was transformed into a Commission with significant norm-setting powers. However, while there has been some incremental growth in the powers of the ECOWAS Parliament, there appears to be some reluctance to strengthen the ECOWAS Parliament, whose role remains largely that of an advisory institution.

How then does SADC fare? Among all the organisations covered in this study, SADC is clearly an aberration. The SADC Summit, after suspending and effectively disbanding the SADC Tribunal, seem still to prefer an institutional framework where power is concentrated in itself, and is apparently not ready to create an institutional framework underpinned by the democratic credentials—especially separation of powers and the rule of law.

This study has demonstrated that there is a need for institutional reform in SADC which should result in the creation of a democratic framework of governance that is subject to the rule of law. While the best possible design of an REC may itself not guarantee that the values of democracy and the rule of law will be promoted and protected by the REC and its Member States in practice, just as the best-crafted commercial contract may not guarantee that it will be respected by the parties to it, at least there will be a good starting point for the parties (and stakeholders in the case of an REC) to call upon those who deviate to account. From a lawyer's perspective at least, this is different from advocating 'good behaviour' on the part of an international organisation or its member states in the absence of a predetermined democratic and rule of law-based treaty framework.

The next chapter seeks to demonstrate the applicability of the shared governance model in SADC, and is informed not only by the study's own innovation, but also by what has been recognised as good practices in the other three RECs discussed in this chapter.

CHAPTER 7

Applying Shared Governance in SADC

7.1   INTRODUCTION

So far, particularly in Chaps. 1, 3, and 4, it has been demonstrated that
there is a serious democratic deficit in the governance framework of SADC
which remains steeped in classical inter-governmentalism where the executive branch of government holds sway in international affairs. The overarching powers of the Summit and the absence of an institution with
effective judicial control mean that SADC still has a long way to go in
terms of separation of powers and the rule of law. While the preamble and
the objectives and principles of the SADC Treaty are alive to and incorpo-
rate democratic and constitutionalist principles including the rule of law,
the design of the SADC institutional framework does not accommodate
these, thereby creating a gap between the normative values set out in the
Treaty and the institutional framework.

The absence of internal democracy and the rule of law in SADC, other
than being the result of lack of political will to embrace these principles, is
intrinsically tied to the nature of the institutions created by the SADC
Treaty and the way they relate to each other.[1] Thus, in the absence of real
and autonomous norm-setting powers bestowed upon the other SADC
institutions, especially in light of the absence of legislative and judiciary
organs with meaningful powers, the subordinate executive institutions in
SADC do no more than prepare the landing ground for the ultimate

---

[1] It can also be argued, conversely, that the design of SADC institutions itself reflects lack
of political will to accommodate democracy and the rule of law in SADC processes.

© The Author(s) 2019   179
M. Nyathi, *The Southern African Development Community
and Law*, https://doi.org/10.1007/978-3-319-76511-2_7

institution, the Summit. They are, for lack of a better term, the forerun-ners—more like advisory committees of the Summit.

In addition to the inherent risk of breeding an institution that is too powerful and unaccountable, the present institutional framework of SADC burdens Summit with too much responsibility. Instead of focusing on broad policy and political direction, the Summit involves itself in matters that can effectively and efficiently be dealt with by the other institutions.[2] The views of Ng'ongo'la in this regard are worth quoting:

> The last round of reforms and the restructuring have not succeeded in dis-tancing the political governors of the region from the mundane technical aspects of integration. This creates the challenge of securing political com-mitment at the highest level for technical aspects of integration that at any particular moment might not be in political vogue.[3]

Despite the institutional shortcomings of SADC (and its predecessor SADCC), some have noted that the organisation has made some limited positive contribution to the region, for example, in the field of infrastruc-ture development.[4] The other benefit has been, arguably, the forging of a regional identity and a sense of a common destiny among the countries and peoples of Southern Africa.[5] It has also been argued by some that without SADC, its Member States might be worse off. Others, however, view this line of assessment as nothing but a 'counterfactual possibility' and that the SADC leaders should not view it as a measure of success.[6]

---

[2] These include the adoption of protocols for the various integration areas and the adop-tion of the budget.

[3] C. Ng'ong'ola 'The framework for regional integration in the Southern African Development Community' (2008) *University of Botswana Law Journal* 32.

[4] J. Isaksen 'Restructuring SADC—progress and problems' Development Studies and Human Rights, Chr Michelsen Institute Report R 2002: 15: Norway 1 http://www.cmi.no (accessed 12 December 2013).

[5] G.H. Oosthuizen *The Southern African Development Community: The organization, its policies and prospects* (2006) 69; Isaksen (Footnote 4 above) 1; E.N. Tjønneland 'Making SADC work? Revisiting institutional reform' in Hansohm D et al. (eds) *Monitoring regional integration in Southern Africa yearbook* (2005) 5, 166, 181.

[6] B. Sirota 'Sovereignty and the Southern African Development Community' (2004–2005) 5#1 *Chicago Journal of International Law* 346. See also E.N. Tjønneland 'Making sense of the Southern African Development Community' (2013) 22 # 3 *African Security Review* 196. Tjønneland makes the same point (while dismissing pessimists) that Southern Africa would be worse off without SADC and that the organisation has made some progress over

The value of the mere existence of SADC should, however, not be underestimated, its current shortcomings as identified so far in this study notwithstanding. It has been observed that mere membership of an international organisation has a behavioural dividend since states would, upon assumption of, and during the currency of their membership of an international organisation, ordinarily recoil from undemocratic tendencies at the domestic level, as they would want to build and maintain a reputation of 'good standing.'[7]

Arguably, another notable achievement in the area of promotion of democracy has been the adoption of SADC Principles and Guidelines Governing Democratic Elections, and the SADC election observation missions based on these principles and guidelines.[8] These have most probably played a role in the development of a democratic culture, although questions abound regarding their substance and effectiveness.[9] In addition to their substantive shortcomings, there has been sharp criticism of the failure by SADC to respect the letter and spirit of its own principles and guidelines, resulting in SADC validating evidently flawed electoral processes in Member States, thereby militating against the democratisation efforts in the SADC region.[10]

Whatever the contested and contestable achievements of SADC (especially in the democratic arena) might be, this study has so far demonstrated that the design of SADC's institutional architecture puts the destiny of SADC largely in the hands of one institution—the Summit. There has been some evident reluctance to develop strong, professional supranational institutions that are autonomous and able to formulate a regional agenda and enforce agreed decisions and programmes.[11] A view has been expressed that the state of affairs in SADC represents a continuing

time; and that it is in a far better shape than it was in 1980 and in 1995 (at p. 195). Some may argue, as does Sirota, that this is nothing but a counterfactual assessment.

[7] G. Ulfstein 'Institutions and competencies' in J. Klabbers et al. *The constitutionalizaion of international Law* (2009) 45.

[8] These Principles and Guidelines were adopted in 2005.

[9] Oosthuizen (Footnote 5 above) 306.

[10] A case in point is the well-documented Zimbabwean example where there were significant flaws in the 2002, 2008 and the 2013 electoral processes where SADC either endorsed the outcomes or failed to act decisively where it was clear that the electoral process was far from being free and fair.

[11] G.M. Khadiagala 'Historical legacy' in C. Saunders (ed) *Region-building in Southern Africa: Progress, problems and prospects* (2012) 35.

tension between 'narrow nationalisms and supranationalism.'[12] So far, and to the extent that this may be a valid view and judging by the institutional architecture of SADC, the former (narrow nationalisms) seem to be holding sway.

An argument has been advanced by some that the rule of law at the national level constitutes a proper foundation for the rule of law at the international level and that in the absence of the rule of law at the national level, it is difficult to construct the rule of law at the international level.[13] Thus, states that are not governed per dictates of the rule of law cannot be expected to sincerely pursue the rule of law at the international level.[14] While this could arguably be true,[15] it does not mean that there is nothing positive that could come out of a grouping of non-liberal states that do not respect the rule of law at the national level, or for that matter, a grouping that includes a significant number or whose majority is such states.

As stated above, the desire for 'good standing' in the eyes of the international community may work as an incentive for non-democratic states to be seen to be embracing the rule of law at the international level. There is, therefore, a possibility of such states being reformed, even unwittingly, from above. Indeed (even if only in theory) it can logically be argued that where, for instance, there is a sufficiently strong and independent judicial body at the regional level that makes progressive decisions that are habitually complied with by some of the member states, emulated conformism (even if grudgingly) by otherwise non-democratic member states (and thereby respect for the rule of law at the national level) may result.

This chapter proposes an alternative SADC institutional design anchored in the shared governance model. Although this study is not the first of its kind to provide a critique of the institutional framework of SADC and to suggest institutional reform,[16] it could be so far, as indicated

---

[12] Khadiagala (Footnote 11 above). While Khadiagala expresses this as a tension between narrow nationalisms and supranationalism, Nathan explains the situation in somewhat different terms. According to Nathan, the reason for the current state of affairs in SADC is the subordination of the values of human rights and the rule of law to the principles of regime solidarity and sovereignty. See generally L. Nathan 'Solidarity triumphs over democracy – The dissolution of the SADC Tribunal' (2011) 57 *Development Dialogue* 123.

[13] A. Nollkaemper (2012) *National courts and the international rule of law* 2.

[14] Nollkaemper, as above.

[15] Even in the absence of empirical evidence, it would be difficult to contest this kind of conclusion since it seems to rest on sound deductive reasoning.

[16] Ng'ong'ola, for example, is critical of the SADC institutional design. He criticises, among other things, the dominance of the Summit in SADC and he also challenges the rel-

in Chap. 1, be the first to recommend far-reaching treaty-based institutional changes. The recommendations made in this book are largely confined to rule-making/norm-setting and oversight institutions that are discussed in Chaps. 3 and 4. Each section will be dedicated to each of the institutions, clearly setting out the composition and functions of each institution and how it should relate to other institutions within the broader proposed framework. For those institutions where a recommendation is made for their jettisoning, such is clearly stated in the relevant section dealing with the relevant institution. For reasons of economy and the need to confine the recommendations to the major themes of this study, the recommendations do not contain every detail as would a draft model treaty.

The recommendations carried below are meant to democratise decision-making in SADC and hopefully lead to a more efficient integration project. However, the proposals would not be the sole panacea to all the challenges faced by SADC. Indeed, the challenges faced by SADC are many and require multifaceted solutions. Some of the challenges noted in scholarship include SADC's fixation with sovereignty and regime solidarity at the expense of democratic governance and regional integration; political instability in the region; and the general disregard by SADC leaders of the letter of legal instruments that they sign up to, among other things.[17]

The section on the Summit has specific thematic sub-sections on major policy areas. This is to ensure coherence and to set the tone for the overall recommendations covering other institutions as well. The recommendations on the other institutions are in the form of omnibus narratives, since adopting thematic sub-sections would lead to unnecessary repetitions and incoherence due to the many cross-cutting issues involved.

---

evance of the SCMCs as, according to him, the functions of the latter overlap with those of the CoM. Another criticism raised by Ng'ong'ola is the SADC lawmaking regime. His view, especially with regard to protocols, is that there is too much discretion accorded to SADC Member States when it comes to the ratification of Protocols and this defeats the purpose of integration since it amounts to the right to make reservations, something that the SADC Treaty itself prohibits with regards to its provisions. See Ng'ong'ola (Footnote 3 above) 3.

[17] See, for example, the cumulative, although not necessarily congruent, contributions by Sirota (Footnote 6 above); L. Nathan 'Solidarity triumphs over democracy...' (Footnote 12 above) 57 *Development Dialogue* 123; L. Nathan *Community of insecurity: SADC's struggle for peace and security in Southern Africa* (2012); L. Nathan 'The disbanding of the SADC Tribunal: A cautionary tale' (2013) 35 # 4 *Human Rights Quarterly* 870.

7.2   The Summit of Heads of State or Government

There does not appear to be any disagreement on the role of national executives, particularly heads of state or government, in international organisations in which their countries are members. They, in fact, are in the forefront when it comes to the creation of these organisations, and they also play a major role in the amendment of their constitutive treaties and indeed in their dissolutions.[18]

Original constitutive documents are ordinarily negotiated and signed by the heads of state or government or their authorised representatives, although there is now a trend of involving legislatures of their respective countries in the ratification of the treaties in accordance with their domestic constitutions or legal traditions. There is also an emerging participatory approach when it comes to the amendment of treaties. For example, in some of the Member States of the EU, it is no longer necessarily the direct representatives of the citizens of each EU Member State, in the form of their legislatures, who have a say, but the citizens themselves. Indeed, it was the exercise of this power by the citizens of France and the Netherlands through the 2005 negative votes in the two countries' referenda that saw the stillbirth of the EU constitutional treaty.[19]

The following sub-sections carry a model that advocates a shift in the functions of the Summit in the areas of general decision-making; adoption of the SADC budget; and admission of new members.

General Decision-making Powers

When it comes to rule making or norm setting in international organisations, there is growing evidence of a desire by a number of international organisations, especially, RECs, to limit the role of the heads of state or government to that of providing general policy direction. In the EAC, for instance, while the Summit is at the top of the policymaking hierarchy, there are other institutions with far-reaching powers and autonomy in the area of lawmaking. As has been shown in the previous chapter, the EAC Council has power to initiate and submit Bills to the EALA. Its other

---

[18] As evidence of the role of heads of state or government in the amendment or revision of constitutive treaties see generally; art 150 of the EAC Treaty; art 90 of the ECOWAS Treaty; art 36 of the SADC Treaty; and art 48 TEU.

[19] N. Walker 'Reframing EU Constitutionalism' in L. Dunoff & P. Trachtman (eds) *Ruling the world? Constitutionalism, international law and global governance* (2009) 149.

autonomous powers include the making of general binding regulations and adopting staff rules and regulations and financial rules and regulations of the community. This does not mean that the other institutions cannot interfere with the manner the EAC Council discharges its function. It is simply an illustration that it has sufficient autonomy in the various areas given to it by the EAC Treaty. Intervention by, for example, the Summit or the EALA, for whatever reason, would in fact be welcome as it will increase the incidence of conversation (and ensure checks and balances) between and among these institutions before the final decision is taken.

In the EU, while the European Council is in overall charge of EU in that it is the institution that provides the necessary impetus for the development of the EU and that defines the political direction and priorities of the EU, it is specifically prohibited from entering some of the autonomous policy/lawmaking zones allocated to the other institutions of the Union. For example, as has already been indicated in Chap. 6, the European Council is specifically prohibited from exercising legislative functions. Even in those areas that are quite clearly political, like security, defence, and foreign policy in general, while the European Council's powers are far-reaching, the exercise of such powers is not exclusively within the domain of the European Council but is shared with other institutions.[20]

In SADC, the current position regarding the powers of the Summit is both unsatisfactory and unworkable. While power is centralised in this institution, decisions emanating from the exercise of that power do not carry the force of law against which policies and actions of Member States and institutions of SADC can be measured. In this regard, the observation by Habermas, made in the context of the EU, is instructive:

[L]egally non-binding agreements concluded by the heads of government are either ineffectual or undemocratic and must therefore be replaced by an institutionalization of joint decisions with irreproachable democratic credential.[21]

It is, therefore, recommended that there should be a provision giving the Summit the general power to define the general political policy and strategic direction of SADC, subject to the treaty and other applicable

[20] See particularly arts 22 & 26 of the TEU.
[21] J. Habermas 'The Crisis of the European Union in the light of a constitutionalization of international law (2012) 23 # 2 *The European Journal of International law* 336 http://www.ejil.org/pdfs/23/2/2211.pdf (accessed 16 July 2013).

instruments. Such a provision should also state that in the discharge of their functions, the executive organs of SADC should be guided by the political directions and strategic priorities as defined by the Summit, subject to the treaty and other applicable instruments. Limiting the powers of the Summit to general political policy and strategic direction would not only broaden the space of decision-making within SADC and thus increase the legitimacy of SADC norms, it is also likely to result in the unlocking of governance efficiency, since the capacity of the Summit will be freed from operational and implementation matters that can be more efficiently handled by other institutions so that it concentrates more on providing general leadership.[22] The following sections deal with specific major policy areas where the Summit should have the final say.

Adoption and Amendment of Treaty

Constitutive treaties of international organisations ordinarily lay down broad policy frameworks within which decisions are to be taken. Thus, the treaty becomes both a procedural and substantive reference point for any decision taken. A constitutive treaty is thus a primary and significant document whose adoption and amendment should involve a broad spectrum of institutions. Because of a treaty's primacy, and because the Summit, as proposed, would be the ultimate institution to provide overall policy and strategic direction to SADC, it follows that the Summit should have the ultimate say in the adoption and amendment of the treaty.

However, before the Summit reaches its ultimate decision, there should be input into the content of the draft of such an instrument and adequate inter-institutional conversation before its final adoption or amendment. But over and above the internal institutions of SADC, there is also a need for the legitimation of the process by the Member States through ratification processes as determined by their respective constitutional provisions or legal traditions.

Over and above the involvement of a broad array of stakeholders in the process, there is also need for the treaty to be clear and detailed enough so

---

[22] For a similar view, see Tjønneland (Footnote 5 above) 170. Tjønneland points out, with reference to the relationship between the SADC Secretariat and what he refers to as the 'governing structures,' that '[i]t is often claimed that the governing structures are spending too much time on administrative details and too little on leadership.' It is most likely that Tjønneland is here not just referring to the Summit but to such other institutions as the CoM. See also Ng'ong'ola (Footnote 3 above) 32.

as to limit the incidence of discretion. All institutions and organs should be aware of the exact nature and actual extent of their responsibilities and those of the other components as well. The importance of having clearly and narrowly defined predetermined rules is that it tends to limit arbitrariness and guarantees the reviewability of decisions that are not taken in line with the agreed guidelines.

Arguably, the legitimacy earned through ratification by Member States would most likely lead to an increase in the incidence of compliance with, and the acceptance and domestication of not only the Treaty, but also of the secondary implementation instruments adopted pursuant thereto. In line with these arguments, it is recommended that the power of the Summit to act alone (with or without recommendations from the CoM) be done away with. Further, for meaningful integration, legal instruments adopted pursuant to the Treaty should have legal effect in all Member States unless there are clearly defined exceptions based on objective criteria.

Admission of New Members

The SADC Treaty does not lay down the qualifications for admission into SADC membership or the application procedure. These are left to the discretion of the Summit.[23] Although the Summit is enjoined to act on the recommendations of the CoM in the admission of new members, its power in this regard is unfettered, since it can easily change the admission criteria and procedures through ordinary decision-making.

At its meeting of 28 August 1995 in Johannesburg, the Summit adopted the criteria and procedure for the admission of new members which had been drawn up by the Secretariat and had been adopted by the CoM for consideration by the Summit.[24] The criteria to be fulfilled by a prospective candidate were adopted as follows:

- geographical proximity of the applicant to the SADC region
- commonality of political, economic, social, and cultural systems of the applicant with the systems of the SADC Region

---

[23] Art 7(2) of the SADC Treaty.
[24] Items 2.5.1 & 2.7 of the minutes of Summit proceedings available in the SADC library (accessed 10 March 2014).

- feasibility of cost effective and efficient coordination of the applicant's economic, social, and cultural activities under the SADC framework of cooperation
- absence of a record of engagement in subversive and destabilisation activities, and territorial ambitions against SADC, or any of its Member States
- must be a democracy, observing the principles of human rights and the rule of law
- must share SADC's ideals and aspirations

However, these criteria were later revised by the Summit of 25–26 August 2006, held in Dar es Salaam.[25] The new criteria are as follows:

- the applicant should be well versed with and share SADC's ideals and aspirations as enshrined in the SADC Treaty
- commonality of political, economic, social, and cultural systems of the applicant with the systems of the SADC region, as well as the observance of the principles of democracy, human rights, good governance, and the rule of law in accordance with the African Charter on Human and People's Rights
- should have a good track record and ability to honour its obligations and to participate effectively and efficiently in the SADC Programme of Action for the benefit of the Community
- should have levels of macro-economic indicators in line with targets set in the RISDP
- should not be at war and should not be involved or engaged in subversive and destabilisation activities, and have territorial ambitions against SADC, any of its Member States or any Member State of the African Union

The new criteria are relatively clearer and broader in scope than the earlier ones.[26] They also remove the requirement of geographical proximity which gives the possibility of SADC's future enlargement beyond the

---

[25] Items 4.4.3 of the minutes of Summit proceedings available in the SADC library (accessed 10 March 2014).

[26] There are some obvious drafting lapses though. For example, the criterion that an applicant state should not be at war should have been framed in a much clearer and narrower manner to make it clear that such war, in order to disqualify an applicant, should be an illegal one. For example, it does not make sense to disqualify an applicant that is involved in a UN

Southern African region. However, leaving the criteria of admission of new members to the discretion of the Summit exercised through ordinary decision-making procedure means that a significant policy area like the enlargement of SADC is not subjected to inter-institutional discourse and evaluation. This is not to say the Summit should not have a final say on the matter—this final say should not only be predicated on a justiciable treaty basis, but should also come after giving stakeholders an opportunity to debate in an environment where all the information is available. This is to guard against arbitrary exercise of discretion by a few.

There is need to involve more institutions in the procedure for the admission of new members. This would serve to enhance the credibility and legitimacy of the process. While there could be no compelling reason to disallow the Summit from having the ultimate say in the matter, it is desirable to have a peremptory involvement of an executive organ (there is a proposal elsewhere in this chapter for the transformation of the present Secretariat into a full-fledged executive organ of SADC) in the process.

A preferable arrangement, and the one being proposed here, would be to have the proposed commission receiving the application for membership and making an assessment based on the economic factors and the CoM making its recommendations based on political factors, and the two institutions thereafter submitting their recommendations to the Summit for final decision-making. The objective criteria setting out these economic and political qualifications should be clearly set out in the Treaty itself. The same procedure should apply, with the necessary modifications, on the question of suspension of a Member State that is in breach of the Treaty or that falls short of the qualification requirements during the course of their membership. In order to curtail arbitrariness and to limit the incidence of discretion, the Treaty should provide that the recommendations made by the commission and the CoM should be made public.

Budgetary Powers

Generally, the need for different voices within an organisation in the budgeting process is crucial in order to ensure that, among other things, competing interests are accommodated and balanced. The EU model presents something of a collaborative attempt in the budgeting process involving

sanctioned war, or in a lawful war in pursuit of SADC's (or for that matter the African Union's) legitimate interests.

the Commission, the Council and the EP. But over and above these institutions, the starting point in the budgeting process is the involvement of all the institutions of the EU, save for the Central Bank.[27]

For SADC, it is recommended that the proposed commission should come up with a draft budget for submission to the standing committee of CoM and that the latter should then seek the proposed parliament's approval, which should be by a simple majority.[28] However, in order to involve as many institutions as possible, the Treaty should provide that the proposed commission's draft budget should be sent to all institutions of SADC, without exception, for their comments and inputs. This should be before the draft budget is sent to the standing committee of CoM for its consideration. There should be a further provision obligating the proposed commission to take into account the comments and inputs of the institutions and to include a document concisely stating the comments and inputs it received from the institutions and whether or not it incorporated them in the draft budget and the reasons why it did or did not do so.

In reality, in so far as involving all the institutions of SADC in the budget formulation process is concerned, there is not much of a difference between this proposed framework and the EU one where different institutions come up with their own different estimates. There is a slight, but significant, variation though. Because the proposed commission would be the overall implementer of the budget, it would be in a position to tell, on a historical basis, the expenditure trends of the various institutions. Other than being overly cumbersome, the EU model has the risk of creating a budget initiation process that is defined more by individual institutional subjectivity and egos.

7.3   COUNCIL OF MINISTERS

Any public international organisation is bound during the course of its life to make decisions. Indeed, the actual act of coming up with a treaty framework, including revisions of that treaty, entails the exercise of decision-making powers. The same is the case with the adoption of secondary implementation instruments. As stated elsewhere in this study, the nature of these decisions should not determine whether democratic principles of decision-making should be present before the decisions are made. Whether

---

[27] Art 314 (1) of TFEU. See Chap. 6, Sect. 6.4 for a detailed discussion.
[28] See Sect. 7.3 below for the proposal for a reconfigured CoM.

the decisions are classified as 'policies,' 'legal instruments,' 'laws,' 'directives,' 'regulations,' or 'guidelines' should not matter.[29] This is more so because over and above the intended outcomes, some decisions may, as has already been stated before, eventually play themselves out in a manner that was not initially intended by the decision makers.

However, having said that, and without any contradiction whatsoever, it is imperative, if SADC is sincere about integration in all the areas encapsulated in the Common Agenda, to have a treaty framework that broadly spells out those decisions that are binding on Member States upon adoption by the relevant policy/legislative organs. The nature and extent of such decisions would obviously be informed by the relevant social and political considerations and can only be shaped by political bargaining involving a wide range of stakeholders.

For purposes of efficacy, the proposed framework of lawmaking should do away with lawmaking through protocols as currently obtaining or similar instruments, and instead provide for adoption of directly applicable legislative acts, regulations, and directives or some such similar instruments. The only 'treaty' should be the constitutive instrument, against which all other legal instruments, decisions, and actions would have to be tested, more like a constitution in a domestic legal order. Subsidiary lawmaking through treaties or protocols has serious limitations. As noted by Killander, even where a treaty has been widely ratified, national courts are usually hesitant to apply treaties directly; state accountability mechanisms (including the monitoring of such mechanisms) are generally weak; and 'national implementing legislation based on treaties adopted by regional or sub-regional organisations is rare.'[30]

There is need, therefore, the nature and intended effect of the decisions notwithstanding, to have identifiable institutions within SADC with varying degrees of lawmaking powers. The CoM is the ideal institution, together with the Commission as proposed in this study, to play such a role. The current functions of the CoM, as stated elsewhere in this study, are enmeshed and subsumed within those of the Summit. There is no clear autonomous zone allocated to the CoM. The disadvantage of the current

---

[29] For a detailed discussion of the nature of legal instruments adopted by international organisations, see J. Klabbers, *An introduction to international institutional law* (2009) 178–203.

[30] M. Killander 'Legal harmonization in Africa: Taking stock and moving forward' in L. Fioramonti (ed) *Regionalism in a changing world: Comparative Perspectives in the new global order* (2013) 88.

norm-setting regime is that the Summit will always have the ultimate say even on minor decisions that should be handled by other institutions. Where the Summit feels that it has treaty power to come up with a decision in any area of integration, it may do so without even being conscious of its own capacity constraints and may thus come up with hastily made and ill-conceived decisions.

Adoption of legal instruments pursuant to the treaty should thus be left to the CoM, working in collaboration with the proposed commission, under the oversight of SADC parliament as proposed in this study. Giving such functions to the CoM is advantageous in a number of respects including that interaction between the CoM and the proposed commission in the legislative sphere would be far much easier in terms of protocol, thus enhancing the volume and quality of reasoned dialogue. As long as the treaty framework is clear and detailed enough, lawmaking, including that of an implementation nature, in all the areas covered by the SADC Common Agenda can be more effectively made at the level of the CoM and the proposed commission.

But in order to address the imperatives of shared governance, a number of institutions should be involved, in an environment characterised by an unencumbered flow of information, before the ultimate decision is taken. The best way to achieve this would be for the treaty to categorically state that decisions of the norm-setting institutions other than those that are purely procedural and administrative should be in the form of legislative acts. This would entail a requirement for comments on the draft forms of such decisions as proposed in the section dealing with the proposed SADC parliament below. Such a requirement would not only serve to enhance the transparency (and legitimacy) of lawmaking through disclosure of information in the form of draft legislation, but it would also serve to ensure added value arising from input from a broad range of stakeholders in decision-making.

This proposed legislative process would be more open and transparent than what is obtaining in the EAC and ECOWAS, for example. In the EAC, the Secretary General is obligated by article 64 to cause every Act of the Community to be published in the *Gazette*. In ECOWAS, just like in the EAC, article 9(5) of the ECOWAS Treaty provides for the publication the decisions of the Authority. These are published 30 days after their signature by the Chairperson of the Authority and they enter into force 60 days after their publication in the Official Journal of the Community.[31] There is a further requirement that these decisions should be published in the *National Gazette* of each Member State.[32] While the EAC and the ECOWAS frameworks ensure communication of the organisations' decisions even within the Partner/Member States, which framework should be emulated by SADC, such communication is, unfortunately, only *ex post facto*. It does not necessarily guarantee the involvement of a broad spectrum of the components of the organisation, let alone the generality of the citizens in these communities, in the decision-making process since the decisions would have already been made.[33]

On composition, the current CoM consists of one minister from each Member State with the preference given to ministers of foreign affairs. However, in order to make the CoM an effective institution with the capacity to deal with all matters that fall under the SADC Common Agenda, it is recommended that the CoM should have, as is the case in the EU, various configurations. This is more so in light of the recommendation made below for the abolition of the SCMCs.

In order to ensure the free flow of information between and among the various institutions, more so because of the fragmented (although hopefully more effective) proposed CoM, there would be a need for a constant communication channel and a clearing house for all CoM-related matters. Under the EU framework, there is, in addition to the various configurations of Council, the General Affairs Council. The General Affairs Council is meant to ensure consistency in the work of the Council in its different configurations, and is the link between the 'overall' Council and the European Council and the Commission.

It is recommended that for SADC, a similar institution be adopted but instead be called the standing committee of the CoM. The term 'standing committee' is more descriptively appropriate because it conveys the actual purpose of the committee.[34] 'General Affairs Council,' on the other hand, may give an impression of a separate institution with more general powers

---

[31] Art 9(6) of the ECOWAS Treaty. See also Chap. 6, Sect. 6.3 for a discussion of the new ECOWAS lawmaking regime.

[32] Art 9(7) of the ECOWAS Treaty. See also Sect. 7.10 below on access to information.

[33] A more detailed discussion of this is made in Sect. 7.10 below on access to information.

[34] It should be noted that the standing committee of CoM proposed here is distinguishable from an institution with the same name established by art 71 of the Treaty on the functioning of the European Union.

over the various configurations. For the composition of the proposed standing committee of the CoM, there would be nothing wrong with giving preference to ministers responsible for foreign affairs, and it is accordingly recommended.

7.4   SECTORAL AND CLUSTER MINISTERIAL COMMITTEES

A lot has been said already about the SCMCs. It is recommended that the SCMCs be abolished and their functions (at least those that are clearly articulated) be subsumed under the proposed new look CoM.

7.5   THE SECRETARIAT

International organisations generally have regular organs including executive organs (e.g. the Security Council of the UN which 'meets and may take decisions on shorter notice') and administrative organs which are ordinarily limited to administrative tasks.[35] However, it has been observed that some Secretaries General, like that of the UN, sometimes play some political roles, and others may, in the exercise of their otherwise non-political administrative role, 'push boundaries.'[36]

It has been asserted, in relation to the League of Nations, that the name 'secretariat' was intentionally chosen 'to indicate a purely administrative, secondary organ,'[37] and that the founders 'did not want the Secretariat to perform independent functions, but merely to assist the activities of the principal organs.'[38] However, the nature (and effectiveness) of the secretariats of international organisations differ, depending in the main on the kind of formal powers they are given by their different constitutive treaties, resources at their disposal, and the competency of their staff.[39]

While called 'executive' institutions, the secretariats of the EAC and SADC are, strictly speaking, merely administrative institutions. While nothing much should be read into a name, at times inter-institutional relations and perceptions are informed by names. An institutional name that does not convey a sense of autonomy and independence may compromise

---

[35] Klabbers (Footnote 29 above) 155–156.
[36] Klabbers (Footnote 29 above) 155–157.
[37] H.G. Schermers & N.M. Blokker *International institutional law: Unity within diversity* (2011) 321.
[38] As above.
[39] Schermers & Blokker (Footnote 37 above) 323.

the effectiveness of an institution. Accordingly, it is recommended that the SADC Secretariat be transformed into a commission, or some such appropriately named similar institution.[40]

Where a secretariat of an international organisation is placed under the constant guidance and supervision of the political organs, it cannot be expected to effectively implement the policies of the organisations since its powers of interpretation (implementation entails interpretation of the instruments to be implemented) are constrained by those institutions that have a supervisory role above them. As Tjønneland rightly notes with reference to the SADC secretariat, '[t]he SADC Treaty and the mandate of the secretariat, however, restrict it to being an administrative unit with no political decision-making powers.'[41]

Even with regard to those powers that are *prima facie* in the domain of the Secretariat, or for that matter the Executive Secretary, this might not be exactly the case in practice. For example, the current practice in the recruitment of those officials below the Deputy Executive Secretaries is that in the event of a vacancy, applicants submit their applications to their respective SADC National Contact Points.[42] The influence of Member States in the recruitment process cannot be underestimated. There is no guarantee that the process may not be abused through, for example, some 'unofficial' vetting processes meant to perpetuate political patronage that favours the political parties in power and their supporters or sympathisers. Even worse, there is also a real likelihood that personnel at the SADC National Contact Points might destroy or not forward applications of some of the applicants either because of corruption or outright political hostility. At the end of the day, the Executive Secretary might be deprived

---

[40] Interestingly, the former Belgian Prime Minister, Guy Verhofstadt, is said to have suggested that the name of the European Commission should be changed to 'European Government' since, in his view, the former was ridiculous. See A. Saurombe 'The European Union as a model for regional integration in the Southern African Development Community: A selective institutional comparative analysis' (2013) 17 *Law Democracy and Development* 468 and the reference thereunder.

[41] Tjønneland (Footnote 5 above) 169, 170.

[42] See, for example, the vacancy announcement in http://www.sadc.int/files/5213/9962/0216/ADVERT_-_6__SADC_REGIONAL_POSITIONS_MAY_2014.pdf (accessed 15 October 2014).

of a wide pool of potential candidates from which to choose from, thereby adversely affecting the quality of personnel at the Secretariat.[43]

Giving the proposed commission adequate autonomy and independence is in line with the overall recommendation of adopting a shared governance model. The specific functions of the proposed commission are set out in the relevant sections in this chapter.

7.6   STANDING COMMITTEE OF OFFICIALS

As indicated in Chap. 3, the SCO's remit is rather short: it serves as a technical advisory committee to the CoM. It should be noted that in addition to the article 9 institutions, there is also a Committee of SADC Ambassadors/High Commissioners (CoA) that was established by way of a decision of the CoM in February 2005.[44] The functions that were initially given to the CoA included advising the CoM on issues related to the implementation of SADC programmes and activities; facilitating interaction and consultations between Member States and the Secretariat; and participating in the preparations for meetings of the CoM and the Integrated Committee of Ministers (read SCMCs), including the preparation of the agenda.

Generally speaking, there are no dissimilarities between the functions of the SCO and those that were initially earmarked for the CoA. Be that as it may, in response to these initial terms of reference, the CoA argued, among other things, that it was not appropriate for the CoA to advise or make recommendations directly to the CoM as its members report to their respective countries and not to the CoM. It further argued, somewhat contradicting itself, that issues that are reported to the CoM should first

---

[43] A similar argument seems to be implied in the observation made by Saurombe in his paper 'The role of SADC institutions in implementing SADC Treaty provisions dealing with regional integration' (2012) 15 # 2 *Potchefstroom Electronic Law Journal* at p. 475 https:// doi.org/10.4314/pelj.v15i2.16 (accessed 15 October 2014). After noting that '[t]he biggest challenge for the Secretariat is still the apparent reluctance on the part of Member States to surrender national initiative and active representativeness to the principle of supranationalism[,]' (sic) he states, after making some other relevant observations (the poor funding of the Secretariat and the filling of some of the positions at the Secretariat through a system whereby Member States second their own employees to the Secretariat), that '[w]hen jobs are advertised, interested candidates have to apply through each Member State's national contact point and applications made directly to the Secretariat are not considered.'

[44] Item 4.5.1 of the minutes of meeting of the CoM of 11–16 August 2011, Luanda available in the SADC library, Gaborone (accessed 10 March 2014).

be 'cleared' by the SCO, and that this would be impossible to achieve since they had no *locus standi* in the SCO to present their issues. They also indicated that not all ambassadors accredited to Botswana are based in Botswana as some of them were stationed in South Africa.[45] The CoM then approved the revision of the terms of reference of the CoA, specifically the removal of the reference of the CoA reporting to the CoM.

The CoA was initially modelled along the Permanent Representatives Committee (PRC) of the African Union (AU).[46] Indeed, in its early stages, there was confusion regarding the name of the CoA as the names 'Committee of Ambassadors/High Commissioners' and 'Committee of Permanent Representatives' were being used interchangeably.[47] In the context of the AU, the PRC's remit is to prepare the work of the Executive Council of the AU.[48] The Executive Council is very much similar to the CoM: it comprises the Ministers of Foreign Affairs or such other Ministers or Authorities as are designated by the Governments of AU Member States; it is responsible to the Assembly of Heads of State or Government; and it considers issues referred to it and monitors the implementation of policies formulated by the Assembly.[49]

A similar institution exists within the EU in the form of the Committee of Permanent Representatives of the Governments of Member States (Coreper). Coreper is established in terms of article 16(7) of the TEU and its functions as expressed in both the said article and article 240 of the TFEU are the preparation of the work of the Council and carrying out functions assigned to it by the Council.

In practice, Coreper has evolved into an important institution in the work of the Council. It is said to be 'pivotal' as it is both a forum for dialogue (among the permanent representatives and between them and their respective national capitals) and as a means of political control (guidance

---

[45] For these arguments by the Ambassadors/High Commissioners, see item 4.5.1, particularly items 4.5.1.3 (i), (ii), (iii), and (vii) of the minutes of the meeting referred to in Footnote 44 above.

[46] Established by art 21 of the Constitutive Act of the African Union available at http://www.africa-union.org/root/au/aboutau/constitutive_act_en.htm (accessed 13 March 2014).

[47] See item 4.5.1.3 (iv) of the minutes of meeting of the CoM (Footnote 44 above).

[48] Art 21(2) of the Constitutive Act of the AU.

[49] Art 10(1) and 13(2) of the Constitutive Act of the AU.

and supervision of the work of expert groups).[50] Coreper scrutinises proposals and draft legislative acts tabled by the Commission as carried on the Council's agenda.[51] Its role in this regard is to seek to find common ground on each matter tabled for discussion, failing which it may then 'suggest guidelines, options or suggested solutions to the Council.'[52] Coreper significantly reduces the workload of the Council—by the time matters reach the Council, the agenda would clearly indicate, on the one hand, those matters which should be approved without discussion since there would have been an agreement within Coreper, and on the other hand, those matters submitted for discussion by the Council owing to lack of agreement at the level of Coreper.[53]

Coreper deals with almost all the matters falling within the remit of the Council as provided for in the Treaties. It carries out its work in its two configurations: Coreper I, consisting of deputy permanent representatives (dealing with technical matters), and Coreper II which consists of ambassadors who deal with political, commercial, and institutional matters.[54]

It is difficult, therefore, to appreciate the argument by the ambassadors accredited to Botswana that it would not be appropriate to advise or make recommendations to the CoM as they report to their respective countries. In light of similarity of functions of the SCO and the CoA, and also of the tenuous argument by the ambassadors, there is no rationale remaining justifying the existence of these two institutions. For the sake of efficiency, especially in light of their physical and functional proximity to the SADC headquarters (this covers even those based in neighbouring South Africa), it is recommended that the CoA be reconstituted into a Treaty body and continue to discharge the functions it is currently seized with, together with those, to the extent that they are different, of the SCO. This would assist in institutional streamlining that would enhance efficiency and save on resources.

Unlike the AU and the EU, the EAC has a slightly different institution. But the difference is more in terms of composition than functionality. This

---

[50] http://europa.eu/legislation_summaries/glossary/coreper_en.htm (accessed 17 March 2014). The latter institution, the expert groups, does not form part of this study.
[51] As above.
[52] As above.
[53] As above.
[54] As above.

is the Co-ordination Committee.[55] The functions of the Co-ordination Committee include submission of reports and recommendations to the EAC Council on the implementation of the EAC Treaty; and implementation of the decisions of the Council as directed by the Council. This committee consists of Permanent Secretaries responsible for EAC affairs in each Partner State and such other Permanent Secretaries of the Partner States as each Partner State may determine.

It is important to note that by establishing an office of permanent secretary responsible for EAC affairs, each EAC Partner State has a dedicated senior officer with close functional proximity to the EAC. These are national officers with a 'supranational' responsibility. As indicated above, not only does the Co-ordination Committee provide policy advice to the Council, it also implements the decisions of the Council. Therefore, although somewhat similar to the SCO in terms of composition on the face of it, the EAC Co-ordination Committee is very different from the SCO, since the members of the latter have predominantly national duties that they are seized with on a daily basis, with the SADC functions constituting an additional 'burden.' On the other hand, in ECOWAS, no similar body exists but instead there are several technical committees (discussed in Chap. 6) responsible for different integration areas.[56]

It is proposed that the CoA should act as the link between the proposed commission and the CoM. While on its own it would not be a norm-setting/rule-making institution in the strict sense of the term, such an institution would serve the purpose of increasing the flow of information and conversation between the proposed commission, and the CoM. In order to enhance the transparency of inter-institutional engagement, the Treaty should, instead of deferring issues of internal procedures to the relevant institutions as is currently the case, spell out clear rules of procedure for the meetings of the appropriate institutions of SADC including the CoA. Such rules should encompass, among other things, that the meetings are as a general rule accessible to the public and that due notice (including the agenda) is given, not only to the other institutions of SADC, but to accredited CSOs that would also be allowed, at the minimum, to make written contributions on matters under discussion.

[55] The composition, functions, and procedures of the Co-ordination Committee are set out in arts 17–19 of the EAC Treaty.
[56] The composition and functions of these committees are provided for in arts 22 & 23 of the ECOWAS Treaty.

Locating the CoA between the proposed commission and the CoM is likely to enhance the quality of decision-making by the CoM.[57] Because of the relative physical and functional proximity of the CoA to the proposed commission, there is the possibility of more time being dedicated to debating issues, including exchange of documentation so that by the time an issue reaches the CoM it would have undergone meaningful debate and refinement. Regarding 'technical' matters that may be beyond the grasp of an ambassador, they can, by virtue of their position, get proper guidance from relevant people in their respective offices and in their home countries. The same would be the case anyway with permanent secretaries (and their equivalents) since they may not necessarily be 'technical' people and even if they were, they would not be expected to know everything within their broad areas of expertise.

7.7   THE SADC TRIBUNAL

The rationale for establishing a judicial organ in an international organisation has been discussed in detail in Chap. 4. In a governance framework underpinned by shared governance, the role of a judicial institution is not only that of umpire. The judicial body is part of the overall institutional matrix and is involved in the institution's normative discourse.

In order to ensure the effective recognition and protection of the role of a judicial body, there is need for its establishment and broad jurisdiction to be set out in the Treaty itself. Deferring these matters to a separate protocol, even if it is said to be an integral part of the treaty, as has been shown by the SADC experience, is problematic. There is absolutely no reason why the composition, functions, and procedures of the other institutions are spelt out in sufficient detail in the Treaty, and when it comes to the Tribunal there is a wholesale deference of everything to a protocol. Other than the risk of subjecting the protocol to a different amendment procedure, there is also the possibility of creating the impression, within the other institutions, that the judicial body is a lesser institution compared to the other institutions. Deferring the operationalisation of a judicial body to a protocol to be adopted at a later stage might, like was the case when the SADC Tribunal was initially established, inculcate the idea that the business of the organisation can carry on in the absence of judicial

---

[57] The term 'locating … between' here is used not to imply a hierarchical order but rather refers to operational interface.

oversight.[58] There is no escaping the conclusion that the Summit might have been guided by these impressions when it took its decisions initially suspending and eventually disbanding the SADC Tribunal.

The composition of the judicial body including the actual number of judges; their qualifications; terms of office; the method of their appointment; and the functions of the judicial body; and the full extent of the basis and scope of its jurisdiction should thus be clearly spelt out in the Treaty itself. A lot can be learnt from the relevant provisions of the EAC Treaty (discussed in detail in Chap. 6) in this regard. The rules for the efficacious discharge of the mandate of the judicial body may, as is generally the norm in both domestic and international courts, be deferred to a subsidiary instrument adopted by the judicial body itself within guidelines clearly set out in the Treaty.

In line with current trends in regional integration schemes, the scope of jurisdiction should cover such matters as actions brought by Member States, other institutions of SADC and natural and legal persons. National courts should also be allowed to refer matters to the regional court for a preliminary opinion where Treaty provisions and other regional instruments/norms are implicated in any proceedings before them. Indeed, the very nature and extent of the SADC Common Agenda makes the denial of access to the Tribunal to natural and legal persons a mockery of the very integration ideal SADC is purportedly founded on. Wide jurisdictional powers clearly serve to give an impetus to the regional integration project and they also assist in the process of harmonisation of laws within Member States. This is particularly so because in the final analysis, it is the private SADC citizen (including legal persons) who should be the ultimate beneficiary of the integration project. It is the SADC citizen, therefore, who is better able to assist, including through seeking judicial review, the development of the integration project.

As already indicated, qualifications of judges should be set out in clear and sufficient detail in the Treaty itself. Only highly qualified persons of unquestionable integrity and independence acknowledged throughout

---

[58] The SADC Tribunal was established by the 1992 SADC Treaty and the Tribunal Protocol was adopted in 2000. The judges were appointed in 2005 and the Registry was set up in 2006, with the Tribunal starting operating in 2007, some 15 years after its 'establishment.' See S.T. Ebobrah 'Litigating human rights before sub-regional courts in Africa: Prospects and challenges' (2009) 17 *African Journal of International and Comparative Law* 83; Nathan '*Community of insecurity...*' (Footnote 17 above) 124, 134 and the reference on the latter page; http://www.sadc-tribunal.org/ (last accessed 24 August 2014).

the region should assume the office of judge. Their nomination and appointment should, in line with the values of shared governance, be a matter of inter-institutional dialogue and bargaining involving nomination by the CoM, assessment of qualifications by the proposed new commission, approval by a majority in the proposed parliament and finally appointment by consensus, failing which by a special majority by the Summit.

For dialogue within an organisation to be effective, it should not just be inter-institutional, but intra-institutional as well. A two chamber judicial body ensures that before an ultimately binding legal position is reached, a number of legal minds would have been involved at various stages of adjudication. Thus, creation of a first instance division (with jurisdiction also over administrative matters) and an appellate division, allows for further reflection, especially on points of law, before the final legal position is eventually settled, unlike when there is just one chamber whose decisions are not subject to appeal.

Another matter that might appear insignificant, when in fact it is not, is the name of the judicial organ. 'SADC Court' or 'SADC Court of Justice' conveys an impression of significant stature. While linguistically there is no significant distinction between a court and a tribunal, the latter term is usually (although not exclusively) associated with administrative quasi-judicial bodies, and might not inspire much confidence especially in the SADC citizen who is desperately in need of an additional layer of judicial protection (over and above their domestic courts) especially in the area of human rights.

7.8   THE SADC PARLIAMENTARY FORUM

A clear case for a proper SADC regional parliament has been made elsewhere in this study. The breadth of the SADC Common Agenda and the concomitant need for policies and regulations in the various areas of integration require decision-making by those institutions of SADC charged with norm setting. This calls not only for a much broader norm-setting framework but also a framework to ensure that there is oversight over lawmaking/norm-setting institutions.

Other than being merely an oversight institution solely meant to reign in the norm-setting institutions, a SADC Parliament should actually be involved in policy formulation through a variety of ways, including playing a significant role in the amendments to the Treaty. It is recommended in this regard that proposals for Treaty amendment should be open to Member States and all the institutions of SADC. Broadening the scope of proposers gives impetus to conversation. Member States and indeed executive SADC institutions themselves may be too constrained by comity and other diplomatic considerations to propose radical and progressive amendments.

It is further recommended that any proposed amendment should be directed to the proposed commission for its comments. The commission should then send a copy of the proposal to the CoM for its comments before the proposed amendment is tabled in Parliament for debate and approval. If the commission is the proposer, then it should send its proposal to CoM for its comments subject to the same procedure outlined above. If the proposal is from CoM, then it should go straight to Parliament via the commission for the latter's comments. A simple parliamentary majority should be enough to carry the proposal, subject the unanimity of the Summit or simple majority if the amendments are not substantive, with the ultimate responsibility of adopting substantive amendments resting with Member States through parliamentary ratification.

It is, however, proposed that secondary implementation legislation should be left to the proposed commission subject to a requirement that drafts of these should be tabled before CoM and Parliament for the latter's comments. In the event that the comments are adverse, the commission should be obligated to take into account such comments, failing which it should provide written reasons for not accommodating the comments. It should be noted here that with regards to implementation legislation, there is a further safeguard of judicial review in the event that the legislation so adopted is alleged to be *ultra vires* the Treaty or is for some other reason impugned.

The other significant area for the involvement of Parliament should be, as already recommended in Sect. 7.2 above, the adoption of the budget.

In addition to functions, another significant matter is the composition of the proposed parliament. In the EU, for example, some of the perceived advantages of direct elections were initially thought as the following: increase in the influence of the parliamentary institution; development of a sense of regional citizenship through a regional civic duty to vote; stimulation of the formation of regional parties; and devotion of all the members' energies to the regional parliament.[59]

[59] Schermers & Blokker (Footnote 37 above) 419–421.

However, the validity of some of these assumptions has been questioned. For example, voter apathy in European elections has been increasing over time, although it is admitted that this could also be attributable to other causes.[60] There are also a number of disadvantages that have been pointed out as emanating from a directly elected international parliament, including lack of prestige of international parliamentarians and their inability to act in the national field on behalf of the international organisation.[61]

In order for a regional parliament to be a truly representative body, it might appear as if directly elected representation would be ideal. Unfortunately, there are some other considerations that may militate against this apparently ideal situation, for example, resource constraints and efficiency. Moreover, in a region where there are serious concerns about the credibility of the electoral processes at the national level, direct representation at the regional level might actually skew representation at the regional level in favour of a dominant, but not necessarily legitimate and progressive, political current in the region and thus exclude other political views.[62] The best solution would be to have an indirectly elected, ultra-lean,[63] and hopefully, efficient, regional parliament with adequate political clout to inspire confidence in the regional decision-making process. Indeed, it has been suggested by some scholars that the direct election framework of the EP makes it lack 'the authority that the previous European Parliament derived from the fact that its members were members of national parliaments with some influence in national politics.'[64]

It is recommended that the proposed regional parliament should have, based on current membership of SADC, 32 members—two from each Member State. Of course, this number would increase or decrease

---

[60] Schermers & Blokker (Footnote 37 above) 419–420.

[61] Schermers and Blokker (Footnote 37 above) 423.

[62] Schermers & Blokker (Footnote 37 above) assert (at p. 406) that the distribution of seats of international parliamentary organs should be influenced by the need to include the most important national opinions and the need for equitable representation of the populations of participating states.

[63] Any design of SADC institutions should, in addition to considerations of effectiveness, democracy and rule of law, take into account financial considerations. This is more so in view of SADC's dependency on donor support. For the information on donor support, see G.A. Dzinesa et al. 'Introduction' in C. Saunders et al. (eds) *Region-building in Southern Africa: Progress, problems and prospects* (2012) 17. The size of the proposed parliament should therefore be lean enough so that it can be financed by SADC's own resources.

[64] Schermers & Blokker (Footnote 37 above) 420.

depending on the Member States joining or leaving SADC. For a broad representation of interests, national representation should include a speaker of Parliament of each Member State or that of the main legislative chamber/house (in cases where there are more than one chambers/ houses of parliament) and the leader of the opposition in the same chamber/house. The whole body would then choose their speaker and deputy speaker from among themselves and have the power to divide themselves into separate committees, preferably, but not necessarily, modelled along the SADC Common Agenda.

Having a speaker and a leader of opposition from each Member State should ensure coherence between regional and national interests which might result in easy harmonisation of policies. The model where Member State parliaments choose representatives outside Parliament to be regional representatives runs the risk of delinking regional issues from national discourse, yet they should in fact go together.

For the sake of efficiency, the sittings of the regional parliament should be as limited as possible to ensure that members have time for their national duties as well. It is also recommended that in the event of clash of commitments, regional business will take precedence.

7.9   SADC National Committees

As illustrated in Chap. 4, the SADC Treaty framework on SNCs is not satisfactory. Not only were they ill-designed, but they also clearly lack the support of the other institutions of SADC. The stakeholder participation in SNCs' work that the Treaty seeks to encourage would be difficult to realise. In any case, as acknowledged in Chap. 4, the value of civil society participation does not lie in them being embedded in policymaking and implementation, but rather in them playing the watchdog role. Making them formal partners in policy formulation and implementation weakens their strategic position. While they should have a say in matters to do with norm formation and implementation, they should do so as external stakeholders. In fact, their participation should be a peremptory right that is justiciable—but only as contributors, not the actual decision makers.

In light of the foregoing, it is recommended that the SNCs be jettisoned from the SADC institutional framework. However, to make the contribution of civil society a reality, there should be peremptory provisions in the Treaty that provide for the accreditation of CSOs subject to liberal and objective criteria. In addition to this, the Treaty should obligate the proposed commission to publish all legislative drafts, including those of secondary or implementation nature on the official website(s) and such other similar communication platforms and call for comments (open to all stakeholders, including SADC citizens and CSOs) before inter-institutional deliberations on the drafts and their adoption or otherwise by the relevant institutions. As noted by Mbuende, '[a] successful regional integration scheme must be rules-based, and the involvement of non-state actors cannot be an exception.'[65] This should ensure, among other things, that NGOs 'systematically, and continuously ... provide their input into regional integration efforts.'[66]

7.10   ACCESS TO INFORMATION

Access to information by all internal stakeholders in an organisation is one of the core elements of shared governance. However, the value of a liberal access to information regime goes beyond the narrow inter-institutional relations. The interest of the SADC citizen, both natural and legal, cannot be ignored. Indeed it has been stated in a number of places in this book that the model herein proposed is not disruptive of other democracy-enhancing principles already acknowledged in international institutional law and is in fact in harmony with them. While the model proposed in this study is predicated on the free flow of information between the institutions of SADC, it is necessary to propose, not by way of an epilogue but as part of the overall treaty-based shared governance package, an access to information regime that does not only ensure an inter-institutional free flow of information but also ensures access to SADC information by the ultimate beneficiary of the SADC integration project—the SADC citizen.

[65] K. Mbuende 'The SADC: Between co-operation and development—an insider's perspective' in C. Saunders (ed) *Region-building in Southern Africa: Progress, problems and prospects* (2012) 57.
[66] Mbuende (Footnote 65 above). Mbuende's proposal is for the establishment of an Economic and Social Council in the mould of similar institutions in the UN and the AU. While Mbuende's proposal would be an improvement to the current situation, its value is by far limited when compared to the model proposed in this study which bestows clear rights on CSOs that are justiciable and thus enforceable through judicial review. Also, as stated above in connection with the size of the proposed regional parliament, financial considerations (the establishment and operations of an economic and social council will obviously have serious budgetary implications) should also be a factor in the design of SADC institutions.

The SADC Treaty does not have any provision on access to information. This is a matter that is dealt with by way of secondary norms. The first formal attempt to formulate an access to information framework appears to have been made by way of a decision of CoM that was taken in Dar es Salaam, Republic of Tanzania, in 2003.[67] It would appear that prior to the Dar es Salaam meeting, the CoM 'had directed the Secretariat to determine the categories of information to be posted on the SADC website, taking into account the need for confidentiality of certain documents.'[68]

The access to information 'Guidelines for the SADC Secretariat Library' that came out of that meeting are as follows[69]:

- Classified documents will be marked either confidential or restricted. These classifications extend beyond the SADC institutions, as they should be observed by the SADC Member States. The number of copies printed will be an absolute minimum. This classification is applicable to all electronically based and computer-generated information,
- Confidential documents would be those that contain particularly sensitive information for limited use of SADC or documents deemed to be prejudicial to the interest of SADC. These are Summit, Council, and ICM (read SCMCs) records. These documents will automatically be declassified and made public after two years and posted on the SADC website,
- Restricted documents would be those that contain sensitive information for the internal use of SADC. These include internal and regional studies, which contain sensitive information about SADC as determined by the executive secretary. These documents will be automatically declassified and made public after one year and posted on the SADC website,
- Information on SADC studies which do not contain sensitive information on SADC will be made public and posted on the SADC website, after approval by Summit, Council, or ICM (read SCMCs).

[67] Item 5.9 of the minutes of CoM meeting of 23–24 August 2003. The minutes are available in the SADC library, Gaborone (accessed 14 March 2014).

[68] This is captured as a recollection in item 5.9.1 of the Dar es Salaam meeting. See note 67 above.

[69] See Footnote 68 above, item 5.9.6 and the bullets thereunder. Save for some minor changes to do with such things as form, the guidelines are captured almost verbatim as adopted.

As indicated above, prior to the adoption of the above guidelines, the CoM had directed the Secretariat, at its meeting in Luanda on 9–11 August, to 'determine the categories of information to be posted on the website, taking into account the need for confidentiality of certain documents.'[70] The practice of the Secretariat then, as noted by the CoM, was to classify Summit and CoM documents as restricted documents for a period of up to five years. Even then, such documents could only be accessed as 'reference' documents which could not be photocopied, and thus could not even be posted on the website.[71]

While the Dar es Salaam guidelines marked a significant improvement in the SADC access to information regime, they still remain too broad in scope and can easily be subjected to arbitrary abuse. It is not enough, for example, to leave the categorisation of 'sensitive' to the discretion of the Executive Secretary without any narrowly defined guidelines.

In coming up with the guidelines, the CoM was guided by, among other things, what it might have deemed as 'best practice' obtaining in some organisations some of which do not fall under the same typology as SADC, for example, the Bank of Botswana Library.[72] Access to documents in a library of a national central bank should surely differ from that of access to documents of a regional integration organisation like SADC which is undergirded by such values as democracy and the rule of law and whose treaty acknowledges the centrality of the involvement of the SADC citizen and key stakeholders in the regional integration project.

In addition to lack of a justiciable right of access to information in the SADC Treaty itself and a restrictive subsidiary policy regime on access to information, there is also apparently no culture that is sympathetic to access to information in SADC. For example, at the height of the 'negotiations' over the future of the SADC Tribunal, discussed at length in Chap. 4, there were two reports that were prepared in connection with the issue: the Bartels report and the report by the Committee of Ministers of Justice/Attorneys-General. During a press briefing, the then Executive Secretary of SADC, Dr. Tomaz Salomão, when asked whether the reports

---

[70] As above, item 5.9.1 of the minutes.
[71] As above, item 5.9.3.
[72] As above.

would be made public, is alleged to have responded that 'neither the media nor SADC citizens needed to know.'[73]

In the EU, the right to access to information is enshrined in article 15 TFEU. Article 15(1) provides that the EU institutions, bodies, and agencies shall conduct their work as openly as possibly. In terms of article 15(2), the EP is obligated to meet in public. The same article provides that the Council, when considering and voting on draft legislative acts should do likewise. Thus, in the EU, unlike in the case of EAC and ECOWAS, it is not just the output of the legislative process (through publication of legal instruments) that is made public but the process itself.

It is, however, article 15 (3) TFEU that is more specific when it comes to access to information. This article gives every citizen of the EU, including any natural or legal person residing or having a registered office in a Member State of the EU, the right of access to documents of the EU institutions, bodies, offices, and agencies, whatever their medium.[74] This article further provides that the general principles and limits on grounds of public policy or private interest governing the right to access to documents are to be determined by the EP and the Council through ordinary legislative action. The EP and the Council are, on their part, specifically obligated to ensure the publication of the documents relating to their legislative procedures as provided for in the said regulations.

---

[73] See H. Melber, 'Promoting the rule of law: Challenges for South Africa's policy' Open Society Foundation for South Africa SAFPI Commentary No. 5, 13 August 2012 http://www.safpi.org/publications/promoting-rule-law-challenges-south-africas-policy (accessed 18 July 2013). See also F. Cowell 'The death of the Southern African Development Community Tribunal's human rights jurisdiction' (2013) *Human Rights Law Review* (advance access March 12 2013) 10 http://hrlr.oxfordjournals.org/ (accessed 26 April 2013) where mention of the same statement by Dr. Salomão, with reference to Melber, is made. See also Tjønneland (Footnote 5 above) 182. One of the recommendations made by Tjønneland is that '...SADC has to change its secretive and bureaucratic mode of operation and become more transparent.' On access to information generally in international organisations, see the Report of the International Law Association (ILA), Berlin Conference (2004) pp. 8–9 www.ila-hq.org/...cfm/.../6B708C25-4D6D-42E2-8385DADA752815E8 (accessed 2 September 2014); E de Wet 'Holding international institutions accountable: The complementary role of non-judicial oversight mechanisms and judicial review' *German Law Journal* (Special Issue: Public authority & international institutions) (2008) 9 # 11 1990 where she makes reference to the same ILA Berlin Conference (2004) Report.

[74] However, with regard to the CJEU and the European Central Bank, the right to access to documents is limited to when these institutions are exercising their administrative tasks.

The right of access to documents is also provided for in the Charter of Fundamental Rights.[75] Article 42 of the Charter gives every EU citizen the right of access to EP, Council, and Commission documents. This right extends with equal force to natural and legal persons residing or having a registered office in an EU Member State.

The EP and the Council adopted a Regulation on access to documents (Regulation on access).[76] The rationale for adopting a regime of access to documents is well captured in the second paragraph of the preamble to the Regulation on access:

> Openness enables citizens to participate more closely in decision-making process and guarantees that the administration enjoys greater legitimacy and is more effective and more accountable to the citizen in a democratic system. Openness contributes to strengthening the principles of democracy and respect for fundamental rights as laid down in Article 6 of the EU Treaty and in the Charter of Fundamental Rights of the European Union.

In Chap. 6, an observation is made that the EU system of governance is quite elaborate when it comes to dialogue between and among the EU institutions themselves. It is thus unsurprising that the regime of access to information expounded in the Regulation on access focuses more on the right of access to documents by EU citizens and residents. It is indeed in line with the rationale of the generality of freedom of information laws. However, in SADC, it is not only the SADC citizen who is deprived of information. As is clearly indicated in the policy framework adopted by the CoM above, internal stakeholders are equally constrained. Indeed, it is difficult to imagine a robust policy dialogue taking place either between or among SADC institutions themselves or between the SADC institutions and the SADC citizen and CSOs if such policy debate is related to information access to which is restricted. Therefore, by adopting a liberal access

[75] The Charter was adopted by the EP, Council and the Commission at Nice on 7 December 2000 and is available at http://www.europar/.europa.eu/charter/pdf/text_en.pdf (accessed 18 March 2014). In terms of art 6(1) of TEU, the Charter as subsequently proclaimed in 2007 by the same institutions has the same legal value as the Treaties. SADC also has a Charter of the Fundamental Social Rights that was signed in 2003. The SADC Charter, however, is largely confined to employment and labour relations within the SADC region. See http://www.sadc.int/documents-publications/show/837 (last accessed 2 October 2014).

[76] Regulation (EC) 1049/2001 of 30 May 2001 http://eur-lex.europa.eu/LexUriServ/LexUriServ.do?uri=OJ%3AL%3A2001%3A145%3A0043%3A0048%3AEN%3APDF (accessed 18 March 2014).

to information regime for the benefit of the regional citizen, this would also translate into access to and unconstrained use of the same information by the internal institutions of SADC and institutions of Member States as well. This would certainly serve to improve the quality of debates on SADC policy, both its formulation and implementation, by a broad range of stakeholders.

The current SADC policy on classified documents—those marked 'confidential' or 'restricted' is too broad in scope. Not only does it apply to Member States but also to SADC institutions. In any access to information regime, it may indeed be legitimate to set out restrictions on the right to access to information. Such a restriction should, however, be narrowly defined in terms of the public and the private interest, similar to what is obtaining in the EU. To cast the restriction in overly broad terms creates a real likelihood of abuse of discretion.

When it comes to the so-called confidential documents, the breadth of the policy is even more discomforting. This classification includes all Summit, Council, and SCMCs records. The content of such documents does not matter. In addition to this over breadth, these documents are accessible after two years. For an organisation that aspires to involve the SADC citizens 'centrally in the process of development and integration' as proclaimed in the preamble to the SADC Treaty, this policy is a negation of such an aspiration. Involvement of the SADC citizen should mean participation in the processes of norm setting as well, through access to draft policy documents, not just debating, *ex post facto*, norms that have already been adopted.

Even the requirement of approval by either the Summit, Council, or the SCMCs before a non-sensitive document is made public or posted on the SADC website is an unnecessary restriction on access information, considering the length of time it might take to get the necessary approval, in view of the limited number of meetings of these institutions as prescribed in the Treaty. This would be so even assuming that a round robin approval is possible.

There should thus be a treaty-based general right of access to any document held by SADC unless there are legitimate restrictions imposed on the basis of well-defined and narrowly construed public and private interest considerations. There should also be a right to both administrative and judicial recourse (another reason for the need for an independent, impartial, and accessible judicial organ in SADC) in the event of delay or refusal.[77]

---

[77] See, for example, the framing of arts 7 & 8 of the Regulation on access (Footnote 76 above).

7.11   Conclusion

The intention of this chapter was to not only make a proposal for the democratisation of the SADC institutional framework, but also to illustrate that such a reform proposal can be based on a determinate model with identifiable elements. A realistic alternative SADC institutional framework anchored in the shared governance model, benefitting from progressive elements in the institutional frameworks of the three organisations selected as comparators—the EAC, ECOWAS, and the EU, and also based on this study's own innovations, has been sufficiently sketched out in this chapter.

The ultimate proposal that has come out of this chapter is 'constitutional change' in SADC. This includes, among other things, the transformation of the Secretariat into an effective body that proposes and implements SADC policy; creation of a legislative arm with a say over proposed policies, amendment of the SADC Treaty and in the adoption of the SADC budget, among other things; an independent judicial organ with significant powers of review; and a liberal and robust access to information regime.

In adopting the shared governance framework, SADC should not ignore the imperatives of continual self-assessment. Challenges of governance will always exist in any polity. What is important is how those challenges are addressed, especially through the creation or realignment of institutions in line with the dictates of democracy and the rule of law.

CHAPTER 8

Conclusion

The future of SADC as an international organisation (and indeed that of any other international organisation) is difficult to predict. The possibilities are just too many. The worst-case scenario is disintegration either out of irreconcilable differences between Member States or out of a mutual recognition that the regional integration agenda is no longer in the interests of the Member States.[1]

There is also another possibility that SADC might be gradually subsumed under a bigger regional integration scheme comprising COMESA, EAC, and SADC.[2] Whether the COMESA-EAC-SADC tripartite arrangement

---

[1] The recent pronouncement by the government of Botswana that it might consider not taking part in SADC led election observation missions in SADC Member States because of the concerns surrounding the credibility of such processes, although that threat has been reversed, is something that should be taken seriously. See http://en.starafrica.com/news/botswana-in-sadc-poll-observation-boycott-u-turn.html (accessed 4 May 2014). SADC is not the only REC that may be facing an existential threat. In the period immediately following the British referendum to exit the EU, the EU Commission President Jean-Claude Juncker spoke of existential threats to the EU in his State of the Union address to the European Parliament. See 'State of the Union Address 2016: Towards a better Europe – a Europe that protects, empowers and defends' European Commission Press Release Database, available at http://europa.eu/rapid/press-release_SPEECH-16-3043_en.htm (accessed on 15 September 2016).

[2] These three RECs have already signed a tripartite Memorandum of Understanding with a view to working together in a wide range of matters. See http://www.comesa-eac-sadc-tripartite.org/sites/default/files/documents/Tripartite-Triparrtite%20MoU%20Signed%20Version.pdf (accessed 19 June 2014). For an interesting discussion of the histori-

© The Author(s) 2019
M. Nyathi, *The Southern African Development Community and Law*, https://doi.org/10.1007/978-3-319-76511-2_8

will transform into a reality, and what the eventual nature and scope of the envisaged scheme would be, are matters that are difficult to predict.[3] It would appear though that the arrangement has been or is being consummated: a website is now in place and some positions have been advertised.[4] Interestingly, the execution section of the MoU appears like an intra-SADC agreement, since all the three signatories are heads of state or government of SADC countries—Namibia, Swaziland, and Tanzania, only that for the occasion they were representing SADC, COMESA, and EAC respectively. Needless to say, this shows the overlapping membership of RECs and reflects a *prima facie* inefficient duplication of efforts.

The other possibility is the realisation, in practical terms, of an African Economic Community (AEC) (an institutional ideal whose realisation is partly envisioned through the African RECs as its building blocks). The assumption, as expressed in the relevant instruments, is that once the AEC is functional, there would not be any need for the smaller sub-regional RECs.[5] Whether this is a valid assumption is debatable. Yet, some see as another possibility the development of two main regional blocs in Africa: one covering West and Central Africa; and the other comprising states in Eastern and Southern Africa.[6]

---

cal background and other matters in connection with the tripartite arrangement, see generally B. Lunogelo & V.A. Mbilinyi 'Convergence of COMESA-SADC-EAC regional frameworks' (2009) *The Economic and Social Research Foundation*, Dar es Salaam, Tanzania, a paper presented during the Annual Forum for Private, Public and Academia Partnership on Trade Policy and Negotiations organized by the Tanzanian Ministry of Industry and Marketing http://www.tzonline.org/pdf/convegenceofcomesa.pdf (accessed 4 May 2014).

[3] Based on the current membership of the three organisations, the COMESA-EAC -SADC arrangement would cover 26 states and more than half of Africa in terms of population. See http://www.sadc.int/about-sadc/continental-interregional-integration/tripartite-cooperation/ (accessed 2 February 2016).

[4] See http://www.comesa-eac-sadc-tripartite.org/; http://www.comesa-eac-sadc-tripartite.org/Latest from the Tripartite, respectively (both accessed 23 June 2014).

[5] Art 5(1)(d) of the Protocol on Relations between the African Union and the Regional Economic Communities (RECs) http://www.afrimap.org/english/images/treaty/AU-RECs-Protocol.pdf (accessed 30 May 2014); S.T. Ebobrah 'Legitimacy and feasibility of human rights realisation through regional economic communities in Africa: The case of the Economic Community of West African States' unpublished LLD thesis, Faculty of Law, University of Pretoria (2009) 128–129; M. Killander 'Legal harmonization in Africa: Taking stock and moving forward' in L. Fioramonti (ed) *Regionalism in a changing world: Comparative perspectives in the new global order* (2013) 95.

[6] Killander (Footnote 5 above) 88.

This book has, however, been written on the basis of SADC as a 'going concern,' and on the assumption that it will endure as a public international organisation for some time to come. Based on that assumption, the possibility of organisational change is inevitable. Indeed, SADC is in transformation, although the direction and implications of this transformation are not clear—for example, there is still uncertainty surrounding the fate of the SADC Tribunal. This study, therefore, seeks to advocate a SADC institutional transformation informed by the need to infuse democracy and the rule of law into SADC processes.

This study has sought to prove that the current institutional framework of SADC is not democratic and is not underpinned by the rule of law. This is largely because of the concentration of uncontrolled power in the institution of Summit. The clearest example of this concentration of power in the Summit and its arbitrary use has been the suspension and disbandment of the SADC Tribunal.

The other three RECs that have been chosen for comparative purposes in this study—the EAC, ECOWAS, and the EU have been able, to differing degrees, to address their respective democratic deficits through the creation and empowerment of institutions within their governance frameworks. None of these three RECs represents a perfect democratic model, and indeed a lot still has to be done in terms of their democratisation. For example, the EACJ is still without human rights jurisdiction; the ECOWAS Parliament has but a superficial role in ECOWAS policy formulation; and in the EU there are concerns that the powers of the EP are limited as compared to those of the Council. However, in trying to find an alternative institutional framework for SADC, a lot can be learnt from each of the three.

This book has presented incontrovertible shortcomings of the SADC governance framework. Indeed, there appears to be no current literature that persuasively says otherwise. Scholars and commentators alike seem to acknowledge the state of affairs. However, despite the clear and acknowledged shortcomings of the SADC institutional architecture, there are some in scholarship who seem to be against progressive institutional reforms in SADC, their reasoning being that a more integrated and democratic framework is beyond the capacity of SADC. There are also some who believe that progressive change is not feasible in view of the current political reality in the region. There is also the view that the current institutional design is adequate for the attainment of SADC's objectives. In fact, as indicated earlier in this book, some even call for more limited ambitions for SADC. They suggest that SADC should rather confine itself to such matters as trade facilitation and security. Unfortunately, just what capacity is lacking (and needed), and how advocating a more integrated, democratic, and rules-based regional governance framework underpinned by the rule of law raises 'capacity' challenges does not come out of the writings of these sceptics. The 'lack of capacity' argument is extremely unfortunate in that by pointing this out as a challenge and yet at the same time recoiling from elaborating on the capacity challenges that supposedly always accompany SADC and Africans in general, a crude innuendo is created.

As things stand, SADC remains steeped in classical intergovernmental-ism dominated by the collective executive will of the heads of states or government of its Member States. Under the current framework, the nor-mative outcomes can hardly achieve the goals of the Common Agenda that SADC set for itself in the 2001 amended Treaty. Also, with no frame-work for the adoption of general supranational legal instruments that are directly applicable in Member States and whose implementation is coordi-nated at the SADC supranational level, SADC will continue to churn out ineffective norms whose reception in Member States remains optional. In such an environment, policy harmonisation and implementation and indeed regional integration itself, can only be a dream.

Over and above these shortcomings, there is limited respect for the fundamentals of democracy, the rule of law and good governance as dem-onstrated by, among other things, the suspension and disbandment of the SADC Tribunal and the failure to unequivocally insist on free and fair electoral processes in SADC Member States.

Reform proposals cannot be made in abstract. They can only be informed by the need to change the current state of things. For reform proposals to be valid, they should, except in the case of untried new inno-vative ideas, be guided by acceptable standards in similarly placed organ-isations, or what may be deemed to be current 'best' practice. The EAC and ECOWAS have both taken the more integrated supranational route, with their respective regional institutions/organs-setting norms that are directly applicable in Member States. Also, ECOWAS has over time made efforts to strengthen its judicial institution, the ECCJ.

On the other hand, the EU has over the years been evolving into a highly integrated organisation with significant supranational powers. In doing so, it has always tried to accommodate and entrench democracy in its governance architecture. The European Parliament now has increased powers; and civil society participation has continued to grow in a number of sites in the EU governance architecture. These are matters to do mostly with political will and loyalty to democratic principles of governance, rather than undefined 'capacity' issues.

This book contributes to the growing academic literature in both international law and international relations on the constitutionalisation of international law. However, the significance of this book is in its uniqueness. It focuses more on the 'internal' dimension of the democratic deficit rather than on the 'external' one. Current literature seems to focus more on the latter—in particular how to accommodate the interests of the individual through 'representative' institutions.

With reference particularly to the literature on SADC, the nature of the democratic deficit in SADC has so far not been clearly and exhaustively defined. Also, scholars and commentators alike have so far not put forward clearly articulated and far-reaching reform proposals. Proposals for reform have largely been focused on selected institutions and limited in scope—for example, some have suggested that the SNCs (and by default civil society organisations) have the potential to contribute positively to the SADC integration project and thus should be empowered. Others have called for the establishment of a proper regional parliament with some lawmaking and oversight powers. There also have been calls (probably the loudest of them all) for the reinstatement of the SADC Tribunal in its previous form. While these proposals and calls should be lauded, they fail to recognise that it is the design of the whole institutional architecture of SADC that should be addressed, something which this study proposes.

Informed by the shortcomings of the SADC institutional architecture, and taking into account lessons learnt from other RECs that are used as comparators, among other things, a model of shared governance is offered as an alternative institutional framework for SADC. The concept of shared governance is not radically different from other democratic theories like constitutionalism and the rule of law. It shares a number of elements with these other theories and should in fact be seen as complementing them rather than seeing it as a completely new and exclusive governance model. In fact, in the final analysis, shared governance goes beyond merely complementing these other democratic principles, but rather accommodates them. And (for argument's sake) to the extent that some may view shared governance as an expression of already existing governance principles (e.g. constitutionalism and institutional balance) in other terms, at least it is (or would be) a more grammatically appropriate description of what may already be obtaining elsewhere.

In order to demonstrate the applicability of the shared governance model in SADC, this study has come up with a practical narrative model on how the SADC institutional architecture can be transformed. This model allows for the involvement of a number of institutions in all the stages of decision-making; provides an obligation for the free flow of information between and among institutions so that all institutions have access to all relevant information in their decision-making processes; creates autonomous lawmaking zones for different institutions subject to checks and balances to be exercised by the other institutions so that the final decisions taken are products of meaningful inter-institutional dialogue which helps to improve the quality of decisions and limit arbitrary exercise of power, among other things.

There is enough empirical evidence to validate the view that a representative regional parliament and a directly accessible regional judiciary with a broad jurisdictional mandate (including that of human rights) do have the potential to serve the interests of the SADC citizen better than what is currently obtaining. As has been shown in this study, the SADC Tribunal did just that before its disbandment. The SADCPF, on the other hand, although not exactly part of the SADC institutional family, has been able to condemn most of the post-2000 Zimbabwean elections that were evidently not in accordance with SADC's own instruments governing elections. There is, however, no empirical evidence yet on what an empowered regional bureaucracy can do in SADC since such has ever been in place. But based on the above empirical evidence on the Tribunal and on the SADCPF, it can be assumed, reasonably, that it can also deliver better public goods that would accelerate the pace of regional integration.

While this book focuses on the internal dimension of the democratic deficit in SADC, it also addresses, by default, other 'constitutionalist' concerns and the 'external' democratic deficit. For example, the model proposed includes an indirectly elected regional parliament and peremptory participation by civil society organisations through, for example, the notice and comment procedure. These address two important dimensions of the usual democratic deficit narrative—the need for representative institutions at the international level and participatory democracy.

This book offers a bold and precise call for the wholesale redesign of SADC's governance framework. The shared governance framework proposed here can and should lead to the creation of democratic and legitimate institutions of SADC that would result in democratic decision-making, respect for the rule of law and the good governance practices of transparency and accountability, and hopefully an efficient and effective execution of the SADC integration project.

However, while the need for a democratic and rule of law-based SADC governance architecture cannot be overemphasised, there can be no guarantee that it will immediately translate into democratic practice. But it would be far much easier to at least call the SADC leadership to account where there is a clearer democratic and rule of law-based treaty framework of governance than is currently obtaining. However, even assuming that both the formal institutional framework and practice are democratic, there can never be a guarantee, as conceded elsewhere in this book, that the SADC integration project would suddenly become a success. Achievement of SADC's many objectives will never be an easy task and cannot be achieved by the presence of democratic institutions and processes alone. However, even so, an inclusive, open, and democratic regional governance framework where leadership is shared and accountable and subject to the rule of law as proposed in this book would most likely accomplish more, than one where the destiny of SADC is largely in the hands of a single, overarching, and largely unaccountable institution—the Summit of Heads of State or Government.

And while the current general political climate in the majority of SADC Member States and at the regional level may make the proposals made in this study appear unrealistic to some as they may be viewed as difficult to achieve in the near future, it should be noted that scholarship should not resign itself to the apparent practical realities of the present day. Other than the advocacy value of scholarship, it should be acknowledged that no one can predict the future when it comes to political change, in both nature and timing, at both the national and international levels. What may appear as unthinkable today may well be the case tomorrow. It should also be noted that the proposals made in this book, although far-reaching in terms of their combined scope, are not outright radical and impracticable. Not only do they mostly have to do with the reform of already existing institutions, but they are made within a broader global perspective and empirical reality of a democratising international order. Constructing a new SADC that is envisioned here through the lens of shared governance is thus something achievable even in the short term.

BIBLIOGRAPHY

Acharya, A. 2013. Comparative regionalism: A field whose time has come? In *Regionalism in a changing world: Comparative perspectives in the new global order*, ed. L. Fioramonti. London and New York: Routledge.

Adjolohoun, H.S. 2013. *Giving effect to the human rights jurisprudence of the Court of Justice of the Economic Community of West African States: Compliance and influence*. Unpublished LLD thesis, University of Pretoria.

Akande, D. 1998. The competence of international organizations and the advisory jurisdiction of the International Court of Justice. *European Journal of International Law* 9: 437.

Archibugi, D. 1995. From the United Nations to cosmopolitan democracy. In *Cosmopolitan democracy: An agenda for a new world order*, ed. D. Archibugi and D. Held. Cambridge: Polity Press.

———. 1998. Principles of cosmopolitan democracy. In *Re-imagining political community: Studies in cosmopolitan democracy*, ed. D. Archibugi et al. Stanford, CA: Stanford University Press.

———. 2008. *The global commonwealth of citizens: Toward cosmopolitan democracy*. Princeton and Oxford: Princeton University Press.

Barron, J.A., and C.T. Dienes. 2013. *Constitutional law in a nutshell*. St. Paul, MN: West Group.

Baudenbacher, C., and M.-J. Clifton. 2013. Courts of regional economic and political integration agreements. In *The Oxford handbook of international adjudication*, ed. C.P.R. Romano, K.J. Alter, and Y. Shany. Oxford: Oxford University Press.

© The Author(s) 2019   221
M. Nyathi, *The Southern African Development Community and Law*, https://doi.org/10.1007/978-3-319-76511-2

Besson, S. 2009. Whose constitution(s)? International law, constitutionalism and democracy. In *Ruling the world? Constitutionalism, international law and global governance*, ed. J.L. Dunoff and J.P. Trachtman. Cambridge: Cambridge University Press.

Boré, L., and F. Henkel. 2015. Disturbing a cosy balance? The ECOWAS Parliament's rocky road to co-decision. *International Policy Analysis*, Friedrich Ebert Stiftung. http://library.fes.de/pdf-files/iez/11185.pdf. Accessed 16 April 2016.

Bosire, C.M. 2011. Local government and human rights: Building institutional links for the effective protection and realization of human rights in Africa. *African Human Rights Journal* 11: 147.

Brownlie, I. 1972. *Principles of public international law*. Oxford: Oxford University Press.

Christiansen, E.C. 2010. Transformative constitutionalism in South Africa: Creative uses of Constitutional Court authority to advance substantive justice. *The Journal of Gender, Race & Justice* 13: 575.

Conway, G. 2011. Recovering a separation of powers in the European Union. *European Law Journal* 17 (3): 304.

Costa, O., and N. Brack. 2013. The role of the European Parliament in Europe's integration and parliamentarization process. In *Parliamentary dimensions of regionalization and globalization: The role of inter-parliamentary institutions*, ed. O. Costa et al. Basingstoke: Palgrave Macmillan.

Costa, O., C. Dri, and S. Stavridis. 2013. Introduction. In *Parliamentary dimensions of regionalization and globalization: The role of inter-parliamentary institutions*, ed. O. Costa et al. Basingstoke: Palgrave Macmillan.

Cowell, F. 2013. The death of the Southern African Development Community Tribunal's human rights jurisdiction. *Human Rights Law Review*. http://hrlr. oxfordjournals.org/. Accessed 12 March 2013.

Craig, P. 2011a. Integration, democracy and legitimacy. In *The evolution of EU law*, ed. P. Craig and G. De Búrca. Oxford: Oxford University Press.

———. 2011b. Institutions, power, and institutional balance. In *The evolution of EU law*, ed. P. Craig and G. De Búrca. Oxford: Oxford University Press.

Craig, P., and G. De Búrca, eds. 2011. *The evolution of EU law*. Oxford: Oxford University Press.

Curtin, D.M., and I.F. Dekker. 2011. The European Union from Maastricht to Lisbon: Institutional and legal unity out of the shadows. In *The evolution of EU law*, ed. P. Craig and G. De Búrca. Oxford: Oxford University Press.

D'Aspremont, J. 2011. The rise and fall of democratic governance in international law: A reply to Susan Marks. *The European Journal of International Law* 22 (2): 549.

Dahl, R.A. 1999. Can international organisations be democratic? A skeptic's view. In *Democracy's edges*, ed. I. Shapiro and C. Hacker-Cordon. Cambridge: Cambridge University Press.

De Búrca, G. 2007–2008. Developing democracy beyond the state. *Columbia Journal of Transnational Law* 46: 221.

De Wet, E. 2004. The direct administration of territories by the United Nations and its Member States in the Post Cold War era: Legal bases and implications for national law. *Max Planck UNYB* 8: 291.

———. 2006. The international constitutional order. *International Comparative Law Quarterly* 15: 53.

———. 2008. Holding international institutions accountable: The complementary role of non-judicial oversight mechanisms and judicial review. *German Law Journal* 9 (11): 1987. (Special Issue: Public Authority & International Institutions).

———. 2013. The rise and fall of the Tribunal of the Southern African Development Community: Implications for dispute settlement in Southern Africa. *ICSID Review* 28 (1): 45.

De Witte, B. 2011. Direct effect, primacy, and the nature of the legal order. In *The evolution of EU law*, ed. P. Craig and G. De Búrca. Oxford: Oxford University Press.

Den Brande, V., and M. Delebarre (rapporteurs). 2009. *Committee of the regions.* White Paper on Multi-level Governance' 80th plenary session, 17 and 18 June 2009.

Dingwerth, K. 2014. Global democracy and the democratic minimum: Why a procedural account alone is insufficient. *European Journal of International Relations* 20: 1124.

Doyle, M.W. 2009. The UN Charter – A global constitution? In *Ruling the world? Constitutionalism, international law and global governance*, ed. J.L. Dunoff and J.P. Trachtman. Cambridge: Cambridge University Press.

Draper, P. 2012. Breaking free from Europe: Why Africa needs another model of regional integration. *The International Spectator: Italian Journal of International Affairs* 47 (1): 67.

Dugard, J. 2011. *International law: A South African perspective.* 4th ed. Cape Town: Juta & Co Ltd.

Dunoff, J.L. 2009. The politics of international constitutions: The curious case of the World Trade Organization. In *Ruling the world? Constitutionalism, international law, and global governance*, ed. J.L. Dunoff and J.P. Trachtman. Cambridge: Cambridge University Press.

Dunoff, J.L., and J.P. Trachtman. 2009. A functional approach to international constitutionalization. In *Ruling the world? Constitutionalism, international law, and global governance*, ed. J.L. Dunoff and J.P. Trachtman. Cambridge: Cambridge University Press.

Dzinesa, G.A., et al. 2012. Introduction. In *Region-building in Southern Africa: Progress, problems and prospects*, ed. C. Saunders et al. London and New York: Zed Books.

Ebobrah, S.T. 2009. *Legitimacy and feasibility of human rights realisation through regional economic communities in Africa: The case of the Economic Community of West African States.* Unpublished LLD thesis, University of Pretoria.

———. 2010. Tackling threats to the existence of the SADC Tribunal: A critique of perilously ambiguous provisions in the SADC Treaty and the protocol on the Tribunal. *Malawi Law Journal* 4 (2): 199.

———. 2012. Human rights developments in African sub-regional economic communities during 2011. *African Human Rights Law Journal* 11: 216.

———. 2013. Human rights developments in African sub-regional economic communities during 2012. *African Human Rights Law Journal* 13 (1): 178.

Fassbender, B. 2009. Rediscovering a forgotten constitution: Notes on the place of the UN Charter in the international legal order. In *Ruling the world? Constitutionalism, international law and global governance*, ed. J.L. Dunoff and J.P. Trachtman. Cambridge: Cambridge University Press.

Forere, M., and L. Stone. 2009. The SADC Protocol on Gender and Development: Duplication or complementarity of the African Union Protocol on Women's Rights? *African Human Rights Law Journal*: 434.

Fox, G.H., and B.R. Roth. 2001. Democracy and international law. *Review of International Studies* 27: 327.

Franck, T.M. 1992. The emerging right to democratic governance. *American Journal of International Law* 86: 46.

———. 2009. International institutions: Why constitutionalize? In *Ruling the world? Constitutionalism, international law, and global governance*, ed. J.L. Dunoff and J.P. Trachtman. New York: Cambridge University Press.

Freestone, D. 1983. The European Court of Justice. In *Institutions and policies of the European Union*, ed. J. Lodge, 43. London: Frances Pinter.

Gardbaum, S. 2009. Human rights and international constitutionalism. In *Ruling the world? Constitutionalism, international law and global governance*, ed. J.L. Dunoff and J.P. Trachtman. Cambridge: Cambridge University Press.

Giuffrida, L., and H. Müller-Godde. 2008. Strengthening SADC institutional structures – Capacity development is the key to SADC Secretariat's effectiveness (chapter six). In *Monitoring regional integration in Southern Africa Yearbook*, ed. A. Bösil et al., vol. 8. Stellenbosch, South Africa: Trade Law Centre for Southern Africa. http://www.kas.de/upload/auslandshomepages/namibia/MRI2008/MRI2008_06_Giuffrida.pdf. Accessed 8 May 2014.

Habermas, J. 2012. The crisis of the European Union in the light of a constitutionalization of international law. *The European Journal of International Law* 23 (2): 335.

Halberstam, D. 2009. The constitutional heterarchy: The centrality of conflict in the European Union and the United States. In *Ruling the world? Constitutionalism, international law and global governance*, ed. J.L. Dunoff and J.P. Trachtman. Cambridge: Cambridge University Press.

Held, D. 1995. Democracy and the new international order. In *Cosmopolitan democracy: An agenda for a new world order*, ed. D. Archibugi and D. Held, 96. Cambridge: Polity Press.

———. 1998. Democracy and globalisation. In *Re-imagining political community: Studies in cosmopolitan democracy*, ed. D. Archibugi, D. Held, and M. Kohler. Stanford, CA: Stanford University Press.

Hess, R. 2004. From bedside to boardroom – Nursing shared governance. *Online Journal of Issues in Nursing* 9 (1). http://gm6.nursingworld.org/MainMenuCategories/ANAMarketplace/ANAPeriodicals/OJIN/TableofContents/Volume92004/No1Jan04/FromBedsidetoBoardroom.html.

Hestermeyer, H.P. 2014. *The implementation of European Union law*. An unpublished paper presented at the workshop *The Implementation of International Law in South Africa – Strengthening the Rule of Law by Following the German Model?* 16–17 May 2014, Faculty of Law, University of South Africa in cooperation with the Max Planck Institute for Comparative Public and International Law, the Konrad Adenauer Stiftung/Foundation & the Alexander von Humboldt Stiftung/Foundation.

Hildreth, R.W. 2012. Word and deed: A Deweyan integration of deliberative and participatory democracy. *New Political Science* 34 (3): 295.

Himler, J.D. 2010. The state of participatory democratic theory. *New Political Science* 32: 43.

Horeth, M. 2001. *The European Commission's White Paper on Governance: A 'toolkit' for closing the legitimacy gap of EU policymaking?* This paper was presented at the Workshop "Preparing Europe's Future. The Contribution of the Commission's White Book on Governance", Centre for European Integration Studies Bonn & Europe 2020, in cooperation with the Representation of the North Rhine Westphalia to the European Union in Brussels, November 2001. www.zel.uni-bonn.de/dateien/discussion-paper/dpc94-hoereth.pdf. Accessed 14 June 2013.

Isaksen, J. 2002. *Restructuring SADC – Progress and problems*. Development Studies and Human Rights, Chr Michelsen Institute Report R 2002: 15, Norway. www.cmi.no. Accessed 12 December 2013.

Kennedy, D. 2009. The mystery of global governance. In *Ruling the world? Constitutionalism, international law and global governance*, ed. J.L. Dunoff and J.P. Trachtman. Cambridge: Cambridge University Press.

Keohane, R.O., et al. 2007. *Democracy-enhancing multilateralism*. New York University School of Law, Institute for International Law & Justice Working Paper 2007/4.

Khadiagala, G.M. 2012. Historical legacy. In *Region-building in Southern Africa: Progress, problems and prospects*, ed. C. Saunders. London and New York: Zed Books.

Killander, M. 2013. Legal harmonization in Africa: Taking stock and moving forward. In *Regionalism in a changing world: Comparative perspectives in the new global order*, ed. L. Fioramonti. London and New York: Routledge.

Killander, M., and M. Nyathi. 2015. Accountability for the *Gukurahundi* atrocities in Zimbabwe thirty years on: Prospects and challenges. *Comparative and International Law Journal of Southern Africa* 48 (3): 463.

Klabbers, J. 2009a. *An introduction to international Institutional Law*. Cambridge: Cambridge University Press.

———. 2009b. Setting the scene. In *The constitutionalization of international law*, ed. J. Klabbers et al. Oxford: Oxford University Press.

Klabbers, J., et al. 2009. *The constitutionalization of international law*. Oxford: Oxford University Press.

Kommers, D.P. 1997. *The constitutional jurisprudence of the Federal Republic of Germany*. Durham and London: Duke University Press.

Krisch, N. 2010. *Beyond constitutionalism: The pluralist structure of postnational law*. Oxford: Oxford University Press.

Krisch, N., and B. Kingsbury. 2006. Introduction: Global governance and global administrative law in the international legal order. *European Journal of International Law* 17 (1): 1.

Kufuor, K.O. 2006. *The institutional transformation of the Economic Community of West African States*. England: Ashgate Publishing Company.

Kumm, M. 2004. The legitimacy of international law: A constitutionalist framework of analysis. *The European Journal of International Law* 15 (5): 907.

———. 2009. The cosmopolitan turn in constitutionalism: On the relationship between constitutionalism in and beyond the state. In *Ruling the world? Constitutionalism, international law and global governance*, ed. J.L. Dunoff and J.P. Trachtman. Cambridge: Cambridge University Press.

Langenhove, L.V. 2013. Why we need to "unpack" regions to compare them more effectively. In *Regionalism in a changing world: Comparative perspectives in the new global order*, ed. L. Fioramonti. London and New York: Routledge.

Leal-Arcas, R. 2003. Exclusive and shared competence in the Common Commercial Policy: From Amsterdam to Nice. *Legal Issues of Economic Integration* 30: 3.

Lunogelo, B., and V.A. Mbilinyi. 2009. *Convergence of COMESA-SADC-EAC regional frameworks*. The Economic and Social Research Foundation, Dar es Salaam, Tanzania, A paper presented during the Annual Forum for Private, Public and Academia Partnership on Trade Policy and Negotiations organised by the Tanzanian Ministry of Industry and Marketing. http://www.tzonline.org/pdf/convegenceofcomesa.pdf.

Maduro, M.P. 2009. Courts and pluralism: Essay on a theory of judicial adjudication in the context of legal and constitutional pluralism. In *Ruling the world? Constitutionalism, international law and global governance*, ed. J.L. Dunoff and J.P. Trachtman. Cambridge: Cambridge University Press.

Marchetti, R. 2008. *Global democracy: For and against: Ethical theory, institutional design and social struggles*. London: Routledge.

Marks, S. 2011. What has become of the emerging right to democratic governance? *The European Journal of International Law* 22 (2): 507.

Matlosa, K. 2012. Elections and conflict management. In *Region-building in Southern Africa: Progress, problems and prospects*, ed. C. Saunders. London and New York: Zed Books.

Mkandawire, C. 2012. *Perspective on the parliamentary transformation agenda*. Regional Parliamentary Seminar on 'Africa's Regional Parliaments: State of Development, Cooperation and Potential', Southern Sun Hotel, Johannesburg, South Africa, 17–18 May 2012.

Moravcsik, A. 2002. In defence of the "democratic deficit": Reassessing legitimacy in the European Union. *Journal of Common Market Studies* 40 (4): 603.

———. 2004. Is there a "democratic deficit" in world politics? A framework for analysis. *Government and Opposition* 39 (2): 336.

———. 2008. The myth of Europe's "democratic deficit". *Intereconomics: Journal of European Public Policy*: 331.

Motsamai, D. 2013. SADC's review of its Principles and Guidelines Governing Democratic Elections: Need for civil society inputs? *Institute for Global Dialogue*, Issue 102, October.

Moyo, B. 2007. *Civil society organisations' engagement with regional economic communities in Africa, people friendly or people driven?* Final Report Submitted to the UNDP Regional Service Centre for Eastern and Southern Africa.

Musavengana, T. 2011. *The proposed SADC parliament: Old wine in new bottles or an ideal whose time has come?* Pretoria: Institute for Security Studies.

Mvungi, S.E.A. 1995. *Constitutional questions in the regional integration process: The case of the Southern African Development Community with reference to the EU*. Unpublished doctoral thesis, Hamburg University.

Nathan, L. 2011. Solidarity triumphs over democracy – The dissolution of the SADC Tribunal. *Development Dialogue* 57: 123.

———. 2012. *Community of insecurity: SADC's struggle for peace and security in Southern Africa*. Surrey, GBR: Ashgate Publishing Group.

———. 2013. The disbanding of the SADC Tribunal: A cautionary tale. *Human Rights Quarterly* 35 (4): 870.

———. 2014. *Sovereignty rules! Human rights regimes and state sovereignty*. Unpublished draft paper presented on 8 August 2014, Centre for Homan Rights, Faculty of law, University of Pretoria.

Neyer, J. 2003. Discourse and order in the EU: A deliberative approach to multi-level governance. In *European governance, deliberation and the quest for democratisation*, ed. E.O. Eriksen et al., 240. Oslo: ARENA. http://www.arena.uio.no. This work is also available as a paper in Volume 41 of the *Journal of Common Market studies*, 2003.

Ng'ongo'la, C. 2008. The framework for regional integration in the Southern African Development Community. *University of Botswana Law Journal* 8: 3.

Ngwenya, S. 2009. Regional integration in Africa. In *Advocates for change: How to overcome Africa's challenges*, ed. M. Moeletsi. Johannesburg: Picador Africa.

Nkhata, M.J. 2012. The role of regional economic communities in protecting and promoting human rights in Africa: Reflecting on the human rights mandate of the Tribunal of the Southern African Development Community. *African Journal of International and Comparative Law* 20: 87.

Nwauche, E.S. 2013. The ECOWAS Community Court of Justice and the horizontal application of human rights. *African Human Rights Law Journal* 13: 30.

Nzewi, O., and L. Zakwe 2009. *Democratising regional integration in Southern Africa: SADC National Committees as platforms for participatory policy making.* Research Report 122, Centre for Policy Studies, Johannesburg 7–8.

Onoria, H. 2010. Botched-up elections, treaty amendments and judicial independence in the East African Community. *Journal of African Law* 54 (1): 74.

Oothuizen, G.H. 2006. *The Southern African Development Community: The organization, its policies and prospects.* Midrand, South Africa: Institute for Global Dialogue.

Osode, P.C. 2003. The Southern African Development Community in legal historical perspective. *Journal for Juridical Science* 28 (3): 1.

Ozanne, J.L., C. Corus, and B. Saatcioglu. 2009. The philosophy and methods of deliberative democracy: Implications for public policy and marketing. *Journal of Public Policy and Marketing* 28 (1): 29.

Paulus, A.L. 2009. The international legal system as a constitution. In *Ruling the world? Constitutionalism, international law and global governance,* ed. J.L. Dunoff and J.P. Trachtman. Cambridge: Cambridge University Press.

Peters, A. 2009a. Membership in the global constitutional community. In *The constitutionalization of international law,* ed. J. Klabbers et al. Oxford: Oxford University Press.

———. 2009b. Dual democracy. In *The constitutionalization of international law,* ed. J. Klabbers et al. Oxford: Oxford University Press.

Robert, R. 2004. The social dimension of regional integration in ECOWAS. Working paper No. 49, Policy Integration Department International Labour Office, Geneva.

Šabič, Z. 2013. International parliamentary institutions: A research agenda. In *Parliamentary dimensions of regionalization and globalization: The role of inter-parliamentary institutions,* ed. O. Costa et al. Basingstoke: Palgrave Macmillan.

Salih, M.A.M. 2013. African regional parliaments: Legislatures without legislative powers. In *Parliamentary dimensions of regionalization and globalization: The role of inter-parliamentary institutions,* ed. O. Costa, C. Dri, and S. Stavridis. Basingstoke: Palgrave Macmillan.

Sandholtz, W., and A. Stone Sweet. 1998. Integration, supranational governance, and the institutionalization of the European polity. In *European Integration and supranational governance,* ed. A. Stone Sweet and W. Sandholtz. Oxford: Oxford University Press.

Saurombe, A. 2011. An analysis and exposition of dispute settlement forum shopping for SADC Member States in the light of the suspension of the SADC Tribunal. *South African Mercantile Law Journal* 23: 392.

————. 2012. The role of SADC institutions in implementing SADC Treaty provisions dealing with regional integration. *Potchefstroom Electronic Law Journal* 15 (2): 454. https://doi.org/10.4314/pelj.v15i2.16.

————. 2013. The European Union as a model for regional integration in the Southern African Development Community: A selective institutional comparative analysis. *Law Democracy and Development* 17: 457.

Schermers, H.G., and N.M. Blokker. 2011. *International institutional law: Unity in diversity*. Leiden and Boston: Martinus Nijhoff Publishers.

Sirota, B. 2004–2005. Sovereignty and the Southern African Development Community. *Chicago Journal of International Law* 5: 343.

Smits, J.M. 2009. Redefining normative legal science: Towards an argumentative discipline. In *Methods of human rights research*, ed. F. Coomans et al. Antwerp, Oxford, and Portland: Intersentia.

Stone Sweet, A. 2009. Constitutionalism, legal pluralism, and international regimes. *Indiana Journal of Global Legal Studies* 16 (2): 621.

————. 2011. The European Court of justice. In *The evolution of EU law*, ed. P. Craig and G. De Búrca. Oxford: Oxford University Press.

Timmer, A., et al. 2014. *Critical analysis of the EU's conceptualisation and operationalisation of the concepts of human rights, democracy and rule of law*. Report prepared under the *Fostering human rights among European policies (Frame)* project running from 1 May 2013–30 April 2017. The report is available at http://www.fp7-frame.eu. Accessed 23 June 2015.

Tjønneland, E.N. 2005. Making SADC work? Revisiting institutional reform. In *Monitoring regional integration in Southern Africa yearbook*, ed. D. Hansohm et al. Windhoek, Namibia: Namibian Economic Policy Research Unit.

————. 2013. Making sense of the Southern African Development Community. *African Security Review* 22 (3): 190.

Trachtman, J.P. 2009. Constitutional economics of the World Trade Organization. In *Ruling the world? Constitutionalism, international law and global governance*, ed. J.L. Dunoff and J.P. Trachtman. Cambridge: Cambridge University Press.

Ulfstein, G. 2009. Institutions and competences. In *The constitutionalization of international law*, ed. J. Klabbers et al. Oxford: Oxford University Press.

Vitale, D. 2006. Between deliberative and participatory democracy: A contribution on Habermas. *Philosophy & Social Criticism* 32 (6): 739.

Volcansek, M.L. 2002. Courts and regional integration. In *Regional and global regulation of international trade*, ed. F. Snyder. Oxford and Portland: Hart Publishing.

———. 2005. Courts and regional trade agreements. In *Courts crossing borders: Blurring the lines of sovereignty*, ed. J.F. Stack Jr. and M.L. Volcansek. Durham, NC: Carolina Academic Press.

Von Bogdandy, A. 2006. Constitutionalisation in international law: Comment on a proposal from Germany. *Harvard International Law Journal* 47 (1): 223.

Walker, N. 2009. Reframing EU Constitutionalism. In *Ruling the world? Constitutionalism, international law and global governance*, ed. L. Dunoff and P. Trachtman. Cambridge: Cambridge University Press.

Weiler, J.H.H. 2004. The geology of international law – Governance, democracy and legitimacy. *ZaöRV* 64: 547.

Wheatley, S. 2010. *The democratic legitimacy of international law*. Oxford and Portland, Oregon: Hart Publishing.

Wincott, D. 1996. The Court of Justice and the European policy process. In *European Union: Power and policy making*, ed. J. Richardson, 180. London and New York: Routledge.

Worley, J.J. 2009. Deliberative constitutionalism. *Brigham Young University Law Review* 2009: 431.

Zondi, S. 2009. *Governance and social policy in the SADC region: An issues analysis.* Working Paper Series No. 2, Planning Division Development Bank of Southern Africa, Midrand. http://www.lead4change.org/downloads/module_2/Zondi%20 DBSA%20Paper%20on%20SADC%20-%20Governance%20and%20Policy.pdf. Accessed 14 December 2013.

Index[1]

[1]Note: Page numbers followed by 'n' refer to notes.

© The Author(s) 2019   231
M. Nyathi, *The Southern African Development Community
and Law*, https://doi.org/10.1007/978-3-319-76511-2

CPSIA information can be obtained
at www.ICGtesting.com
Printed in the USA
LVOW13*1917190518

577815LV00011B/81/P